Dedicated to Warren and Jimmy Buffett

Contents

Introduction

Tom Ecker was a teenager and needed a job. So he learned to balance an old push lawnmower on his chin, and people paid to see that.

Tom Ecker was put in charge of athletics programs in Iowa's second largest public school district. He came up with a five-year plan to begin offering girls' sports, showing the parents of daughters—and the nation—the way of the future.

Tom Ecker was captivated by word puzzles. So he created his own game, calling it Wuzzles, and spent the next fifteen years flogging the idea, trying to get someone to buy it. Finally, one newspaper did, then a syndicate. Thirty-five years later, the puzzles still are seen every day by millions of people around the world.

In reading this memoir, you'll get to know a man who was a high school and college track star and who never quit running during his long, productive life.

You'll meet the energetic showman who pursued challenges and packed enough living—and fun—into his eighty-plus years to merit a memoir twice the size of this one. In fact, the original manuscript was twice this long. An editor suggested it should be shortened, noting it was longer than President Bill Clinton's memoir. "Well, I'm older than Clinton," he shot back.

That's our Tom, the toast on many a continent. He did cut the manuscript—with enough left over for a Volume II—but he still succeeds, in magnificent fashion, in summing up a life filled with energy and accomplishment and a great deal of cleverness and wit.

This is the small-town Iowa boy who grew up to visit sixty-six countries on all seven Continents, who's been at ten Olympic Games, leading tours to some, writing about others, and who, when he retired, figured out a way he and his wife, Carol, could cruise the world, for free.

This is the man who, as a college sophomore, bet a friend $10 he could hitchhike from Iowa City to South Carolina over the weekend and be back in time for class on Monday. He succeeded, of course, collecting the bet and a ton of news coverage along the way.

Ecker has those clippings, and thousands more, chronicling his adventures. He has the twenty books he's written, the interviews and anthems he's taped, the slides and pictures he's taken. And, of course, the note a train conductor wrote for him in 1954 directing him to another train.

A history professor at Western Kentucky University, where Ecker transformed the track program, wrote this: "The renaissance of track and field came with the 1962 appointment of Tom Ecker, the twenty-seven-year-old coach at Elizabethtown High School. Brash, energetic, unpredictable, and controversial, Ecker was a winner."

Every life has its low points, and Ecker includes those, too, along with the surprising reason he has been able to get so much done. You'll learn his thinking on religion—and the loss that prompted it—as well as his work on behalf of an Indian health clinic in rural Mexico. And you'll find the mischief, the general merriment and creativity of clubs and bars, and a great story about an early, key moment with Bruce Jenner (now Caitlyn Jenner).

An attorney once called Ecker a Renaissance man. Ecker's response: "I'd rather not be something I can't spell."

Humor, love, and good jokes fill this joyful book but cannot disguise a life well and fully lived. It holds a takeaway for all of us: Grab life and wring every bit of laughter and fun out of it that you can, all while working hard and following that long brown path wherever you choose.

Mary Sharp
Cedar Rapids, Iowa
October 2019

x—

1

Forks in the Road

Over the years, I've learned that life is a long series of forks in the road. Deciding which fork to take changes your life and leads you to the next fork. Over the period of a lifetime, there are countless decisions to be made, many of which will completely change a person's life. Some of them are probably not very important, like deciding what to have for lunch. Others are more likely to be life-changing, like deciding to get a divorce and moving to Sweden, which I did at the age of thirty-one.

Often, the forks in the road lead to either risk-taking or risk-avoidance decisions. In my case, as will be evident in the following pages, I have usually chosen the risk-taking forks.

My father said I had chutzpah, a Yiddish word that some say means brazen nerve. Others say it means unmitigated gall. Actually, there are no definitions that adequately describe chutzpah. It is better to give an example: If a young boy murders his mother and father, and then asks the court for clemency because he's an orphan, that's chutzpah.

I approached my first major fork in the road in 1953, at the age of eighteen. I had finished high school in Waverly, Iowa, had just completed a very successful track season, and had decided to enlist in the military, as my three older brothers had done. To learn more about the Army, I had even lined up a summer job at Fort Devens, Massachusetts, a military base where my oldest brother Don was stationed.

But my father didn't want me to go into the Army. "I've sent three sons off to wars," he said, "and I don't want to send another one." He asked me if I would consider going to college, something I had never considered before.

I had not really enjoyed going to school up to that point, and I barely had a C average, so I really didn't think college would be for me. Besides, no one from our family had ever gone to college.

But my father was insistent. He didn't want me to go into the Army, so he hit me with a surprise. Would I go to college if it didn't cost anything? It turned out he had been in touch with the track coach at the University of Iowa, Francis Cretzmeyer, who had offered me an activity scholarship that would pay for four years of college. All I had to do was attend classes, stay eligible, work some odd jobs, and run.

I had chatted with Coach Cretzmeyer during the previous track season, and we had talked about my attending Iowa, but I wasn't sure I could even get in. For one thing, I had to have a letter of recommendation from my high school principal, which I thought would be impossible to get. Somehow, my father had managed to get the principal to send the letter, and I had been accepted. So I decided to go to college, which

Francis Cretzmeyer, University of Iowa track and field coach

—1

also made me ineligible for the military draft.

But I still had the summer job waiting for me in Fort Devens, Massachusetts. After graduating from high school, I took trains from Iowa to Chicago and on to Fort Devens, where I bused tables at the PX (Post Exchange) snack bar five days a week for eighty-two cents an hour. For lodging, I stayed in the Fort Devens guest house for a dollar a day. On weekday evenings, I performed for the USO in various theaters in the area, doing a balancing act I had learned four years earlier. The weekends were spent seeing the sights of New England.

The cafeteria where I worked on weekdays was managed by a man named Ned Maestri. I told him he should be in the bakery business. He could name his bakery Ned's Breads or Maestri's Pastries. He told me to get back to work.

In July, a military couple I had met at Fort Devens said they would pay my bus fare back to the Midwest if I would take their four-year-old son with me. They needed to have the boy accompanied to the Midwest, and the parents had no other way to get him there.

It wouldn't be a direct bus ride to Iowa for me, however. I first had to deliver the four-year-old to his grandparents in Omaha, Nebraska. I wanted to get home anyway, so I took the assignment. (Why a young couple would trust a flighty eighteen-year-old with their four-year-old son for several days is difficult for me to fathom now, but it seemed to make good sense at the time.)

I had a book of Greyhound timetables, so I scheduled our trip through places I'd never been, including New York City and Washington, D.C. In New York, we even stopped by the NBC studios to watch *The Today Show* with Dave Garroway. My four-year-old friend and I appeared briefly on national television as we watched the show from the street through a large picture window.

We rode on buses for three days and three nights, from Massachusetts through Rhode Island, Connecticut, New York, New Jersey, Pennsylvania, Maryland, Delaware, Virginia, West Virginia, Ohio, Indiana, Illinois, Iowa, and into Nebraska.

My little friend was a good sport about the entire experience. He took everything in stride. His only failing, in my opinion at the time, was that he was always asking questions. Finally, after I had to answer the question "Why?" a few thousand times, we arrived in Omaha. The boy's grandparents met us at the bus station. Then I took buses back to Waverly, Iowa, where I began making preparations to go off to college.

Taking the fork in the road that led me to college instead of to the Army was one of the best decisions of my life.

Now, so many years later, I'm taking another fork in the road by writing this book. For most of those years, I've been told by friends and relatives that they would like to read a book about my charmed and crazy life. Usually those who encourage creating such a book know only a small portion of just how charmed and crazy a life it has been. My closest family members will be surprised by some of this book's revelations. While digging through old files, even I have been surprised to learn of events that had long been forgotten.

Not everything that could be included in this book will be. I'm not going to include much about my girlfriends, wives, or children, for example, unless their involvement helps to tell a story. Their many experiences and accomplishments could fill several books.

This book, instead, is the story of my endless struggles while coping with a little-understood malady called ADHD (attention deficit hyperactivity disorder), and the difficulty I've had in trying to live a "normal" life while dealing with the problem.

In most autobiographies, the authors have trouble remembering all of the details of their lives. But in my case, that isn't a big problem. I have notes, files, letters, photographs, and clippings that can really jog the memory. Believe it or not, I have records of almost everything I've ever seen, heard, said, read, written, or done.

My wife calls me a pack rat. In our basement, there are seventy-six large storage boxes and nineteen legal-size file drawers stuffed with thousands of "memories." One of the boxes contains forty years of calendars with details of daily activities. There are files with brochures, schedules, and notes for every big trip I've ever taken. And there is a storage box with the dates and notes for all of the speeches I've delivered. There is a box that contains the punch lines of every good joke I've ever heard. And I even have the swizzle stick from my first-ever alcoholic drink, from Lindy's Restaurant in New York City, in August of 1960, when I was twenty-five years old.

There are boxes containing all of the important letters anyone has sent me. There is even a box of all the postcards and letters I sent my parents over the years, detailing various experiences and adventures. They were saved by my parents in a large desk drawer and were given to me before they died. My mother also saved all of my report cards, from first grade through high school, complete with teachers' comments on my deportment.

I've since discovered another great source of information to jog the memory—my daughter Wendy's amazing penchant for saving souvenir items from the past. She has, for example, the souvenir program from the night in 1969 when she and her two brothers were invited to sit on the bench with the Harlem Globetrotters during one of their basketball games. The great thing about Wendy is how organized she is. She not only has countless reminders from the past, she knows where to find them immediately.

My plan is to go through all of the storage boxes and file cabinets to get the most accurate information possible for this book. It may take weeks, months, or even years, but if I can stay alive, the task will be completed. I'll do my best not to follow the advice of W.C. Fields: "If at first you don't succeed, then quit. There's no use being a damn fool about it."

2

Bob and Fred

My parents were born Robert Orson Ecker and Winifred Bachtell. Informally, they were Bob and Fred. They lived long enough to celebrate their seventy-first wedding anniversary, which is quite a feat. After my father died, I asked my mother if she had ever considered divorce during those seventy-one years. She told me she had considered murder a few times, but never divorce.

My parents left me an inheritance of a lifetime. I inherited Reynaud's Disease, a circulation disorder, from my mother and gout from my father. Nothing of monetary value. Just two incurable, but non-life-threatening, ailments.

My father started his adult working career as a "printer's devil" and then as a Linotype operator at the Waverly Publishing Company in Waverly, Iowa, beginning in 1921. The publishing company, with twenty-five employees, was larger than most. My mother was a high school student in Arlington, Iowa, when they met. They were married in 1922 after mother graduated from Arlington High School.

Bob and Fred on their wedding day in 1922.

Besides the usual types of commercial printing, the Waverly Publishing Company produced a weekly newspaper and three poultry magazines: *Plymouth Rock Monthly, Rhode Island Red Journal,* and *Leghorn World.* In 1927, the company de-cided to produce a new magazine, *Wayside Salesman,* to offer advertising opportunities for all the small roadside restaurants that were opening all over the country.

There was a search for an editor for *Wayside Salesman,* and Frank Gruber, a twenty-three-year-old struggling writer living in Chicago, was hired. Gruber aspired to be a writer, as did my father, but up until that time neither of them had had anything published.

My father and Frank Gruber became friends because of my father's interest in poetry. In fact, some of the poetry my father created was featured in several issues of *Wayside Salesman,* always with a roadside motif. The June 1930 issue featured one of my father's poems, "Song of the Wayside," and an article by Frank Gruber, "Red's Barbecue Sells 2,700 Chickens Per Week." Both of the budding writers had suddenly become published authors.

Everything was going well at the publishing company until the effects of the Great Depression engulfed the country in the early 1930s. The publishing company went bankrupt and closed in 1933, leaving my father and Frank Gruber out of work. The company owed its employees several weeks of back wages at the time.

Frank Gruber moved to New York to try his hand at full-time writing. It was a great struggle for him, but he finally sold his first story to a pulp fiction publication, *Underworld Magazine,* in late 1933. That was the beginning of an amazing writing career for Gruber. Over the next thirty-five years, he wrote more than 300 stories for some forty pulp magazines. He also wrote sixty novels and more than 200 screenplays and television scripts.

My father's writing career had to be put on hold for a time. In fact, he was eighty-seven years old when his first and only book was published. It was called *No Greener Pastures,* an account of his recollections about life in small town America.

The Depression was hard on my parents. My father did manage to find employment during the next few years, first working for a short time for his friend, Jack Wright, at Wright's Greenhouse, earning one dollar a day. Then he got more lucrative jobs, managing gas stations for two dollars a day.

Bob and Fred in Wright's Greenhouse in the 1950s.

In order to make additional money or to cut costs, my parents became real entrepreneurs. They had a large garden and canned various vegetables, to help get the family though the winters. They raised and sold chickens. They chopped firewood in nearby forests to help heat the house in the winter. They tapped the maple trees in our yard for maple syrup. They even started chain letters for dimes, putting their names at number three or four on a list of ten names, to be sure there would be some profits.

They managed to butcher a quarter of a hog for the various pork cuts, at no cost, although they did it the hard way. They had accepted a gift of two runt pigs from a farmer friend who lived close to town. The pigs were too weak to nurse, so they had to be bottle-fed until they were old enough to eat on their own. As they grew, the two pigs became the family pets. We named one of the pigs Porky, so, of course, the other pig had to be named Beansy.

By the end of the summer, Porky and Beansy had grown too big to be pets, so they had to be returned to the farm. It was a sad day at our house. A few months later, after the slaughtering season, the farmer provided our family with a quarter of a hog in appreciation for our nurturing the two pigs. He was quick to assure us the meat had not come from either Porky or Beansy.

Late in the Depression, the publishing company reorganized and hired my father back at his old job as a Linotype operator. He was happy to have a real job again, but as it turned out, he wasn't going to be there long.

On Memorial Day 1944, Jack Wright told my parents he was tired of the greenhouse business, and he was going to sell it. My father tried to talk him out of it, but Jack was determined to sell the place. When my father told him he was sure the greenhouse had a good future, Jack said, "If you feel that way about it, why don't you buy it?"

The possibility of financing such a project seemed impossible to my parents, but Jack insisted it could be done. He only wanted to be out of the retail business, so he made my folks the following offer: He would lease them the retail end of the business, sell them all of the current stock of flowers, and sell them whatever flowers he grew as they needed them.

There was also an option for my parents to buy the entire operation later, if they chose to do so. The local bank loaned my parents $900 to buy the stock and they suddenly became florists. Within a year, the business was doing so well, they borrowed another $15,000 and were able to exercise the option to buy the entire business. Wright's Greenhouse, which later became Ecker's Flowers, is still in operation as of this writing.

Once, when I was about ten years old, I asked my father what nationality we are. "We're Americans," he answered, and that was the end of the conversation. I'm not sure if he didn't know our European heritage or if he didn't care.

However, he did tell me later that he was a descendent of Rob Roy McGregor, the famed Scottish outlaw. But whenever he'd mention Rob Roy to anyone, my mother would say, "Rob Roy was a damned cattle thief." Then my father would respond, "He was the Robin Hood of Scotland. He stole from the rich, and he kept it."

A scotch drink called a Rob Roy, which is made with Scotch whiskey, sweet vermouth, and bitters, was named for our ancestor, Rob Roy McGregor. A gin drink called a Bob, which is made with gin and Pepsi-Cola, was named for my father, Bob Ecker. We always joked that gin and Pepsi was a delightful mixture of depressant and stimulant drugs.

There was a family story about an ancestor of ours who was an Indian from the Abenaki tribe. According to the story, a French-Canadian named Peter Demo, who was an ancestor, had married an Indian woman after the French and Indian War. Friends have often suggested to me that my Native-American heritage should qualify me to have my own Indian riverboat casino. However, even if I had Indian blood, it would be only 1/256th, which would barely qualify me to have a canoe with a slot machine aboard.

When I was in grade school, my parents would occasionally take me to the Nautical Club (which I called the Naughty Club), a classy supper club on the northwest edge of Waverly. The Nautical Club was the inspiration of a local farmer, Jack Deinema, who had been a sailor and had a strong love for the sea, even though we were a thousand miles from the nearest one. He built the club on a hillside of his farm, overlooking Wartburg College.

In those days, any liquor consumed in a restaurant had to be brought in from the outside. There were state-run liquor stores where alcohol could be purchased, but in a restaurant, you could only buy a setup, a drink consisting of anything but alcohol. My parents' drink of choice was gin and Pepsi-Cola. So, at the Nautical Club, they ordered bottles of Pepsi, and my assignment was to drink the "tops," taking the level of the cola down far enough so a shot of gin could be added. It was an important assignment.

Although there are many things about my parents for which I am thankful, I treasure their senses of humor the most. There was always happy banter and storytelling, wherever we were. Usually my father was the storyteller, but my mother, the quiet member of the family, often got off some good lines. She was in a department store one day to buy a new pair of shoes. When she took off her shoes, the salesman commented that she had one blue and one brown sock on. She responded, "I have another pair just like these at home."

When I was sixteen years old, I announced to the family that I was planning to write a book, *My 16 Years as a Straight Man.* One of the many straight lines that I fed my father was about English literature. I would ask him, "Do you like Kipling?" He would answer, "I don't know. I've never Kippled." And there was a reference to a nearly extinct community, Artesian, some eight miles east of Waverly. I would say, "Do you know Artesian?" and he would answer "Yes, I know Artesian well."

My father came up with what he called an international way of saying goodbye to someone. He would simply say "carbolic acid." He explained that carbolic acid means goodbye in any language.

He claimed he once walked into a bar and said, "I'd like a drink. I'm thirsty." When the bartender brought him a glass of water, he said, "I'm thirsty, not dirty."

Fortunately, the sense of humor was passed on to me. It has gotten me through some pretty rough times.

In the foreword for my first book, which came out in 1961, George Gibson, president of the Kentuckiana Cinder Club, wrote about me: "Of course, into even such a sunny, active life, some disappointments must come. When they do, they bring a shake of the head, a quick grin and gesture of hand, and he is organized to attack the revised or new objective."

One of my obvious passions throughout my life has been for travel, the result of a lack of available transportation when I was young. I knew there were things to see beyond my hometown of Waverly, Iowa, but there was little hope of ever seeing them. Our family did not even own a car until I was eleven years old. We simply didn't go anywhere.

My father bought a 1939 Ford in 1946, and we began to travel, even into adjoining states Minnesota and Illinois. I was eager to see other places—even places in Minnesota and Illinois.

We took one trip to Minneapolis in 1948 to take a look at two things my father simply had to see. One was the new Tucker automobile, which was definitely ahead of its time. The other was television. The Tucker and the small television set were both on display, in tents, in a Minneapolis park.

My father thought the Tucker was interesting, but he was completely taken with the idea of watching television. He had been a radio buff for many years, pulling in stations from all over the country. But television was about to add a new and exciting dimension to his world.

There were two TV stations in Minneapolis—KSTP and WTCN. Father thought he might be able to put up a tower tall enough to pick up those two stations in Waverly, some 150 miles away, as the TV signal flies.

So, he became a television pioneer. He had a tall tower built on the roof of our second-floor apartment, with a TV antenna on top of it. He then bought a small TV set. Between long periods of "snow," we were able to catch glimpses of Perry Como, Roberta Quinlan, and Earl Wrightson. We would even stay up at night, trying to catch parts of Jerry Lester's Broadway Open House, the forerunner of The Tonight Show.

I can't complete a chapter about Bob and Fred without mentioning that they were lifelong Chicago Cubs fans—first listening to the Cubs' games on radio in the 1930s and later watching their games on television. My mother summarized their fascination with the Cubs one day. She said, "We know they're going to lose, but we just don't know how they're going to do it."

3

A Lifetime of Joking

Over the years, it became a tradition in our family to quote a line from an old joke whenever there was a possibility of doing so. The response makes no sense to anyone who is not familiar with the joke, but it makes perfect sense to family members. Blame my father. He started it.

For example, if someone makes a statement that conflicts with what you're doing, like "That's not the way the joke goes," you respond, "Who's robbin' this train?"

The original joke is about an old-fashioned train robbery. One of the robbers announces, "We're going to take all your money and jewelry, then we're going to have sex with your women." One gentleman stands up and says, "You can take our money and jewelry, but leave our women alone." A little old lady stands up and says, "Who's robbin' this train?"

Another example deals with time. If someone announces, "We don't have time to do that," the response is, "What's time to a pig?"

The original joke is about a pig farmer who was being interviewed by a newspaper reporter about his daily activities. The farmer said, "Well, I start out in the early morning herding the pigs about a mile to the back pasture. Then I herd them back to the barn at coffee time. Then I herd them back out to the pasture. Then I herd them back to the barn for lunch…" "Wait a minute," says the interviewer, "doesn't that take a lot of time?" The farmer answers, "What's time to a pig?"

Another example deals with an occasion where you're being given credit for being intelligent. If someone says, "That was really a smart move," the response is, "I may be crazy, but I'm not stupid."

The original joke is about a man who has a flat tire in front of a mental hospital. One of the hospital's inmates watches through the bars at the front gate as the man changes the tire. The man changing the tire takes all of the lug nuts off the wheel and puts them in the hubcap close to the highway. As the man removes the wheel, a truck comes speeding by, hits the hubcap, and the lug nuts all go flying into the nearby ditch. The man sits staring at the wheel trying to figure out what to do, when the inmate suddenly makes a suggestion. "Why not take one lug nut from each of the other wheels. That will give you enough lug nuts to put the spare tire on and get to a service station." The man was amazed and said, "That was a brilliant suggestion. Aren't you supposed to be crazy?" The inmate answered, "I may be crazy, but I'm not stupid."

One of the better examples deals with one's ability to think. If someone is surprised you know an answer to something, and says, "How did you know that?" you point to your head and say, "Kidneys."

The original joke is about a mental hospital inmate who has to pass a test before he can be released. He has to distinguish between his hand, his wrist, and his elbow. The first time he tries it, he says, "Wrist, hand, elbow." That was wrong, of course. When he came back the next day, he got it right. He said, "Hand, wrist, elbow." The person administering the test asks him, "How did you get it right?" The inmate points to his head and says, "Kidneys."

Another example deals with an occasion when you're not in a big hurry to do something. If someone says, "It's time to mow the lawn," you agree that it is indeed time to do it, but then you add, "But first I'm going to sing a little song."

The original joke deals with one of the great cowboy heroes of the past, Gene Autry. Someone runs up to Gene and says, "Gene, Gene, cattle rustlers are rounding up all the cattle on the south forty." Someone else runs up and says, "Gene, Gene, horse thieves are rounding up all the horses on the north forty." Gene answers, "I'll ride down to the south forty and take care of those cattle rustlers, and I'll ride up to the north forty and take care of those horse thieves. But first I'm going to sing a little song."

If someone makes an obvious mistake, you announce "That's once."

That joke deals with a young newlywed couple leaving on their honeymoon in a horse and buggy. While they are traveling down a country road, the horse stumbles. The husband steps out of the buggy and stands in front of the horse. "That's once," he says to the horse. The man gets back in the buggy, and the couple continues down the road. Then the horse stumbles again. The man reaches under his seat, grabs a shotgun, steps back out of the buggy, stands in front of the horse, and promptly shoots the horse in the head. The man's young bride is horrified. She says to her husband, "That was a terrible thing to do. You are nothing but an evil, nasty man." He looks at her and says, "That's once."

The final example is the one that is used most often. It deals with situations where a result may be in doubt. If someone says, "We can win this game easily," the response is, "We ain't to Memphis yet."

The original joke is about a southern lad who is riding to Memphis on a hay wagon with his girlfriend. He says to her, "I ain't never rode to Memphis on a hay wagon with a pregnant girl before." She responds, "Why, I ain't pregnant." And he answers, "We ain't to Memphis yet."

Another long-running exchange had to do with postcards. My father rarely ever sent me a letter or postcard. That was my mother's job. He might write a poem or limerick intended for me, but mother would have to send it, usually with an attached note referring to another of his "foolishments." It was my job to send postcards to them.

Over a thirty-five-year period, whether I was traveling around Iowa or around the world, I always sent postcards to my parents. Some of them were attempts at humor. Others were just letting them know where I was. On occasion, I would sign them Gulliver or Marco Polo.

For example, when former President Herbert Hoover celebrated his 80th birthday in his hometown, West Branch, Iowa, on August 9, 1954, I was a student at the University of Iowa. I drove the eleven miles from Iowa City to West Branch, bought a postcard and stamp, and wrote on the card: "Dear Bob, Sorry you couldn't make it to the party. – H.H."

In 1954, while hitchhiking through Fort Madison, Iowa, I stopped to buy a postcard to send my father. Pictured on the card was one of the state penitentiaries, which is located there. On it I wrote: "Wish you were here."

One Christmas, while traveling in Fiji, which is near the Equator, I bought a postcard to send to my folks. I drew a picture of Santa Claus on it and had him saying, "HOt HOt HOt!"

While traveling to Toronto in 1953, I went through Michigan, the fortieth state in my collection of forty-eight. I sent my folks a card that just said, "eight to go."

From Coventry, England, I sent a card with a picture of a bronze statue of the nude Lady Godiva riding on a horse, sidesaddle, through the streets of Coventry. On the message side, I wrote, "Why do half the people keep shouting, 'Hooray for our side!'?"

I sent a card from Moscow that I signed with the Russian-sounding name, Rippov. The card said: "This country is a giant. – Rippov"

As funny and fun-loving as he was, my father had a dark side. If he didn't like someone, he would put the "McGregor curse" on them. The McGregor curse, which was a guaranteed death sentence, was reserved for the few people he really didn't like. And it always worked, although sometimes it took many years, sometimes even several decades, for the curse to work.

My father lived a long and fun-filled life. In 1993, when he was on his deathbed, he asked my brother Dick if he was dying. Dick answered, "We're all dying. You just have a head start."

My father couldn't have planned a more fitting ending to his life. On the day before he died, my mother was visiting him in the nursing home where she slipped, fell, and broke her hip. She was rushed to the local hospital where a surgeon performed the needed hip operation.

My father died the next morning at the age of 90, and because my mother was bed-ridden, her hospital room became the site of the visitation before the funeral. Friends and relatives attended the two-day visitation, viewing the body in the casket and visiting with my mother and other family members who were there.

On Friday, the day of the funeral, my mother was in a wheelchair and was taken by van to the Episcopal church where the funeral was to be held. The church was pretty crowded when the funeral director, Jim Corson, realized that my father wasn't there. The funeral had to be delayed as the hearse returned to the hospital to pick up my father in his casket. I know he would have been pleased to know he was late for his own funeral.

4

Finding the Fun in Dysfunctional

My good friend, the late Gus Schrader, who was the sports editor of the Cedar Rapids *Gazette* for many years, once told me the Bible begins with a reference to baseball. He quoted the reference for me: "In the big inning, …"

Speaking of big innings, I was born on Babe Ruth's fortieth birthday, February 6, 1935, in the front bedroom of my parents' home in Waverly, Iowa. I was also born on President Ronald Reagan's twenty-fourth birthday. "Dutch" Reagan, as he was known in those days, was broadcasting a variety of sports events, including the Drake Relays, over WHO radio in Des Moines, Iowa.

I was the fourth of four boys, and the timing couldn't have been worse. The year 1935 was the heart of the Great Depression and finding something to eat was a challenge for almost everyone. My mother's maternity outfits were cloth flour sacks sewn together. Why my parents wanted another mouth to feed at that time in history is a mystery to me. Perhaps they couldn't help it.

When one of my mother's friends asked her how she could possibly take care of four boys, she responded, "Three boys take all of my time, so a fourth one can't possibly take any more."

My parents had already used up all the family's choice names on the first three sons—Donald Claude, Theodore John, and Richard Eugene. One day, almost two weeks into my life, a little girl from the neighborhood, Mary Ann Englebrecht, asked if she could see the baby. As she looked at me, she said, "I think Thomas Robert is a nice name." My parents agreed. My birth was officially registered thirteen days after I was born.

The house we lived in for the first ten years of my life was across the street from Wartburg College. When I was ten, the college needed room to construct a new building, Knights Gymnasium. The property was condemned, and we had to move out of the house.

Before we moved, I measured the distance from a large maple tree in our front yard to the bedroom where I was born. After the gymnasium was built, I measured the distance from that tree to where the bedroom had been. It was the women's restroom. So, I've always told people I was born in the women's restroom of Knights Gymnasium at Wartburg College.

We moved from the Wartburg College neighborhood seven blocks east to a small apartment over the rear part of Wright's Greenhouse, which my parents had just purchased. Brothers Don and Ted were in the military, so Dick and I shared a very small bedroom, sleeping in bunk beds. Dick's was the upper; mine was the lower. I wrote on one of the bed slats above my head: GET UP WHEN YOU WAKE UP! On the next slat I wrote: YOU SAW THE SIGN. GET UP!

All my life, I've had a reputation for being involved

Photo Credit: *The Gazette*

Gus Schrader, long time sports editor of the Cedar Rapids Gazette

in many things at the same time. The standard description has been "jack of all trades and master of none." The truth is I've never had the ability to concentrate on just one thing at a time. And sometimes I haven't had the ability to concentrate on anything at all. It can be very frustrating.

During my working years, I was often asked how it was possible for me to hold down full-time jobs and still have time to do so many other things. My primary secret was getting by with very little sleep. During those working years, I would sleep no more than four hours a night. In a week's time, that added up to an additional twenty-eight hours to do other things. I once told one of my colleagues, "I can call you on the telephone before I go to sleep tonight, and again when I wake up in the morning, and I'll wake you up both times."

In 1964, I was quoted in a newspaper, "Anyone who gets more than five hours of sleep a night is lazy." That was a great line when I was younger, but now I'm the lazy one. In recent years, I've been known to get five hours of sleep before midnight.

My other secret was devoting my free time—Saturdays, Sundays, holidays, and vacation times—to my "enterprises." Most people like to fish or hunt or play golf or bicycle or take part in a host of other hobbies and activities. I did none of these. If I took a vacation, it was a working vacation.

In many respects, I was like my oldest brother Don. The difference was that I married a "rudder," and he did not. Don's wife did nothing to try to steer him in the right direction. My wife was born to steer. And even though Judy and I were later divorced, I'll be forever grateful to her for that.

When I was young, I'm sure I was a lot like Don had been, with lots of ideas and energy, but with very little direction. However, I didn't really know him at that time. He joined the Navy when I was five years old.

Throughout his life, Don demonstrated that he had many talents. Yet, as talented as he was, he could never hold down a regular job. As he jumped from job to job, he had many side projects, but he rarely finished any of them. He wrote books, plays, and songs, and could play every musical instrument you can name. He had many great ideas and worthwhile projects, but as our father used to say, "If the project isn't completed by sundown, he'll be on a new and more exciting project the next day."

Modern-day educators and psychologists would say the culprit for both Don and me was attention deficit hyperactivity disorder (ADHD). Of course, there was no such disorder when I was young, and there certainly were no treatments, unless you count trips to the principal's office.

ADHD victims have difficulty focusing on all but the most engaging or entertaining tasks. Sitting at a desk for long periods of time can be difficult for any child but can be pure hell for one with ADHD.

I had many of the ADHD symptoms when I was in school, such as being easily distracted, not finishing tasks, not paying attention, being easily bored, not stopping to think before acting, being late, being forgetful, and daydreaming. At the time, I thought that was normal behavior.

Like Don, whom I was told had been bored with school, standard schoolwork did not come easy for me. My problems in school were created by my ADHD symptoms, compounded by the successes of my brother, Dick. He was five years older and a model student, excelling in everything he did in school, and I was constantly reminded that I wasn't capable of following in my brother's footsteps. (Dick and I were good friends then, and still are. Years later, I was even the best man in his wedding.)

While Dick was an honors student, I was often in trouble for not finishing assignments and for working on non-school projects during school time. I spent more time writing short stories, radio scripts, and limericks, drawing cartoons, and practicing coin and card tricks than I spent on school work. I never got a failing mark in my entire school career, but I was close a few times.

In junior high, Mrs. Clatterbaugh was the health teacher. Almost from the first day of school, she singled me out to the class as the flightiest student she had ever had. I didn't know what flighty meant at the time, but apparently I was a good example. She wrote on my report card, "Tom is so inconsistent."

Five years later, when I was a senior at the high school, which was in the same building as the junior high, I stopped at the water fountain that served both schools. One of Mrs. Clatterbaugh's seventh-grade health students came up to me and said, "We studied about you today."

I didn't know it at the time, but another reason I was a near-failure in school was because of brain hemisphericity. The human brain is divided into two hemispheres. The left side is concerned with logical and analytic skills. The right side is concerned with artistic and creative abilities.

A few people think with both sides of the brain, but most people are either left- or right-brained. The school subjects that seem to count, such as math and science, are ideal subjects for left-brained people. Right-brained people do better in creative writing, art, and music. Since most school subjects are designed for left-brained people, heavily right-brained people, like me, were left struggling. We all thought I just wasn't very smart.

In fact, I was thirty-two years old before I realized I wasn't really stupid; I just did stupid things. My employer, the Nissen Corporation in Cedar Rapids, sent me to a group of psychologists to take a battery of intelligence, aptitude, and personality tests. My boss at Nissen, "Bus" Klinge, shared the results with me, commenting, "You're not as dumb as we thought."

The scores on the eight tests were: learning ability: 99th percentile; language: 99th percentile; adjustability: 99th percentile; mechanics: 96th percentile; numerical reasoning: 95th percentile; judgment: 95th percentile; analytic visualization: 85th percentile; and assembly: 75th percentile. (Don't ask me to assemble anything!)

One of the psychologists wrote: "Tom needs constant challenge. This is why, we believe, his work history might be characterized as moving from one project to another, as opposed to taking a job and working at it indefinitely. The typical 'steady job' would just not be for him." (He was certainly right about that.)

Fortunately, the "regular" jobs I had in my career, as a sports equipment designer, a teacher, a coach, and a school administrator, allowed me to go from one task to another, without fear of being bored. In fact, I loved all of my jobs through the years. I could be competent in my work and still be creative.

During a television interview, my boss for much of my twenty-six years in the Cedar Rapids school system was asked about me. He said, "He's a human dynamo. The guy is constantly on the move. He has very little need for sleep. He's a creative thinker who has had his hands in as many different things as there are to get them into."

Creativity was an important part of every job I held, but I always tried to inject a little humor, too. For example, when I was the athletics director for the Cedar Rapids schools, I was called as an "expert witness" in a trial involving a sports injury at a school in Ohio.

An attorney for the plaintiff asked me many personal questions about my life, my work, and my interests. Obviously surprised by some of the answers, the attorney tried to flatter me by saying, "You are indeed a Renaissance man." I answered with a smile, "I'd rather not be something I can't spell."

I can't mention being creative without also mentioning my good friend Bob Foley, perhaps the most creative person I've ever known. I met Bob in the early 1970s when we were both administrators in the Cedar Rapids school system. We worked in the same building, the Educational Service Center (which we said were three misnomers), so our paths crossed often.

We would meet after the work day at a local bar, The Fox and Hounds, where we laughed at each other's jokes and stories. Bob once said we were there so much we probably had an endowed booth.

During those meetings, we decided to write a humor book together. It was to be entitled, *The First Book of Affairs (1,001 Meaningful Relationships)*. Its subtitle was *A Practitioner's Guide to Straying*. Although we had many laughs discussing the book's potential contents, we never did finish it. (Most of our ideas were written on cocktail napkins.)

We were very proud of some of the chapter titles: "Should you have your Kate and Edith, too?"; "Guilt without sex;" "Domestic vs. foreign affairs;" "No one is really invisible;" and "Is group sex worth all the phone calls?"

Bob Foley was the brightest and perhaps the funniest person I had ever known. It was always a pleasure to meet and to laugh with him. We were dear friends until he joined Alcoholics Anonymous, and then we parted company.

I guess we were still friends after he joined AA; we just didn't get together anymore. When I once suggested we meet to share some laughter, he told me he had learned one important rule at AA: "If you don't want to slip, don't go where it's slippery."

At one point during the years when Bob and I were working on our book, I asked him if I should try to join Mensa, a high IQ society. I knew Bob had belonged at one time, and I had done well on various sample Mensa tests in recent years. He told me to stay away from the organization. "They're very boring people," he told me. He said I should just tell people I'm a Mensa dropout.

Then we thought perhaps we should start our own organization for right-brained people, calling it Densa.

5

The Tomfoolery Begins

From my earliest recollections, I wanted to be an entertainer. It didn't matter what kind. School plays and variety shows were for me. If there was a speaking or singing part, I'd volunteer for it. Some of the show business allure probably came from attending the Seils-Sterling Circus, a tent and truck show that played Waverly when I was eight years old.

For the first ten years of my life, our family lived across the street from Wartburg College. Grossman

Wartburg College's Old Main

Hall, the men's dormitory, was kitty-corner across the street from our house. Just beyond it was Old Main,

The brick with my name carved into it is still on display.

the college's very old classroom building. When I was nine years old, my older brother Dick and I carved our names into two of the bricks on the front of Old Main. They are still there today. One brick reads "Dick Ecker 1944." The other one just reads simply "Tom Ecker." Over the years, attempts have been made by college employees to smooth over the many names carved into the bricks, but the Ecker names were so deep, they couldn't be effaced. (Fools names and fools faces…)

Neighbor Bill Wiederanders and I formed a neighborhood circus. My arm is in a cast because of a fall from a tree.

While in early elementary school, I put on a neighborhood circus, charging nearby Wartburg College students one cent to attend the performances. The only act I remember now was the appearance of the "elephant," actually my neighbor, Bill Wiederanders, and me under a blanket, with a short hose hanging down in front as the elephant's trunk.

My older brother Don, who was on leave from the

Navy, was writing a book at that time, and he included the circus performance in one of the chapters. He wrote: "Every time the elephant was out of sight, the students would begin chanting, 'We want the elephant. We want the elephant.'"

From grades one through six, I attended Washington Irving Grade School. It was about ten blocks from our home. In those days, grade school teachers had to be female, and they couldn't be married. We had a teacher one year who got married at Christmastime, and we never saw her again.

My first-grade teacher was Miss Carey, who now has an elementary school named for her in Waverly. She wrote on my report card, "Tommy is a keen boy, but must change his attitude. Must improve in conduct."

Miss Carey was not only the first grade teacher, she was also the school's principal. And to all of the students in the school, she was considered an unhappy, evil woman. In retrospect, we now realize why she wasn't married.

Her punishment for a first grader exercising bad conduct was to send the offender to the cloak room, an adjoining room that was used for hanging up coats in the wintertime. Naturally, I became well acquainted with the cloak room. One day, bored with just looking out the cloak room window, I climbed through it, scaled down the side of the building, and walked home. My mother wasn't pleased. Neither was Miss Carey.

Every morning, at the start of school, Miss Carey would have the class stand, face the flag, and recite the Pledge of Allegiance. But the routine of reciting the pledge wasn't the same as it is today. We would begin with our right hands over our hearts. The pledge would begin "I pledge allegiance…" But then we would all straighten our arms toward the flag as the words "to the flag" were spoken. The arm would remain extended until the pledge was finished.

Shortly after December 8 of that year (1941), when the United States declared war against Germany and Japan, the pledge routine was changed. There were those who thought straightening the arm was too similar to the Nazi "Heil Hitler" salute, so the hand remained over the heart.

I still have a copy of our first-grade reading book, *Jim and Judy*. Published in 1939, it used the sight method of teaching reading, emphasizing memorization and repetition. A typical page in the book reads, "This is Jim's birthday," said Mother. "Happy birthday, Jim!" "Happy birthday!" said Father. "This is Judy's birthday, too," said Father. "Happy birthday, Judy!" "Happy birthday!" said Mother.

Looking at the book now, I realize how much better off Jim and Judy's parents were than our parents were at the time. Most of the first graders in my class were poor by today's standards. Jim and Judy's father drove a big new car, and he could afford to take the entire family on an airplane ride. Unlike Jim and Judy's parents, my parents hadn't owned a car since well before I was born. If we wanted to go somewhere, we walked.

In the third grade, there were two class singers— "Tubby" Stafford and me. Because our voices hadn't changed, we were both sopranos. Whenever there was an opportunity to perform on the Irving School stage, we were there. Everybody enjoyed Tubby's singing because he could really belt out a song, even though he was mentally challenged.

World War II was still going strong in 1944. One of the hobbies for the students in my class was collecting and trading military patches. These were cloth identifying patches, such as the 1st Cavalry Division or the 3rd Infantry Division, worn on the upper arm of military uniforms.

One day, one of my classmates came to school with several patches with "IGA" on them. He convinced everyone that the patches were for the Italian-German Army, very valuable for trading purposes. At the time, we didn't realize that IGA stood for Independent Grocers Alliance. (We didn't have an IGA store in Waverly.)

One memory from World War II was rationing. Everything needed for the war effort was rationed at home. Gasoline rationing was one of the most notable of the rationed items, but that didn't affect our family since

Wartburg College's original gymnasium, which is still intact, was home to German prisoners of war in 1944.

we didn't own a car. I remember that every Tuesday was known as "meatless Tuesday," a day on which all of a family's meals had to be prepared without any kind of meat.

On days that weren't meatless, one of my father's favorite cuts of beef was a rump roast. When he ordered one at the local meat market, he always asked for the north end of a cow going south.

The war was on everyone's mind every day, of course, but the conflict was brought closer to home in 1944. About fifty German prisoners of war were sent to Waverly to work at the Marshall Canning Company, a factory which was short-handed because so many young American workers had become part of the U.S. military. The canning company canned string beans and sweet corn to be sold in grocery stores throughout the country.

Since the canning company was only three blocks from our home, it was easy for me to go to the factory and watch the prisoners work. They wore matching gray uniforms, with a large P.W. printed on the back of each shirt.

They appeared to be happy, probably because it was much safer to be stuck in Iowa than to be on the front lines in Germany. And I found them to be very polite. When they walked in front of me as they took their breaks, they always said, "Excuse me."

The prisoners needed a place to sleep, so the dressing rooms of the Wartburg gymnasium were converted to sleeping quarters. The dressing room windows had been painted over, but there were enough "holes" in the paint for us to peer in on them to see how they

Posing for my mother's camera at the swimming pool.

The Waverly Municipal swimming pool

lived. The old gymnasium, which has since been converted to the Players Theatre, is still standing today.

In 1944, when I was in the third grade, my parents purchased Wright's Greenhouse in Waverly. They both had to learn the flower business in a hurry. They even went to a flower design school in Minneapolis for a few days, leaving my fourteen-year-old brother Dick in charge of the greenhouse.

Since the flower business took all of their time, I became what is now known as a "free-range" child. At the age of nine, I quickly learned to be on my own. I usually fixed my own meals, or ate at a local hamburger stand. For breakfast, I often warmed up leftovers from the night before. One day in health class, the teacher asked everyone what they had for breakfast that morning. When it was my turn, I answered, "A bowl of chili." The other students laughed, and it was obvious the health teacher wasn't pleased.

From Memorial Day to Labor Day every year, my primary hangout was the Waverly Municipal Swimming Pool, an ovoid-shaped, above-ground, concrete pool with three-foot and ten-foot diving boards. I spent seventy-five cents for a season ticket each summer, and by the second grade was a good enough swimmer to qualify to swim in the "deep end."

One of the swimming instructors was Mart Brandes, who would later be my high school football and track coach. The local newspaper wanted to get a picture of Coach Brandes teaching someone to swim, and I was picked. In the picture he is holding me as I dog-paddle, but I was already a reasonable swimmer at that time.

I was blond (my nickname was "Cottontop"), had fair skin, and spent as much time in the sun as possible. Of course, no one knew then how damaging the radiation from the sun could be. And the damage is cumulative. I've been suffering from various forms of self-inflicted skin cancer since the age of forty-nine.

Another summer pastime was raising pigeons. I would climb along the beams under the bridge that spanned the Cedar River in downtown Waverly. When I came upon a nest that had baby pigeons in it, I would take the squabs to the greenhouse and hand-feed corn to them until they could fly. The problem was getting rid of them. Whenever I took the mature pigeons back to the bridge where I had found them, they would immediately fly back to the greenhouse. They weren't homing pigeons, but nobody explained that to them.

I walked to school every day, and on warm weekends and during the summer, I often walked to the swimming pool or explored nearby forests and waterways, mostly along the Cedar River. The area of exploration was a remote upstream area I called "the island." It wasn't really an island, of course, since I didn't have to cross any water to get there. It was a heavily wooded area, with inlets from the river and ponds, filled with fish that were trapped there during the annual spring flood season. It was one of my favorite hangouts every summer until I turned sixteen.

One year, I found a small rowboat that had drifted downstream to Waverly during the previous spring flood, and I managed to repair it to working order. It was my river transportation for one summer, until the next year's flood took it farther downstream.

In 1944, my brother Ted, who was a senior in high school, was working as a mechanic in a local garage. He earned enough money to buy a used 1935 Hudson Terraplane for $150. When Ted was drafted into the Army six months later, my parents became custodians of the Terraplane until Ted returned from the war. It was used to make flower deliveries, and on rare occasions it was used for short trips out of town

One of those trips was to Waterloo, twenty-two miles away, where my parents and I saw the new musical, *Carousel,* which was playing at the Paramount

Theatre there. I can still remember the orchestra playing "June Is Bustin' Out All Over" as we left the theater.

While driving out of Waterloo that day, my father noticed a sign at Canfield Airport that read: Airplane Rides—Two dollars. My father pulled the car into the airport parking lot, handed me two dollars, and asked me if I'd like to take an airplane ride. The plane was a single-engine, yellow biplane, or double-winger, as we called them. I rode in the front seat, wearing goggles, and the pilot rode behind me. That short flight was my introduction to the magic of flying, which I continue to enjoy to this day.

When I was at home, I spent more time with my father's sister, Aunt Janet, who had moved to Waverly to help out in the greenhouse business, than with my parents. My one responsibility was shoveling coal in the greenhouse coal bin once a day, making sure there was a pile of coal over the auger leading to the greenhouse furnace and boilers.

When I was about ten years old, my father's oldest brother, Uncle John, visited our family on his way driving back to his home in California. He was intrigued by the "wire-walking" apparatus I had rigged in the backyard. I didn't have any wire, so I had used a piece of half-inch pipe that was about three feet off the ground. When Uncle John saw me performing my "pipe-walking" act, he said he had the perfect circus name for me—Ramundi LaCortella. I was impressed with the name at the time and have never forgotten it. The name was a whole lot better than the act.

Our fifth-grade class produced a mimeographed newspaper called *The Chatterbox* as part of a six-week English project. My job was assistant cartoonist. In one of my cartoons, a young boy named Junior is holding a drum and talking to his uncle. Junior says, "The drum you gave me was the best present I ever got." Uncle replies, "It was? I'm glad to hear that." Junior says, "Yes, Mother gives me a quarter a day not to play it."

Among *The Chatterbox* news items were these press-stoppers: "February 6 was Tommy Ecker's eleventh birthday. He treated each of us to a Life Saver roll." And this one: "The fifth graders have chosen the two spellers who will represent their room in the city contest. We chose the winners through a series of spelldowns. Tom Ecker and Delores Schiller won." Even though I could spell, my name was conspicuously absent from the honor roll.

Spelling was not always one of my strengths. In school, we had a contest where a student would say a letter and then an object. The other students would then try to guess what the object was. When it was my turn, I said the letter is "S," and the object was a vegetable. After my classmates had guessed spinach, squash, and sweet potato, I gave them the answer: "Sparagus."

Another classroom contest had to do with spelling words progressively. A student selected by the teacher would say the starting letter of a word, and then call on a classmate to say the next letter. That person would add a third letter, etc. When no one could think of a letter that would continue in the spelling of a word, the class would call out "Challenge." The student who had said the last letter then had to say what the word was.

Before school one day, I asked a friend to help me with an idea I had. If he was selected to begin the spelling of a word, he should say "L," and then call on me. Sure enough, he was called on that day. He said "L" and called on me. I said "L," and everyone in the class called out "Challenge." I told the class my word was Llama.

In 1946, Waverly staged a citywide musical, called *Rumpelstiltskin,* with hundreds of participants. I had just turned eleven and was in fifth grade. Originally, I was cast in the lead role, probably because of my singing voice, but when the director realized I was too flighty to learn my lines, I was demoted to the role of a non-speaking guard.

That same year, our fifth grade put on a play called *The Proud Princess.* I wasn't in the play itself, probably because I couldn't learn lines, but I drew the cover design for the program.

In the sixth grade, our class put on an epic play with a cast of thirty-five (everybody in the class). The play was *How Boots Befooled the King.* I played the part of Boots. And even though Boots shared the title role with the king, the king was top-billed and Boots was number ten on the list of cast members.

When I was in the sixth grade, I learned how to make hydrogen for launching toy balloons. I got the idea from my older brother Dick, who had sent balloons skyward five years earlier, when he was my age. He used muriatic acid for making hydrogen; I used hydrochloric acid. It turned out they were the same thing. When pieces of zinc were added to the acid, hydrogen was produced.

First, I went to Ed Meyer, the local druggist, and bought a quart of hydrochloric acid. (As dangerous as hydrochloric acid can be, it doesn't seem possible a young kid could have bought it, but no one asked any questions.)

Then my neighbor, Ty Brooks, who was a year younger, and I set up a laboratory in a shed near Ty's house. We poured some of the acid into an empty Coke bottle. Then we cut up some old zinc jar lids and dropped the pieces into the acid. Immediately, hydrogen gas began pouring out of the bottle.

We attached a rubber balloon to the top of the bottle and watched as it filled with the gas. When the balloon was about a foot in diameter, we tied a string around the balloon's neck and removed it from the bottle. Then another balloon was attached to the bottle. While the second balloon was filling up, we tied a note to the string on the first balloon that said: "Please write to Tom Ecker, Waverly, Iowa." We sent several balloons into the atmosphere carrying the same message before calling it a day.

I received letters from a few people, but they were all sent from within our county. But two weeks later, I received a letter from a farm boy in Snover, Michigan, north of Detroit. He had found the balloon in a farm field there. The balloon had traveled more than 500 miles. The next edition of the Waverly newspaper ran a story about the balloon's journey with this headline: "Boy Scientists Contact Michigan." Ty and I were very proud.

In elementary school, I remember an assignment we had one day. We were to memorize and recite a poem in front of the class. I wasn't good at memorizing, but I already knew a poem that my father had taught me, so I didn't bother to try to memorize a new one. I stood in front of the class and said, "I never saw a purple cow, I never hope to see one, but this I tell you anyhow, I'd rather see than be one." It got a big laugh.

I remember a classmate who changed his poem when he was in front of the class. The original version was, "The woodpecker pecked on the henhouse door, he pecked and he pecked till his pecker got sore." When he got up, he said, "The woodpecker pecked on the henhouse door, he pecked and he pecked till the door fell down."

6

The Right Side of the Brain Kicks In

My freelance writing career began at the two newspapers that were published in Waverly, *The Waverly Democrat* and *The Bremer County Independent*. One was printed Tuesday evening and one Thursday evening. Both newspapers were published by the same staff in the same building, but, for some reason, they had different names.

My first effort was an entry in a citywide essay contest when I was in the sixth grade. My essay, which won first prize and was printed in one of the two papers, was "My Flag and What It Means to Me." I still have the original essay, which was written with a pen that had to be dipped in an inkwell.

The essay began with the Pledge of Allegiance as it was recited at that time, without the reference to God:

I pledge allegiance to the Flag of the United States of America, and to the Republic for which it stands, one Nation, indivisible, with liberty and justice for all.

Have you ever stopped to think what these words mean? Can you understand them? Do they mean anything to you? Or are you the kind that just stands with you palm on your heart, just standing, hoping you can hurry and sit down? When you're in a group, maybe you look around and smile at someone.

Most people don't stop to think what the words mean. If you translated the big words they might sound like this. To me, the words "I pledge allegiance to the United States of America" mean "I promise or agree to give loyalty and service which each person owes to his country to my flag of the United States of America." And the words "and to the Republic for which it stands, one Nation, indivisible, with liberty and justice for all" means to me "my nation is not capable of being divided or separated, and strives to make its people free and give justice to all."

Next time, just think what the words mean. It's your country. Think about it. Let's be one hundred percent patriotic.

—Tom Ecker, Irving School, Grade Six

Sixth grade was also the year I was introduced to track and field. In the spring, the high school track coach, Mart Brandes, visited Irving School to announce that there would be a citywide track meet for sixth graders, and Irving would be one of the four participating teams. The other teams would be the eastside public grade school, Lincoln, the Lutheran Children's Home grade school, and St. Paul's parochial grade school.

Because Coach Brandes knew my older brother Dick, who was on the high school track team at that time, he said I would be the team captain. Because of my shortage of sports prowess, some of our school's sports stars weren't very happy that I was the team captain. (One time while batting in an Irving baseball game, I struck out three times in the same inning.)

Since I was the team's captain, I selected the relay team, with me on it. Others selected their favorite events. On the day of the meet, we all showed up at Waverly's half-mile horse track, where the meet was to be held. As we readied ourselves for the big event, it began to rain and the meet was postponed. So far, it hasn't been rescheduled.

At that time, there was only one large truck in Waverly. It was owned by Ray Anderson, who was one of the largest men in town, weighing in at nearly four hundred pounds. If you wanted anything moved from one part of town to another, you called Ray Anderson. The truck had a metal frame behind the cab, with a canvas top and canvas sides, but it was completely open in the back.

During the summers, I would often join my buddies and spend time riding in the back of Ray's truck as it made its rounds around town. No one, including Ray himself, thought it was a dangerous practice. We just knew we had to hang on for dear life.

One day, not realizing it was an inappropriate question, I asked Ray how much he weighed. Without hesitating, he responded, "Two pounds short of a ton." I now realize that was probably his practiced response.

In the seventh grade, I taught myself to play my father's three-string ukulele. It was a tenor uke that he used to play on occasions when he and my mother would harmonize on a tune called "She promised to meet me when the clock struck seventeen." Actually, that probably wasn't the song's title, but I know it was the first line. My father's hands were quite small, so in order to reach all the necessary strings to make chords, he removed the fourth (top) string years before.

Later, when I realized the fourth string could be pretty important with certain chord changes, I added a fourth string to the uke. But since I had already learned to play using three strings, I had to use my thumb to cover the fourth string on many of the chords. It's a very unorthodox way of playing, but it works.

When playing the uke in front of people in later years, I would stop strumming and ask, "What's the difference between an onion and a ukulele?" The answer: "No one cries if you chop up a ukulele."

That year, my father bought an antique pump organ at a yard sale and somehow he managed to find a space for it in our tiny apartment. I used the organ to compose simple melodies by writing numbers on the organ's keys with a pencil. Then I could replay the melodies by following the numbers. Much of my early "composing" began this way.

But more importantly, I learned to play the organ, or any piano, with my nose. The nose-playing became a very popular party stunt. Someone in the crowd would announce that Tom could play a church hymn on the piano, using only his nose. Then I would proceed to play "Jesus Loves Me," which can be played using only black keys. It was a popular stunt that continued until the 1980s.

There was a "unique" business in Waverly at that time—Unique Chicks, which was located on West Bremer Avenue. The business sold newly hatched chickens to area farmers who raised them to maturity. We were told that it was not unusual for travelers to see the Unique Chicks listing in the Waverly telephone book and call the number, hoping for an exciting evening with one of the "chicks."

My seventh-grade year was best summarized by our health teacher, Mrs. Clatterbaugh. She said, "There's nothing ordinary about this class. The girls are all boy-crazy, and the boys are just plain crazy."

In the fall of 1948, I entered the eighth grade, which turned out to be a pivotal year in my life. During that year I developed a balancing act, which would keep me onstage for the next seven years, had my first short stories published in the local newspaper, wrote my first published song, and became serious about the sport of track and field.

During the first days of school, I decided to become a balancing artist. Bob Dotzauer, a student at Wartburg College in Waverly, was gaining all kinds of notoriety

Balancing a pencil on my nose with a rubber ball on top.

Balancing a chair on the chin in front of Wright's Greenhouse.

Balancing a lawnmower on my chin.

—19

because of his balancing act. He had been featured in Ripley's "Believe It Or Not" newspaper feature seven times. "Bobby, the Human Seal," as he called himself, balanced inanimate objects, such as pencils, ladders, and push lawnmowers on his nose or chin.

Balancing objects didn't look that difficult to me, so I taught myself to do all the same tricks Bobby was doing. In March 1949, he even had me come out of the audience to do a simple balancing stunt during one of his appearances at the high school auditorium in Waverly. After that, he was pretty cool to me. I'm sure he didn't think it looked good that a 14-year-old kid could do all the tricks he was doing. Not long after that, Bobby moved from Waverly to Cedar Rapids, where he worked for the YMCA.

The void left by Bobby's disappearance fueled my interest in expanding my balancing act. I added lines of patter and several comedy routines. In fact, the balancing act became the center of my show biz world until I was twenty-one years old.

During the winter, there was an assignment in English class to write a short story. I wrote about a pilot named White who was flying across Lake Michigan in his single-engine airplane.

A dense fog can cover several square miles of lake country in a matter of minutes. One day as White was flying over Lake Michigan, such a fog rolled in. White had nothing to do but keep his course and stay as level as possible. He judged that ten minutes would carry him into Michigan, but he had a slim chance of making a landing in such wooded country. He would just have to wait and hope for the best.

The N.A.A. was giving storm warnings over the radio. "I should be over Michigan now," said White as he decided to go down. He sailed slowly downward for a dead-stick landing but was surprised when he heard a loud splash and felt his plane lurch suddenly. Realizing he had landed in the lake, White climbed out on the wing. The fog was clearing, and his plane was sinking rapidly. To the east he could see Michigan's rough coast.

White decided he'd have to swim for it. The water was icy cold as he plunged in and started swimming toward the distant shore. As White was swimming along, he happened to think, "I can't swim." He drowned.

Miss Chittenden, the English teacher, thought the

ending was so funny that she had me read the story in all four classrooms on parents' night. Then, Charlie Gebhard, a columnist with the Waverly newspapers, printed it as part of one of his columns on December 1, 1948.

Two months later, Charlie Gebhard printed another of "Tommy Ecker's yarns," entitled "The Wildest of Dreams":

Many strange things can happen to the mind at night—strange dreams, visions and nightmares. The midnight wintry wind was howling outdoors like a sick mourning dove. Trapper White had started early to check his traps during the blizzard. He had found it necessary to enter an old abandoned cabin for shelter from the wind and snow.

He found some dry wood and built a cheerful crackling fire, which contrasted brilliantly with the bleak darkness outside. Having devoured a large slab of smoked venison, he sat with his back against a wall of the cabin near the fireplace for a comfortable nap.

White dreamed he was sleeping in the snow outside the cabin and that he was bitterly cold and slowly freezing to death. Waking abruptly from his horrible dream, he screamed, "Where am I?" Naturally, he was still in the cabin. The fire had gone out.

Sheet music for "Someone, Someday,"
which was published internationally in 1957.

My first real attempt at song writing came during that eighth-grade school year. The song was called "Someone, Someday," written originally by using penciled numbers on the keys of the pump organ, and then using the ukulele to create chords to support the melody. Of course, I had no idea at the time that writing the song was destined to become more than just a fun pastime. Eight years later, "Someone, Someday" was recorded and released internationally by Capitol Records in Hollywood.

I went out for the eighth-grade track that spring, with practices held at the half-mile horse track at the fairgrounds. On my first day of practice there, a high jumper named Bobby Campbell was practicing his straddle high-jumping technique. Bobby was a Wartburg College student, but he had to practice there because Wartburg didn't have a track.

I watched Bobby Campbell's every move and began trying to copy his technique. I wanted to become a high jumper. No one told me at the time that Bobby was jumping off his right foot, and that a right-handed jumper is supposed to jump off his left foot. So I was jumping from the wrong side, but it didn't seem to matter.

In early May, I fashioned a crude jumping area in our backyard where I could continue to practice jumping. However, on the first day at the new facility, I didn't see a small stump in the ground. I approached the crossbar and planted my foot on the stump, breaking a bone in my right foot. I was on crutches for six weeks, wearing a knee-high cast on my right leg. Somehow, that didn't keep me from taking Jean Redick to the eighth-grade prom. Her father referred to me as "Step-and-a-half" or "Glass Foot."

That year my parents bought a dog, a Springer Spaniel named Sam. Sam was loyal to the family—perhaps too loyal. One day, after we had had the dog for more than a year, it bit a neighbor. Without a second thought, my father had Sam put to sleep. When I complained, my father explained, "If a dog bites once, that's the dog's fault. If it bites a second time, that's the owners' fault."

During the summer after Bobby the Human Seal left Waverly, Lee Bros. three-ring circus came to town. It was the old Seils-Sterling Circus with a new name. An old-fashioned tent show, it traveled from town to town, with trucks hauling the animals and equipment, and house trailers serving as dressing rooms for the performers. They drove during the night, set up in the morning, did an afternoon and an evening show, and then tore everything down and packed the trucks for the overnight ride to the next town. It seemed like the ideal life to me at the time.

The morning the trucks arrived, the Bremer County Fairgrounds area was a beehive of activity as townspeople watched the tents go up. Boldly, I wheeled my lawnmower to the circus grounds and asked to see the boss. I was directed to a man who said he was the show's foreman. I demonstrated the lawnmower act, and told him I had always wanted to be in a circus. He asked me if I could balance the lawnmower while riding a bicycle. I said no, but I could do it while climbing up a stepladder. He said he'd give me a break, but he couldn't pay me. He had room for a short act in one of the side rings, and he said he'd give me a try.

So I performed the act during the afternoon show, and the circus people seemed to like what they saw. But word spreads fast in a town of 3,500 people. My father found out what I had done, and I immediately "unjoined" the circus. Although my circus life was short, that incident has given me countless opportunities to tell people I performed in a circus when I was fourteen years old.

7

Magic and Merriment

Of course, I didn't know it when I was a freshman in high school, but the sport of track and field was going to become a major part of my life. My sudden successes on the track my junior and senior years were a big surprise for my family and me. In the eighth grade, I was the second slowest boy in my class. When we had neighborhood foot races during the summertime, even the girls beat me. But sometimes it was pretty close.

I credit my athletic turnaround to a job I had at the local newspaper during my freshman and sophomore years in high school. On Tuesday and Thursday evenings, the newspaper would be printed. I had several jobs around the pressroom. One of them was to push a cart, heavy with newspapers, to the post office for mail delivery.

When the day was finished for most of the other newspaper workers, I ran two paper routes with a heavy bag of newspapers on each shoulder. By accident, I was using resistance training and interval training methods that were unknown to athletes at that time. And it was at a time in my life when the androgenic hormones were flowing. I was getting stronger and faster without knowing why.

That year, I became interested in magic when my father took me to Des Moines to see Harry Blackstone, the great illusionist, at the KRNT Radio Theatre. At one point in the show, Blackstone called for volunteers to help him with a card trick. Of course, I was the first volunteer onstage.

During the course of the trick, Blackstone, who was in his mid-60s at the time, suffered a mild heart attack. The curtain was pulled, and I was still onstage, with the other volunteers, amid the confusion as Blackstone's assistants came to his aid. He said he just needed some rest. One of the assistants took the volunteers back into the audience as the announce-ment was made that Blackstone would not be able to complete his show. In a few days, Blackstone had made a full recovery. We were able to see his entire show at a later date. (I still have the program.)

I was hooked on magic. I bought trick cards and other small illusion pieces and began to craft a magic act. I did a few shows, usually in the high school auditorium, for anyone who would attend. My best trick was having someone in the audience volunteer to mark a silver dollar, which I dropped into a glass of water. It disappeared, to the amazement of everyone standing around. Then my assistant, neighbor Ty Brooks, threw me an orange. I cut open the orange, and there was the marked silver dollar. It was my best trick, and it was an original.

At Christmastime, my older brother Dick gave me a present that changed my life in many ways. He presented me with a check. At the top of the check he had crossed out Waverly Savings Bank and substituted "Bogan Gun Shop." (Howard Bogan was a local barber and gun dealer.) The next line read "Waverly, Iowa 12-24-1949." The dollar amount was "1/2 gun," which was written out as "One half 410 shotgun." And it was signed Richard E. Ecker.

Brother Dick owned that single shot .410-gauge shotgun, and he wanted me to use it. That led to several years of tromping through the wooded areas around Waverly, hunting for rabbits and pheasants. It was an ideal gift for a fourteen-year-old.

During that winter, I took a job as an usher at the Waverly Theater. Armed with a flashlight, I would lead people, whose eyes had not yet become accustomed to the dark, to available seats in the theater. The job didn't pay anything, but it provided me with free passes to both the Waverly and the Bremer theaters. The Waverly Theater ran three first-run movies per week. The Bremer Theater ran three last-run double-features per week.

The Waverly track team was really good that spring, winning the Northeast Iowa Conference championship. The school yearbook describes the win as "the first time in many, many years that a Go-Hawk track team has won the title."

I was proud to be a member of the team that year, even though I didn't score any points. I remember that my father gave me some sagely advice. He said, "Run like you've never run before. Run fast."

I was one of only two freshmen who went out for the varsity track team that year. I'm the one who didn't earn a letter. But, fortunately, I didn't give up, largely because my older brother Dick told me I wasn't allowed to.

My sophomore year I went out for the freshman-sophomore football team and was immediately successful because I had suddenly developed a lot of speed. The coach played me at right halfback, and I was able to make big gains with end runs. If the defense moved their ends out to stop the end runs, they would run me inside the ends. I couldn't block or tackle, but I could run. In the first game of the season, I scored five touchdowns. (That sounds like an Al Bundy line from *Married with Children*.)

Our game at Osage was played on the night of October 31—Halloween. As soon as my ankles were taped and my football uniform was on, I put on my football shoes and helmet and left the school building. Then I went "trick-or-treating" all around the neighborhood. Several people commented on my clever costume. Later that night we beat Osage, 40-19.

During a home game against Oelwein, I met Al Baker, who was to become my best friend. Al was a freshman at Oelwein High School, a year behind me in school and thirty-one miles away. On one of Waverly's plays, the quarterback faked the ball to me as I ran straight ahead, and the ball was then pitched to the other halfback, who was running around the end. Al was a linebacker for Oelwein, and he tackled me as soon as I crossed the line of scrimmage. I jumped up, held my arms out wide to show him I didn't have the ball, and said, "Surprise!"

After the game, when Al was dressed in street clothes, he came to our locker room to find me. He said he wanted to meet someone who would say "Surprise" after faking out an opponent. Immediately, we became good friends.

On weekends, I would hitchhike to Oelwein or Al would hitchhike to Waverly. There were even times when Al would make extra money by working part time in Waverly. I taught him to play the ukulele and taught him the balancing act. We were a pretty good team. We even did a dual balancing act, appearing in a show in Monticello, Iowa. (We were billed as Al Baker and Jim Ecker.)

On weekends, we would hitchhike to many places around the state. There would always come a time when we'd reach a point where he'd have to head to Oelwein and I would go to Waverly. When we arrived at the intersection where we would part company, we would always sing, in harmony, "Now is the hour, when we must say goodbye." We would sing the whole song, but we thought the last line was particularly funny. We both pointed to the place where we were standing and sang, "When you return you'll find me waiting *here*."

Although I continued with balancing and magic, I had the opportunity to get into radio when I was sixteen. The radio station at Wartburg College, KWAR-FM, was looking for live programming, so I applied. The station manager, a college student named Bob Snyder, said he wanted me to write and perform in a radio variety show that he named *Super Novelty Revue*. My comedy partner was a Wartburg College student, Dick Camp. Handling sound effects were two other Wartburg students, Bob Gronstahl and Jim Lenguadoro. The deep-voiced announcer was my friend, Bill Wiederanders, who was a junior in high school.

We were broadcasting on FM, a wave length that had been introduced only twelve years earlier and was not yet popular. The station had only fifty watts of

It was easy to determine which homes were able to receive FM radio signals. The FM antennas had a unique look.

power, but our show was on the air, live, once a week. I told people that our signal carried for several miles, straight up, but our horizontal signal barely covered the town of Waverly.

Receiving FM signals required a special rooftop antenna in those days. It was an oval-shaped piece of tubing that was easy to recognize. We drove around town, noting which homes had FM antennas, thus identifying potential listeners. There weren't many.

Bill Wiederanders and I honored our benefactor, Bob Snyder, by forming an organization called "Snyder Radio-TV Productions." On our business cards, it said that we had offices in New York, Chicago and Shell Rock. We often made fun of Shell Rock, which was a town six miles west of Waverly. (Little did we know that someday Waverly High School would become Waverly-Shell Rock High School.)

I was the only script writer for Super Novelty Revue. The show's sketches parodied real-life situations, and we used many different voices and accents. We did song parodies, takeoffs on radio singing commercials, satirical takes on other radio shows, and any kind of sketch where we could use sound effects. My ukulele was the show's only musical instrument.

We modeled our program after two popular network radio shows of the time, *Bob and Ray*, featuring Bob Elliott and Ray Goulding, and lesser-known *Rayburn and Finch*, with Gene Rayburn (later of TV game show fame) and Dee Finch. We tried to get a sense for their humor, but we never copied any of their material.

My favorite Bob and Ray sketch was a takeoff on a radio mystery of the time, *Mr. Keen, Tracer of Lost Persons*, a show that was on network radio for eighteen years. The Bob and Ray version was called *Mr. Trace, Keener than Most Persons*.

There were two other popular mystery programs on network radio at that time. One of the weekly programs, *Mr. Chameleon*, was a series about a police detective who used various disguises to solve crimes. The other was *Hearthstone of the Death Squad*, featuring Inspector Hearthstone, who was always successful in solving murder mysteries. We combined the two ideas and did a program called *Chamelestone of the Hearth Squad*.

Two of the names we used in our scripts were Gladys Glockenspiel and Lou Schmedloe. I thought Glockenspiel and Schmedloe were funny-sounding names. We also used the word Fulano whenever we

could. Fulano is Spanish for "what's his name."

One of our sketches was called "The Question Man." After an introduction, I would ask three questions without providing any answers. For example, I would ask, "Great Scott, who wrote 'Ivanhoe'? Who in the Dickens wrote 'A Christmas Carol'? Who is buried in King Fulano's tomb?"

When I wrote the following sketch, I had never been on a commercial flight, nor had I ever seen an airplane ticket. In the sketch, I sent Lou Schmedloe (Dick Camp) to the airport to buy me a plane ticket. When he returned he said, "They have blue ones and green ones and yellow ones, but they don't have any *plain* tickets."

Another routine involved confusing the names Moran and Moron.

Dick: Let's see, Glockenspiel Insurance, Bates and Ryan Lawyers. My, there are a lot of doors. Hiccups Loan Service, Schmedloe's Finance Company, Gentlemen. (Long Pause) Oh, here it is, P.J. Moran, Private Eye. Walk in. (Door opens and closes) Are you P. J. Moron?

Tom: That's *Moran*.

Dick: Well, I've got a case for you.

Tom: Wait just a minute. I have to answer the telephone. (Telephone rings) Hello (pause). That's *Moran*. (pause) Yes, OK, goodbye.

Dick: What I came in here to say was I'd like you to follow my wife. She's been acting strangely lately, and I'm curious to find out why.

Tom: Consider it done.

Dick: Thank you, Mr. Moron.

Tom: That's *Moran*.

Bill: Two weeks passed and P. J. Moron's client ...

Tom: That's *Moran*.

Bill: P. J. Moran's client came bursting into the office. (Balloon pops)

Dick: You let my wife get away. You're nothing but a stupid, blundering Moran.

Tom: That's *Moron*.

A hit song of that era was "Slow Boat to China." The song begins "I'd like to get you on a slow boat to China, all to myself, alone." Since Waverly is on the Cedar River, I changed the lyrics of the song. "I'd like to get you on a slow boat to Waterloo, but there's a dam at Cedar Falls."

Newspaper columnist Walter Winchell was on

national radio at the time, hosting a news show that began with Winchell saying, "Mr. and Mrs. America and all the ships at sea." Then he would tap randomly on a telegraph key to add authenticity to his program. Our parody began with me saying, "Mr. and Mrs. America and all the ships on the Cedar." Dick would say, "Di-da-dit, di-da-dit." Then I would read some silly news items.

We even joked about our studio engineer, Wartburg student George Hanusa (pronounced huh-NOOSE-uh), at the end of one our shows. Our announcer, Bill Wiederanders, gave the names of everyone who was on the show, finishing with: "Our studio engineer is George Hanusa." I said, "George who?" Bill said, "Hanusa." Then I said, "Gesundheit," and we were off the air.

In our home, we had a piece of "high-tech" equipment—a reel-to-reel wire recorder. It was part of a console that also contained an AM radio and a 78-rpm record player. I used the wire recorder for my early recordings, including one of the earliest radio shows we did. I still have that show on a spool of wire but will never be able to hear it. The wires were thin, and they broke easily, so it was a relief when tape recorders came out.

I saved my money and bought my first tape recorder in 1951 when I was sixteen. I used it for the next ten years, recording just about anything one can imagine. I still have hundreds of tapes that were recorded during those years.

My father purchased an inexpensive second car, an imported Ford Anglia. Apparently, the local Ford dealer had to take two of the British-made Fords, the two-door Anglia and the four-door Prefect. The Anglia had four cylinders, ten horsepower, and a top speed of fifty-seven mph, although it was recommended that it not be driven over thirty-five mph.

Since I had already completed driver education, I got my driver's license on my sixteenth birthday. That evening I took the Anglia on one of many "spins" around town. The car could even make it to Shell Rock, but it was a very slow trip.

My schoolwork and grades continued to be average. Part of it was because I didn't pay attention in class, part of it was never doing any homework, even in study halls, and a large part of it was my terrible attitude. I didn't like school, and it was obvious to everyone.

The Ford Anglia, 1949

I'm not proud now of my attitude toward school at that time. One day I was tardy for school (even though we lived only two blocks away), and I was sent to the principal's office. The principal's secretary told me my punishment was to stay after school for an hour that day. I asked her what the punishment would be for being absent. She said there was no punishment for being absent. So I said, "See you tomorrow," and I went home.

There were twenty-eight on the track team that spring. The track coach, Mart Brandes, decided that I was going to be a hurdler. The high hurdles were thirty-nine inches high, so I would leap over a hurdle, take three bounding steps in between, and then leap again. (Actually there are four bounding steps, but for some reason in the track and field world, the first step isn't counted.) The low hurdles, only thirty inches high, were much easier to negotiate.

In a dual meet against Oelwein, I was walking toward the starting line for the low hurdles when I passed a group of Oelwein runners, including my friend Al Baker, sitting on the grass. I had a pencil behind my ear. I explained that it was my lucky pencil. During the race, I didn't quite clear one of the hurdles, and I tumbled onto the cinder track, causing abrasions on a knee and a shoulder. As I limped back to where the Oelwein runners were sitting, I said, "Anyone want to buy a lucky pencil?"

Waverly qualified eight athletes for the state championships. I barely qualified in both the high hurdles and the low hurdles but lost out in the preliminaries

—25

of both races at the state meet.

Throughout high school, I spent a lot of time writing radio scripts, but there was also time to co-write a humor column with Bill Wiederanders for the high school newspaper, The *Go-Hawk-Eye.* (Waverly's team name was the Go-Hawks. Iowa is the Hawkeye State. Thus the name Go-Hawk-Eye.)

The column was called "Sittin' In with Bill, Tom, and Sam." Bill and I would write short word-gags and would often make reference to Sam, a fictitious character. Sam's full name was Sam Bflspk (pronounced Cob).

After school was out that year, my father announced that the family members who were still at home would be taking a vacation trip. My parents had never had a vacation, so this was a big announcement. My parents, my two-year old sister Janet, and I would be traveling west in our 1949 Ford station wagon.

We left Waverly early on July 7 and took a frantic seven-day loop that took us to the Corn Palace, the Badlands National Park, Wall Drug, the Black Hills, Mount Rushmore, Yellowstone National Park and Old Faithful, Salt Lake City, including a visit to the Mormon Temple and a swim in the lake, and then home through Colorado and Nebraska. Our sixth and final overnight was in North Platte, Nebraska. Even though it was a long way, my father was determined to make it back to Waverly in one day. The total trip covered almost 3,000 miles on two-lane highways. There were no interstates in those days.

One of my best experiences on that trip was during our overnight stay in Steamboat Springs, Colorado. I was working out on the high school track, where I met a local high school student, Tony Montoya, who was just a month younger than I was. After the workout, Tony asked me if I'd like to go porcupine hunting as soon as it got dark.

Tony and a few of his friends picked me up at the motel and drove us deep into the nearby forest. He handed me a flashlight and we proceeded to hunt porcupines, not with guns, but with flashlights. We saw several before we quit "hunting." (Using the internet, I tried to find Tony after fifty-six years, but all I found was his obituary. He died in 2005 at the age of seventy.)

8

Crossing Stages, Finish Lines, and Borders

In my junior year, I was still doing the radio show and writing the humor column for the school paper, and I went out for the football team. But I dislocated my elbow practicing for the second game and was out for the season. This changed my life in two ways: I had to drop out of my typing class because of the injury. And I had to substitute a senior-level speech class, taught by John Nydegger, the drama teacher.

At John Nydegger's insistence, and since I had nothing to do after school each day, I tried out for the junior class play, *Dear Ruth*. I was cast as one of the leads, Lieutenant William Seacroft. Somehow I was able to learn my lines, and the play, which ran for three nights, was a success.

However, after the opening night, we had to make a number of script changes. Classmate Irving Borochoff, who played Ruth's clueless boyfriend, Harold Kobbermeyer, was being upstaged by potential boyfriend, Lieutenant Seacroft. As called for in the script, Kobbermeyer used a great deal of profanity to help voice his frustrations.

The next day we were told by John Nydegger that many of Irving's lines would have to be changed because of "public opinion." I didn't have to change any of my lines, fortunately, but poor Irving had to change many of his. He made the changes with little effort, and the new audiences had no idea that they were seeing a whitewashed version of *Dear Ruth*.

The radio show continued that season, but the name was changed to Variety Time. I still did all the writing, but we no longer used college students. Bill Wiederanders was the announcer, but he also participated in the sketches. And we added a great singer to the show, LaMone Eichler.

We pulled our best stunt that year. There was a freshman at Wartburg named Eddie Fisher. He wasn't the real Eddie Fisher, of course, but that didn't really matter to us. There was virtually no television at that time, so no one knew what Eddie Fisher looked like, but his songs were big hits on the radio.

One night on the show, I played an Eddie Fisher record, then interviewed our Eddie Fisher, and then played another Eddie Fisher record. When we got off the air, there was a carload of young women outside who wanted to meet Eddie. We ended up having a party at my house, with Eddie charming our new friends. But then it all ended. Someone asked Eddie to sing and, unfortunately, he did. We had to explain our prank.

One of our bits on the radio was based on my impersonation of gravelly voiced Louis Armstrong. It was the best impression I could do. Bill Wiederanders would ask me to do my impression of Bing Crosby. I'd sing "... on Blueberry Hill," sounding like Louis Armstrong. Then he'd ask me to do Frank Sinatra. Again, I'd sing "... on Blueberry Hill," sounding like Louis Armstrong. Then he'd ask me to do Louis Armstrong. I'd answer, "I'm sorry. I can't do that one." It wasn't great comedy, but it was typical of our radio humor in those days.

Early that spring, our drama teacher, John Nydegger, asked me to try out for a one-act play, *The Sisters McIntosh*. There were only three people in the play, two old women and one young man. Fortunately, I was cast as the young man.

At that time, the University of Iowa hosted a one-act play festival every spring. High schools from throughout the state entered the competition, which lasted six days, with performances each morning, afternoon, and evening. The sets were brown-colored flats that could be rearranged into the appropriate one-act sets between plays. The judges were drama professors from Midwest colleges and universities.

The Sisters McIntosh was a comedy about a young man who visits his two elderly aunts, but they don't believe he is their nephew. John Nydegger, who was a brilliant director, coached me on body movements and voice inflections that showed me he was a genius in his field.

After we had rehearsed the show for several days, Mr. Nydegger and his cast of three made the drive to Iowa City in Mr. Nydegger's new Dodge. Fortunately, our play was scheduled in the early evening, and we had a lively, responsive audience. Laughter is infectious, and we had an infected crowd that night.

After the play, our judge, who was a drama professor at the University of Omaha, met with John and the cast to discuss his review of the play. There were individual critique sheets for each cast member. On each sheet, there were three categories, with scoring from seven down to zero in each category.

The two girls, a freshman and a sophomore who had to play old women, scored twenty and nineteen. I didn't think it was fair since they had such challenging roles. In my case, I was cast as a nervous young man. I was young, and nobody could have been more nervous.

My score was twenty-one, and the judge had written only these words across the critique sheet: "Congratulations on a wonderful performance." My plaque reads: "1952 Outstanding Acting Award." The judge also asked me if I'd be interested in attending the University of Omaha on a drama scholarship.

On the track, my performances really turned around that year. I won most of my hurdle races and was a pretty consistent winner in the high jump. One day during track practice, our two coaches, Mart Brandes, who was near retirement age, and his rookie assistant, Jack Fisk, were watching the team warm up. Coach Fisk had the starter's pistol in his front pocket, when it suddenly went off, startling everyone, especially Coach Fisk. "That was pretty close to the family jewels," Coach Brandes remarked to all of us. "It's pretty important for Coach Fisk, but it wouldn't really matter much to me."

The big competition for me that season was the district meet held in Charles City, which qualified the first- and second-place finishers for the state meet. The district meet was an all-day Saturday competition. I was entered in three events—the high jump, high hurdles, and low hurdles.

My brother Dick, a second lieutenant on leave from the Army, attended the meet. He was always my biggest booster. Dick was about to be shipped out to Korea, so this was his last chance to see me run.

In the morning, we had qualifying heats in both hurdle races. I qualified for the finals in both. In the afternoon, the high jump competition began. On one of my early jumps, which required falling into wet, packed sand, I cleared the bar, but the side of my left foot hit the sand hard. I got up limping. I didn't know it at the time, but I had broken a small bone on the outside of my left foot. Without consulting with my coach, who was up in the stands, I scratched myself out of the rest of the high jump competition.

Later that day, when the high hurdle race was about to begin, I went to the starting line and scratched myself out of that competition, too. I knew that coming down on my aching left foot after clearing ten thirty-nine-inch hurdles would be unbearable. My coach, Mart Brandes, a rather gruff, no-nonsense person, had a different opinion. He called me over and "explained" to me that it is the coach's job to scratch someone out of a race.

That left only the 180-yard, low-hurdle race—my last chance to qualify for the state meet, which would be held two weeks later. The low hurdles were only thirty inches high, so my goal was to get through this race in either first or second place.

The race was run on a curve, which gave me an advantage, because I led with the left leg, unlike most right-handed hurdlers. It's much easier to hurdle on a counter-clockwise curve when leading with the left leg. My huge disadvantage was that I'd have to land on that aching foot eight times during the race.

When it was time for the low hurdle race, I went to the starting line. I still remember the race vividly. I didn't feel the pain until late in the race. I was in first place throughout the race, but had to cut my stride before coming to the final hurdle, jumping off my left leg, landing on the right. I had never alternated legs while hurdling before. At the finish line, I was still ahead, so I had qualified for the state meet.

There was no hurdling during the two weeks leading to the state meet. In fact, there was no running of any kind. Twice a day, my coach had me sit next to the whirlpool bath with my left foot dangling in the hot, swirling water. I had to miss the conference track meet, which was scheduled on the weekend between the district and the state meets.

The night before the state meet, I went to the junior-senior prom by myself. I stayed until 9 p.m., and then went home and went to bed.

The next morning, the coach drove his seven-year-old son, John, and me to Ames for the state meet. In the morning, I managed to qualify for the low-hurdle final race, which was to be held in the afternoon. I felt no pain in my foot.

When we were setting our blocks for the final, Coach Brandes, who by state meet rules was not allowed to talk to me before the race, sent his son down to wish me luck. I told him I'd do my damnedest. I later learned that he had reported to his dad that I said I would do my best.

As I was taking off my sweat clothes, I noticed a *Waterloo Courier* photographer stationed beside the first row of hurdles. Of course, I decided I had to be leading over that hurdle, in order to get my picture in the paper. The rest of the race didn't matter that much. I was a huge underdog.

When the gun was fired, I ran as hard as I could to the first hurdle. And, as planned, I was leading, but there were still 160 yards to go. I figured I'd stay out ahead as long as I could. I remember I could see runners, peripherally, on both sides of me at different times during the race. Several of us crossed the finish line together. It looked to me like a photo finish.

Here is the story that appeared in the *Des Moines Register* the next day:

A surprise victory came in the 180-yard low hurdles when Tom Ecker of Waverly won in 20 seconds flat. There was no one more surprised than Ecker.

He sped over the finish line and went scooting up the mound of earth on the outside of the track, apparently with a sneaking hunch he might have won the close race.

Then he turned and started talking to spectators near the finish line. He pointed to himself and shook his head from side to side. "Not me?" he said in disbelief. "Not me?"

Ecker, who cut a full second off his previous best time of the year, still was barely convinced when he saw the official placings.

"I couldn't have won," he insisted. "Look at all those good hurdlers in the race."

It was the first state championship ever won by a Waverly athlete. What a great way to end the year. It was a whole lot better than going to the junior-senior prom.

The summer between my junior and senior years was filled with wonderful travel experiences, including my first "international" trip. A neighbor and friend, Allen "Mutt" Miller, said he'd provide his car—a 1936 Ford—if I'd provide the gas and oil money for a trip to southern Minnesota to visit some of his relatives there. The car used more gas than oil, but not by much.

We visited the relatives for a short time and then decided to parlay that trip into a multistate excursion that took us from Minnesota to Wisconsin, and then back to Minnesota for a trek all the way north to Canada—Fort Frances, Ontario. I was hooked on travel, a bug that I knew would never leave my system. I was seventeen and had already been in four states and one foreign country.

I learned the previous year that hitchhiking—common in the 1950s—was the cheapest way to travel. But it could be slow. There were no interstates at that time, and the length of a ride was always unpredictable.

My first serious hitchhiking was later that summer, when a friend, Daryl Jaschen, and I took a trip from Iowa to Mexico to practice my Spanish. (I had taken a year of Spanish my junior year in high school.)

When my mother, who was surprised that I had parlayed a trip to Minnesota into a trip to Canada, heard of the Mexico plans, she said to me, "I hope you don't go too far into South America."

We rode on buses for most of the trip, but we managed to hitchhike some of the way. We were given a ride across the border between Laredo, Texas, and Nuevo Laredo, Mexico, in a pickup truck driven by a cheery Mexican named Rudolfo Garza Amaya. There was a large, new refrigerator in the back of the pickup. Rudolfo told us he was going to try to "smuggle" it across the border into Mexico.

Rudolfo taught us a valuable lesson that day while we were at the border, discussing his contraband with Mexican customs agents. "No matter how serious the situation is," he told us later, "always keep a smile on your face." He got the refrigerator across the border with very little hassle.

Rudolfo drove us through the city of Monterrey all the way to Saltillo, his hometown, where he dropped us off. Daryl and I spent the night in a cheap hotel, and then we began the long trek, hitchhiking and riding buses to get back home in time to begin our senior year in high school.

9

Senior Moments

Variety Time continued on the radio through my senior year. My two partners, Bill Wiederanders and LaMone Eichler, were now freshmen at Wartburg College, so we could continue working together. I still was the only script writer.

In all the time we did the radio show, Bill Wiederanders was never considered a singer. We did sing our opening number, "Side by Side," together, accompanied by my ukulele, but that was it. The irony of that played out ten years later when Bill was invited to sing at New York's Carnegie Hall. He played the part of Jesus in Bach's "St. Matthew Passion." (I told him playing the part of Jesus was like starting at the top. Where do you go from there?) One of the other soloists was Beverly Sills.

I started off my senior year as a football player. Since I was running well and finally had learned to block, the coach had me positioned at right halfback. But it wasn't to be. While warming up for the second game of the season, I received a punt near the sideline and, diving to catch the ball, I fell on one of the three-foot posts that were attached to either end of the ten-yard chain. The posts, which were unattended, were stuck in the turf on the sideline. The post went into my left groin and well into my thigh, and then came back out as I fell and rolled.

At first, I didn't know anything was wrong. But as I jogged back on the field, my left leg felt warm, and it appeared to me that blood was bubbling up from my white sock. I walked up to the coach, who was near the center of the field, and he walked me into the end zone and told me to lie down on the grass. He called for a doctor, and Dr. Vince Carstensen, who was attending the game, came down out of the stands.

When Dr. Carstensen pulled down my pants, I could see blood spurting into the air from the wound. He applied pressure to the area with his finger to reduce the bleeding until a stretcher arrived. I was taken to the nearby Mercy Hospital by ambulance, and I don't remember anything else until the next morning when I woke up.

The surgeon who put everything back together, Dr. Robert Bartel, told me his surgery team had worked well into the night. He also told me how lucky I was that the pole had only bruised the femoral artery. If it had punctured it, I would have bled to death on the football field.

I thought that was the end of my running career, and maybe even of my walking career. But after a week lying in the hospital bed, the doctor came in to see me one night. He told me to get up and walk over to a nearby chair, which I did. What a relief that was for both my father, who was there at the time, and me.

I was able to go back to school, but the football season was over for me. Actually, it was "over" for the rest of the team, too. They lost all of their remaining seven games.

In December, my friend John Chezik, who was an outstanding baseball pitcher for Waverly High, asked me if I would like to go to Florida over the two-week Christmas break. He said another friend, Don Hagemann, would drive his car, and we would all chip in to pay expenses.

John had signed a contract with a professional baseball team, the now defunct St. Louis Browns, and he had to report to training camp in Florida after the first of the year. That gave us two weeks to see a part of the country none of us had seen before.

We drove straight through to Florida, all the way to Key West. There John and Don caught a flight to Havana, Cuba, to spend the night. I couldn't afford the trip, so I slept on a beach in Key West.

On the way back, we stopped in Miami for New Year's Eve. Unfortunately, the Orange Bowl game was the next day, and no hotel rooms were available. A nice woman who was managing a small hotel provided us bedding so we could sleep on couches in the hotel's lobby.

The next day we dropped John off at the Browns' training camp, and we began the long drive back to Iowa.

After the Christmas break, I began running over hurdles in the gymnasium and was surprised there was no pain in my left groin. There were regular practices in the gymnasium, and once a week I drove the fourteen miles to Cedar Falls where I could work out on the Iowa State Teachers College indoor track.

The first track meet of the year was the State Indoor Championships in Iowa City. The coach entered me in four events—the sixty-yard high hurdles, the sixty-yard low hurdles, the long jump, and the high jump.

In the high jump, I passed all the early jumps until the bar reached five feet, six inches. That was cleared on my second jump. The bar was then raised to five feet, eight-and-one-fourth inches, which I cleared on the third try. No one else made that height, which made me the winner.

Next was the long jump competition. Long jumping was a new event for me. These would be my first-ever jumps in competition. The second jump was twenty-one feet, eight-and-a-half inches, good enough to win the event.

Long jumping was a new event for me.

Only two final races to go—the high hurdles and the low hurdles. I won the high hurdles easily in a record 7.7 seconds. The low hurdle race was close, but I pulled that one out, too, in a record 7.3 seconds. The result for the day: Four state indoor titles, all of them state indoor records.

By the end of the evening, I didn't feel very tired. Maybe that's because throughout the day I had run a total of only 360 competitive yards in preliminary and final races, had long jumped twice, and had high-jumped five times. It wasn't much of a workout.

Naturally, there was a lot of newspaper coverage. It turned out that this was the first time since 1926 that someone had won four events in a state track meet. The *Des Moines Register* named me the "Prep of the Week."

Beginning with that meet and throughout the season, the sports editor for the *Des Moines Register* kept referring to me as the "one-man track gang." I think he had used "one-man track team" in a previous year, so he was trying to be different.

A full-page spread in the *Waterloo Courier* had five photographs and the headline "ECKER DOESN'T EXPECT TO TRY FOR ANOTHER FOUR-EVENT SLAM."

The next weekend was the Northeast Iowa Conference indoor meet in Cedar Falls. It was pretty much the same story, except the Waterloo newspaper's headline was "ECKER BREAKS FOUR RECORDS."

The next meet for the Waverly track team was the Comet Relays in Charles City. However, Coach Brandes decided to send me to the prestigious Drake Relays in Des Moines instead, with Assistant Coach Wally Linn.

The Drake event was not just another track meet. Entered would be the best athletes from throughout the state in all four high school classes. In the high hurdles, for example, where other hurdlers had already run full flights of hurdles in competition, the *Des Moines Register* had me listed number nine in their pre-meet rankings.

Coach Linn and I left early Friday morning for Des Moines and arrived in plenty of time for the morning preliminaries in the high hurdles. After qualifying for the final race, to be held that afternoon, we checked in at the Savery Hotel in downtown Des Moines.

In the afternoon we drove back to Drake Stadium. Around noon it began pouring rain. By 2 o'clock, when the high hurdle race was to begin, the water on the cinder track was more than an inch deep. As we took our marks for the start, it was raining so hard I couldn't see the second hurdle, twenty-five yards away. When the gun was fired, I led all the way, winning in 15.5 seconds. It was considered a major upset.

After spending the night at the Savery, I was ready for the long jump, scheduled for 9 a.m. Saturday. The runway was so muddy, the result of the previous day's downpour, it was impossible to get a decent footing. My approach run was on the grass, next to the runway, with the final step on the take-off board before jumping. Somehow, I managed to jump twenty feet, five inches to win the event. (I love telling people that in more than one hundred years of Drake Relays history, counting high school, college, university and invitational athletes, no winning long jumper has ever jumped shorter than twenty feet, five inches.)

Sunday's sports page headlines included "ECKER DOUBLE WINNER" and "WAVERLY'S ACE HURDLER REMAINS UNBEATEN."

Our annual dual track meet with Oelwein was held in Waverly. It was a cold day, so the coach had me leave my sweat clothes on for my four events. We won the meet, 96 to 72. I won my four events without shedding my sweat clothes. My friend Al Baker scored three points for Oelwein when he finished second in the 880-yard run.

The following week, the coach entered me in three events in the Mohawk Relays in Mason City. (There

Winning my eighth and final state championship.

wasn't a low hurdle race in the meet.) The following week's headline in the Waverly newspaper was: "SAME OLD STORY: THREE EVENTS; THREE MORE ECKER TRACK WINS."

The district meet, which qualifies first- and second-place finishers for the state meet, was held in Charles City. I was back in top form, winning all four of my specialties. The *Des Moines Register's* headline was "WAVERLY ACE TOM ECKER AGAIN WINS 4 TRACK TITLES."

The conference meet was held in Osage on a very cold night. Again, competing in sweat clothes, I won my four events, setting three new conference records.

The state meet, held on the Drake University track in Des Moines, was another fun experience. Jack Mathews of Red Oak was favored in the high hurdles, but I was favored in my other three events. I started off my beating Mathews in the highs and setting a new state record. Then I won the long jump and low hurdles but finished second in the high jump. It was a great ending for a special track season.

Bill Wiederanders and LaMone Eichler, my partners in *Variety Time,* and I decided to produce a stage show, sponsored by the Waverly Amvets, to be performed in the high school auditorium in the spring. It was called "Tom Ecker's Variety Show."

One of the newspaper ads for the show read, "The best of local talent has been gathered together by Tom Ecker and molded into a show that promises to be one of the best ever put on by a local group. You can't miss on this one!" It was not only the best of local talent, it was probably the only local talent. We had a large number of performers.

Bill Wiederanders was the master of ceremonies, LaMone Eichler was the primary songstress, and I did my magic, balancing, and comedy acts. Also appearing were The Choralettes, a popular women's quartet from Wartburg College, the comedy team of Bobby Lane and Tiny Sonnenberg, the high school accordion trio, tap dancer Jim Hassman, the Junior Iverson Trio, Wartburg's Fred Voss, and the comedy team of Jerry Edmonds and Dan Stufflebeam. In the orchestra pit, directing pianist Janice Cave, was comedian Jim Ellison. Even my friend Al Baker came over from Oelwein to make an appearance on stage.

The show was well-attended and made some money for the sponsoring Amvets. Best of all, the audience seemed to really enjoy it.

Because we were "Depression[1] children," there were only sixty-two in our graduating class—the smallest number in many years at Waverly High. Our commencement speaker was Dr. Marcus Bach, a professor at the Interfaith School of Religion at the University of Iowa. Dr. Bach's remarks were challenging, and his jokes about religion were very entertaining. I remember that he said the word commencement means the beginning, not the end. He wasn't joking about that.

---

1. The Great Depression started in August 1929, when the economy first went into a recession due to a collapse in the banking system. The Great Depression lasted for approximately ten years.

10

'Hire' Education

In the fall of 1953, I enrolled at what was then called the State University of Iowa (SUI) on an Activity Scholarship. (In my four years in Iowa City, there was a lot of activity, but not much scholarship involved.)

Here's a breakdown on the particulars of the scholarship: The university provided my tuition and fees. I was hired by the university to do some nonexistent job (like winding the electric clocks in the Field House) to pay for my dormitory room. I was hired to peel potatoes at the D&L Grill in downtown Iowa City to pay for my meals. I sold programs (1,000 per game) at home football games to earn spending money. I had to pay for my books, which meant I rarely bought any.

Looking back on the experience, I think I was actually hired by the university to run on the track team.

Selling programs at football games was always a fun experience. My place to sell them was between the main parking lot and the stadium, so I had a lot of traffic. One of my pitches was: "Get your programs here. You can't tell the players and their salaries without a program." I also made reference to the university president, Virgil Hancher, whose picture took up a full page in every program. I would say, "Get your programs here. Every program has a full-size picture of Virgil Hancher, suitable for framing."

During my four years as a student in Iowa City, I was often asked why I selected Iowa. I always answered, "I was actually planning to attend Harvard, but I ran out of gas in Iowa City." (Ironically, sixty-one years later, I had an article, "Olympic Pride," published in the *Harvard Review.* That was the closest I ever came to Harvard.)

The University of Iowa is a member of the Big Ten Conference. There are now fourteen member schools in the Big Ten Conference, which shows we may be very good in sports, but we're not very good in math. Actually, there were only ten schools in the Big Ten

when I was on the track team. Iowa was the smallest, with about 10,000 students. (Today, Iowa is the third smallest, with about 33,000 students.)

My advisor at Iowa was a young professor, Dr. Sam Becker, who would later become a distinguished professor, and even had the Communications Studies Building named for him. Sam must have been a good advisor; I graduated in four years.

When I went off to college, as an entering freshmen, I had to take tests to determine how much skill and knowledge I had in mathematics, writing, and speech. If a freshman scored high enough marks, he could "test out" of the basic course in that discipline. Somehow, even though math was not one of my strengths, I tested out of math. I was considered a competent speaker and writer, yet I didn't pass out of those areas. I had to take Communications Skills (beginning speaking and writing) both semesters my freshman year.

One of my professors that first year was Dr. Russell Ross. His course, which was worth four hours of credit each semester, was called "Man and Society." It was Russell Ross who taught me why it was called the

My advisor, Dr. Sam Becker

34—

College of Liberal Arts. He spent much of his lecture time extolling the virtues of his favorite presidents, Democrats Franklin Roosevelt and Harry Truman. He never mentioned Republican Dwight Eisenhower, who was president at the time.

During the 1970s, long after I thought I'd seen the last of Russell Ross, I got to watch him regularly on local TV stations as he served as one of the experts during election returns.

There were many track and field transitions for me when I went to Iowa. In high school, I had been a high hurdler, low hurdler, high jumper, and long jumper. From high school to college, the high hurdles grew three inches, and I didn't. I could get over the forty-two-inch college highs, but I was too short to be very good at it.

The 180-yard low hurdles became the 440-yard intermediate hurdles—more than twice the distance I was used to, with hurdles that were six inches higher. And my high jumping and long jumping skills were just average by college standards.

My coach, F.X. Cretzmeyer, who insisted we call him Cretz, had a theory about runners: "Everyone is a quarter-miler until he proves otherwise." And, although I continued to practice hurdling and jumping during my freshman year, it was evident that I would eventually be a quarter-miler.

When I enrolled at the University of Iowa in 1953, there was an NCAA rule that freshmen were not eligible for varsity competition. We could practice; we just couldn't participate in competitions. That made for a rather dull year for those of us with more competitive spirit than sense.

The only way freshmen could be in any kind of track and field competition was through "postal meets." On a given day, two schools would run intrasquad meets, keeping track of everyone's times, distances, and heights. Then the two school's coaches would mail the results to each other. The final results would be posted on a bulletin board at each school. It wasn't very exciting, but it was all we had.

Another of Coach Cretzmeyer's ideas was to stage an intrasquad decathlon—a ten-event test of speed, strength, agility, and endurance. If someone wanted to compete in only one or two events, that was fine, but I decided to try them all.

The decathlon event that I knew the least about was the pole vault. When it came time to try it, I barreled down the runway, planted the pole, and managed to muscle my way over the crossbar set at eleven feet, before landing in the pit.

One of the other competitors was our best pole vaulter, Nick Piper. After my vault, Nick said to me, "Ecker, in pole vaulting, there are ninety completely different movements from the time you begin the run-up until you land in the pit. You're doing eighty-nine of them wrong."

We had a great crop of freshman runners that year—the best the school had ever recruited, we were told. We had several state champions from around the country, so the future looked promising for the Iowa track team. Yet, somehow, I was the only member of our class of trackmen who graduated in four years. Several didn't graduate at all.

My roommate was Jack Mathews, a hurdler from Red Oak, Iowa. We shared a large corner room on the second floor of the Quadrangle dormitory. We didn't always get along, so I spent most of my idle time with Whitey Perry, the sprint champion from Marshalltown.

My fields of study were theater arts and television production. The first year I enrolled in as many theater courses as I could, dividing my time between the theater and the television studio. One of my fellow drama students was Jerry Silberman from Milwaukee, Wisconsin. Jerry was an outstanding actor in many shows at Iowa. He later changed his name to Gene Wilder and was an outstanding actor in many movies in Hollywood.

Twice while I was a student at Iowa, I traded autographs with people I thought might become famous someday. (Of course, I thought I would become famous, thus the trade.) One of the students was Jerry Silberman, who indeed became a famous motion picture actor. The other was Frank Miller, who became executive producer of two early TV talk shows, *The Mike Douglas Show* and *The John Davidson Show*.

Of the three of us, I was the only one who didn't become famous. Even Alex Karras, who later lived down the hall from me in Hillcrest Dormitory, and was known mostly as an all-American football player at Iowa, became a noted actor.

I was in theater for only one year. Building sets and rehearsing shows in the afternoons conflicted with track practice, and since running on the track team was paying for my education, the track coach advised me to get out of theater.

So I left theater arts completely to concentrate on television production. I was still doing magic, comedy, and balancing shows in my spare time to earn extra money, but my goal was to become a television director. That way, I could still be in the entertainment business but would be assured of having steady work.

In the fall of my freshman year, I was selected to be a part of a television team that produced an educational program, *TV School Time.* The program was telecast live on WOI-TV in Ames. At that time, WOI was the only TV station in the state with the capability of doing live telecasts. We could do kinescope recordings at Iowa (a process that transferred TV images to 16mm film), but that was all we had.

At 4 a.m. every Wednesday, I would get a wake-up call from the show's director, Dr. Lewin Goff. A half hour later, I was picked up by Dr. Goff, his assistant, and Alice Kemp, a local elementary school teacher, who was the "star" of the show. We drove the 110 miles to Ames, always stopping for breakfast at the King Tower Café in Tama.

TV School Time aired live at 9:30 a.m. every Wednesday and ran for 30 minutes. One of the show's writers and producers was Bob Snyder, who had given me my start in radio when he was a student at Wartburg College in Waverly.

My role in the show was the puppet, Homer. I sat behind Alice's desk, out of the sight of the TV cameras, with Homer on my right hand. As Alice presented the day's lesson, Homer, with a falsetto voice, would make occasional ad-libbed remarks. The director told me Homer was supposed to bring some comedy relief to an otherwise dull program, but I'm not sure if it did or not.

On our trips to and from Ames, there was plenty of time to talk about many different things. One discussion was about a last name for Homer. I suggested he use my last name and be known as Homer Ecker (Home Wrecker). One of the guys thought we should name him Homer Sexual. Anyway, the show ran for ten weeks, and my only cost was missing my Wednesday morning classes.

One of the outstanding freshmen runners on our track team was a Canadian, Donnie Aitken from Toronto. He was an intellectual, had a keen sense of humor, and spoke fluent French. Donnie introduced me to the Englert Theatre and to "art movies," such as

Mr. Hulot's Holiday, The Belles of St. Trinians, and *Captain's Paradise.* Because of *Captain's Paradise,* I became an avid Alec Guinness fan.

Donnie asked me if I'd like to spend the Thanksgiving weekend at his home in Toronto. I had a weathered 1946 Ford coupe and said I would drive. Donnie Aitken, Rich Ferguson, also from Toronto, Al Baker, my friend who was a senior at Oelwein High School, and I made the journey to Toronto, stopping to see Niagara Falls on the way. We had a great weekend in Toronto. I learned that St. Clair is pronounced Sinclair and that you stand and sing "God Save the Queen" when a movie is over. Rich Ferguson decided to take a train back to Iowa City, which turned out to be a wise move. We had six flat tires on the way home.

During Christmas break that year, Alice Kemp, who had been the "star" of the WOI-TV program, and her daughter paid me to drive them from Iowa City to Phoenix and back. They were to visit Alice's son, who was a veterinarian at Arizona Downs, and they said I could stay there, too. I did stay there some of the time but spent most of the two weeks hitchhiking to various places I had never seen.

One of the places was the south rim of the Grand Canyon. What a sight it was. From that moment on, I've said there is no more spectacular sight in the world than the Grand Canyon. Iguazu Falls in South America runs a close second, but the Grand Canyon is still the grand champion.

From the Grand Canyon, I hitched a ride to Las Vegas, arriving on Christmas Eve. One of the young couples giving me a ride said we were headed for Lost Wages, Nevada. Actually, it wasn't a bad substitute name.

There was no Las Vegas strip in those days. What was later to be the strip was a highway with nothing on either side of it but desert. The center of entertainment and gambling was downtown Las Vegas. That's where I went.

I remember losing one dollar playing the roulette wheel at the Fremont Hotel and Casino. As I was leaving the Fremont, at about 11 p.m., a woman dressed in a Salvation Army uniform approached me and asked if I needed a place to spend the night. I told her I did. She said I could spend the night in their shelter and get a free bowl of soup in the morning. (Actually, I thought it would be pretty cool to spend Christmas Eve in a Salvation Army shelter.)

The shelter was within walking distance. When I arrived, I was led to a large, dimly lit room filled with bunk beds, with people asleep in most of them. My assigned bed was a lower bunk. There was no one in the upper bunk. Quietly, I sat on the bed, took off my shoes, and climbed in.

Shortly after falling asleep, I was awakened by an argument between a man and a woman, who were standing in the hallway outside the room. I heard the woman say to the man that he had violated the shelter's curfew. She told him he couldn't stay there if he was out partying and then coming in late.

The man responded that he hadn't been partying. He said he had been working, helping tear down a coin arcade for a man who was moving it to another town. There were further exchanges between the two. Finally, the woman said she would allow him to spend that night at the shelter. But she made it clear it was to be his last.

It turned out that the man was my bunkmate. He was a large black man, with a noticeable scar on his forehead. When he approached the bed, we talked briefly, in whispers, and he told me he had really been working that night, which is the only acceptable reason for coming in late. He had no other place to stay the next night, and he was visibly upset.

In the morning, the man and I had our bowls of soup and we parted company. My goal was to hitchhike back to Phoenix, and then to head south to Nogales, Mexico.

The trips to Phoenix and south to Tucson were uneventful. But then I got a ride from Tucson to Nogales with a man driving a large van. Packed in the back of the van were machines that were part of a coin arcade. When the driver told me he had moved the arcade out of Las Vegas on Christmas Eve, I asked him if a large black man with a scar on his forehead had helped him. He said yes he had, and he seemed surprised that I knew the man.

When I told him the story about the conflict at the Salvation Army Shelter, he stopped at the next telephone booth and made a call to the shelter in Las Vegas. He told the people there the whole story, and we assumed the problem had been solved for my former bunkmate.

I spent the night in Nogales, Mexico, sleeping behind a couch in a hotel lobby. The next day I took a bus one hundred and ten miles south of the border to Hermosillo, Mexico. After exploring the town, I got a room for the night at the Hotel de Anza. In a post-card home, I wrote: "Dear Folks, This is the hotel I'm staying in. Double bed, 4x6' window, dresser, big mirror, bed lamp, all bathroom facilities, closet, telephone—all for 22 pesos ($2.30)—Tom."

The next day I took a bus back to Nogales and then thumbed back to Phoenix.

While staying at the Kemp home in Phoenix that day, I began strumming my ukulele, which was always with me when I traveled. I was trying to write a new song, "Full Moon Above." The song had unusual chord changes, from minor to major and back, which was not easy for me, since I couldn't read or write music.

So the experimental strumming went on until Alice told me to "shut that thing up." That was the end of the strumming that day, but "Full Moon Above" was eventually finished. Three years later, it was published by Palm Springs Music in Hollywood and was recorded and released nationally by Capitol Records.

Another side trip was to Santa Ana, California, for a surprise visit to my Uncle John and Aunt Margaret, two of the greatest hypochondriacs I've ever known. They not only described all of their latest ailments, they took me to the backyard to show me where they each had their most recent heart attacks.

Uncle John told me that he had gone to the City Hall in Santa Ana that week to complain about the winding city streets. He asked a clerk where they kept the snakes. The clerk asked, "What snakes?" Uncle John answered, "The snakes you use to lay out the streets in this goddamn town."

After visiting several fascinating sights, including Disneyland, I arrived back in Phoenix for the long drive back to Iowa City. Those were two fun-filled weeks.

11

'No Underwear, Mr. Giles?'

The winter and early spring of my freshman year were mostly devoted to attending classes, running on the track, performing in a few shows, and going to Waverly on weekends. Whenever I'd arrive at home on a Friday afternoon, there would be a load of laundry for my mother to do. She called our apartment "The Eagle Laundry." I have no idea why.

There were occasional shows and stunts during the spring. Singer Bob Blitz, Al Baker, still a senior at Oelwein High, and I provided the entertainment for the annual MECCA Ball. The dance was for engineering students and their dates. (MECCA stands for Mechanical, Electrical, Chemical, Civil, and Aeronautical engineering.) I played the ukulele while Bob sang, and Al and I traded off doing balancing stunts.

I also provided the entertainment for the Farmer-Businessman's Banquet. I did my usual balancing act, which they called "Feats of Skill."

One of the annual campus activities was the MEBOC (Most Eligible Bachelor on Campus) contest. Each housing unit could nominate one candidate, who would campaign vigorously to try to win the title. Only coeds could vote, and the winner would be crowned during the Spinster Spree dance at the Iowa Memorial Union.

Bob Blitz, who was also a freshman in the television department, was chosen to be in the MEBOC contest by his fraternity, Alpha Epsilon Pi. Bob asked me to help with his campaign. To help publicize his candidacy, Bob asked me to balance a lawnmower on my chin and climb up a stepladder in front of Whetstone's Drug Store on the corner of Clinton and Washington. Of course, the stunt made the newspapers, complete with pictures, but Bob didn't win the contest.

I did take one weekend trip to Chicago because of my fascination with the late Harry Houdini and the possibility of adding "escape artist" to my list of entertainment achievements. I drove to Chicago and visited a private magic shop on Randolph Street, where I bought books on escapes, a set of handcuffs, a straitjacket, and a few other pieces of escape equipment. Escape routines were worked into my ever-evolving stage act.

The final month of the semester was spent preparing for another stage show to be performed in Waverly, this time named "Tom Ecker's All New Variety Show." Again sponsored by the Waverly Amvets, I enlisted the services of some pretty high-level performers who were students at Iowa, plus top entertainers from Wartburg College and Waverly High School.

There were many newspaper articles and ads about the upcoming show, plus placards were placed in store windows throughout town. One of the news articles said, "Tom Ecker, an entertainment favorite in Waverly during the years he was completing his high school career, will be back again on his favorite stage with a variety show Friday and Saturday."

My biggest headliner for the show was Walt Patterson, a sophomore from Nashville, Tennessee, who had won the Big Ten tumbling and trampoline championships that year. Walt was a natural showman. He and I had been making some extra money doing assembly programs at schools in the area, so we knew how to work together.

As an aside, it's interesting to note that Walt and his wife, Ruthie, later became the biggest circus performers in America. As part of the famous Zachinni Family, they were the closing act in the Ringling Bros. Circus for several years. Their act? They were shot out of a cannon twice a day, landing in nets at the other end of the arena. (At the time, I told Walt that it's hard to find a man of his caliber.) The original cannon, mounted on a truck so it could be transported easily, is now on display at the Ringling Museum in Sarasota, Florida.

Walt and Ruthie Patterson were shot out of this cannon twice a day when they performed with the Ringling Brothers Circus. Bruno Zacchini designed the cannon.

The Friday variety show was a bit rough, but we got through it. The Saturday show was going along smoothly until Walt began doing his tumbling and trampoline routines. Suddenly, out of the audience came a University of Iowa gymnast, Bobby Hazlitt, who took over the show. Hazlitt was a great entertainer and had the audience in stitches. I was angry at first but changed my mind when I saw the audience reaction.

The variety show was well received, and the Waverly Amvets made some money for their various projects.

During that summer, I worked as a glazer at my parents' greenhouse during the days, and played left field for a softball team on Tuesday evenings. During one of the softball games, I was chasing a pop fly to short left field and reached out with my right hand to try to catch it. The ball hit the end of my forefinger, breaking it at the first joint.

The next day, the doctor X-rayed the finger and put a cast on my right hand, with the forefinger bent to the palm, but with the other fingers and the thumb free. He told me I wouldn't be able to work for a week and that I should come back to see him the following Wednesday.

I packed a small bag, put a twenty-dollar bill in my billfold, another twenty in my other back pocket, and walked to the south edge of Waverly. My destination was Nashville, Tennessee, where I planned to surprise my good friend, gymnast Walt Patterson, who lived there.

Walt, who had a thick Southern accent, once spent a weekend in Waverly with me. My father asked Walt what his father did for a living in Nashville. "He's in the tar business," Walt drawled. My father thought he was in the road paving business. It turned out Walt was saying, "He's in the tire business."

My goal was to reach Burlington, Iowa, a town on the Mississippi River, by nightfall. My aunt and uncle,

Lavon and Bob Giles, ran the Giles Funeral Home in Burlington. They lived upstairs, over the home, and I knew they'd put me up for the night. Bob Giles was also the county coroner.

There was a long-standing family joke about my Uncle Bob, dating back to the 1930s. A murder case had been featured in a pulp crime magazine, featuring a suspicious drowning case in Burlington. The magazine's stories were based on true cases and used real names.

In the story, the county coroner, Bob Giles, was testifying about a woman whose body had been found floating in the Mississippi River. When he was asked how the woman was dressed, he said, "She wasn't wearing any underwear."

"No underwear, Mr. Giles?" he was asked.

"No underwear," said Mr. Giles.

Whenever a member of our family met my Uncle Bob, the standard greeting was, "No underwear, Mr. Giles?" And he would always answer, "No underwear."

It was after dark when I was dropped off at a gas station at the edge of Burlington. I walked into the station and asked if I could use the phone. The fellow behind the counter pointed to a pay phone on the wall. I didn't want to waste a nickel on a telephone call, so I asked him if I could use the phone on his desk. I explained that I had to call the coroner. Immediately, he handed me the phone.

When my Uncle Bob answered the phone, I said, "This is Tom Ecker, and I have a body for you to pick up." I explained where I was, and before long, Uncle Bob arrived in his car. As I got in the car, I said, "No underwear, Mr. Giles?" And he immediately responded, "No underwear."

We drove to the Giles' residence, where Lavon, Bob, and I spent the rest of the evening talking about family and laughing. So far, the trip was going as planned.

It took me all of Thursday and Thursday night to get across Illinois and Kentucky and into Tennessee. I remember being very tired. It isn't always easy to sleep when you're riding in someone's car.

One driver in southern Illinois dropped me off in the small town of Anna (population: 4,000). I could see a steam passenger train sitting at the railroad station, so I ran over to see if I could buy a ticket. I just wanted to ride far enough to take a nap, so I bought a ticket to Cairo, the southernmost town in Illinois.

As soon as the train started moving, I fell asleep.

When I woke up, the train was coming into Fulton, Kentucky, some forty-five miles past Cairo. That was fine with me, since that put me forty-five miles closer to Nashville. But the conductor was insistent that he get me on the next train going north to Cairo. I still have the note the conductor wrote to get me on a northbound train: "7-27-54, Condr No. 16. Please return psgr to Cairo. Brought by C 717. BPH"

From Fulton, I hitched a ride to Waverly, Tennessee, where I used the bus station's restroom early that morning. But I went into the wrong restroom—not the women's, but the "colored" men's restroom. Everyone in that room stared at me, but no one said anything. That was my first, but not my last, experience seeing racial segregation up close.

I arrived in Nashville, called the Patterson number, and Walt's mother answered the phone. "Walter's not here," she said, "he joined the Shrine Circus." She checked Walt's schedule and told me he would be in Toledo, Ohio, on Saturday. That would give me a couple of days to get to Toledo, in northwestern Ohio, before heading home.

I began thumbing northward and almost immediately got a ride with a trucker from Massachusetts, whose rig included a refrigerated semitrailer. He had delivered half his load of boxes of fish in Nashville. He was headed north for Lexington, Kentucky, to unload the other half. He said I could ride with him to Lexington, and he would pay me if I would help him unload the fish there.

We arrived in Lexington mid-afternoon Friday, drove to the warehouse, and began unloading boxes of fish, under the direction of a warehouse supervisor. When we finished unloading the fish, the driver paid me for my help, and then asked the supervisor for payment for delivering the fish. The supervisor refused, and the two of them got into an argument that turned into a shoving match. I got involved to try to break up the fight, and my only pair of pants were split from the crotch all the way down the pant leg.

I grabbed my bag and left the two, still arguing, as I tried to locate someone who could sew up my pants. I found a small tailor shop, but the front door was locked. I saw someone inside, so I knocked on the door. When the tailor came to the door and saw my dilemma, he sewed up my pants for me and didn't charge me anything.

By the time I got to the north side of Lexington, it was getting dark. It was three hundred miles to Toledo, but I had all night to get there.

There was a small ice cream parlor on the corner where I was hitchhiking. And behind the counter was a beautiful young woman. So I alternated trying to get a ride to Toledo with going into the ice cream parlor to chat with her. The conversation revealed that she was a college student, and this was her summer job.

The minutes turned into hours. It was approaching 10 p.m., and there hadn't been much traffic, so the hitchhiking didn't look very promising. It was nearing closing time, so I went into the ice cream shop once again. The young woman told me her parents were out of town, and, if I couldn't get a ride, I could spend the night at her house. I took her up on the offer, but I agreed I'd go back out for one last hitchhiking try. And wouldn't you know it, I got a ride immediately with a family going all the way to Toledo.

It was early Saturday morning when we arrived in Toledo. I asked the family if they would drop me off at a cheap hotel, where I could freshen up and take a nap. Then I would go to the circus grounds to find Walt. I would keep the hotel room overnight, and then start heading back to Iowa on Sunday morning.

In the afternoon I walked to the circus grounds and immediately found Walt. He told me he got additional money if he would do extra jobs besides the acts he was performing in the show. We had a nice long chat, and he got me a pass to see the show that night. The show was great, and Walt was his usual "hammy" self. Then I went back to the hotel to get a good night's sleep before heading for home.

On Sunday morning, I got a ride from Toledo to Maumee, a suburb of Toledo, just south of the city. After standing by the side of the road for a few minutes, a man pulled his car over and rolled down his window. He told me he was in a hurry to get home, and that he'd pay me to help him drive his car. "OK, where are we going?" I asked. He responded, "Alexandria, Louisiana." It was way out of the way, but I had never been to Louisiana, so I agreed to help him out.

We alternated driving and sleeping in the back seat until we arrived in Alexandria late Monday morning. I had to get back to Waverly to see the doctor Wednesday morning, so I had to head straight back to Iowa. But the only rides I could get kept heading me northwestward instead of due north. On Tuesday morning, I found myself in Oklahoma City.

There I learned from the locals that there weren't many successful hitchhikers in that area at the moment. An ax-murderer had hitched his way through there recently, and hitchhikers were not considered very trustworthy. So I stood by the side of the road for several hours, watching the cars go by.

Finally, a car with Wisconsin license plates pulled over. Obviously, the driver didn't know about the ax-murderer. He told me he was driving back to Wisconsin. He said he usually takes a southern route, through Missouri and Illinois, but if I would help him drive, he would go through Iowa. Just after midnight on Wednesday morning, he dropped me off in Cedar Falls, Iowa, just fourteen miles from Waverly.

I decided to walk the rest of the way home, but as I walked along Highway 218, a high school classmate, Berdine Mehman, was driving from Cedar Falls to Waverly. She recognized me and gave me a ride home. I climbed into bed and slept. My mother woke me up in time for me to go to the doctor. When I arrived at the doctor's office, he checked my finger and asked if I had an interesting week. "Yes," I answered, "a very interesting week."

12

The Ultimate Hitchhiking Trip

There were many changes when I enrolled at Iowa for my sophomore year. My new roommate was Larry "Whitey" Perry, a state champion sprinter from Marshalltown, Iowa, who had a keen sense of humor. And we were moving into Hillcrest Dormitory, across the street from and a step up in quality from the Quadrangle, my home for the freshman year.

My first assignment at Iowa that fall was to be part of the entertainment for freshman orientation. The stage was set up on the north side of the Memorial Union's ballroom, and the freshmen were all seated on the floor. Dressed in gold and black, I did some comedy and balancing, finishing with the lawnmower act.

I had made enough money during the summer that I could afford the additional cost of Hillcrest, which, unlike the Quad, included meals. (My grant-in-aid paid for tuition and room, but not board, so my meals, which I paid for, were in the Hillcrest cafeteria.)

Early in the year, I had a run-in with one of the freshman football players. It was easy to recognize the football jocks on campus. Most were quite large, and many of them, particularly freshmen, wore brown T-shirts with "Property of Iowa Athletic Department" printed on the front.

One evening, I was sitting in the Hillcrest dining room with my photographer friend, L.W. Ward. Across the table from us were two freshmen wearing brown athletic department T-shirts, obviously football players. The larger of the two said, "This fucking food tastes like shit." Then he repeated the line, with more emphasis.

I looked across the table at him and asked, "Are you paying for this food?" Of course, I knew he wasn't.

He glared at me, pushed his chair away from the table, and said, "Let's go outside and settle this."

I turned to Ward, who was slowly inching himself away from me, and I said to him, "This is just like Jack Bremen." (Bremen, also a football player, had been kicked out of school for picking fights.) The angry football player, who obviously didn't know the Jack Bremen story, was even angrier. He again challenged me to join him outside for a fight, which I wasn't about to do.

Finally, the football player cooled off, and he and his buddy left the cafeteria. Later, I learned the angry football player was a freshman, Alex Karras, who later became a two-time All-American football player at Iowa and was three times All-Pro with the Detroit Lions.

As I look back, I find it ironic that Alex Karras was obviously destined to be a big-time jock, and I had my eyes set on making it big in show business. As it turned out, he became a movie and television star, and I became a coach and athletic director.

Whitey Perry and I were pleased that we would finally be eligible for varsity competition that year. But

Sprinter Larry "Whitey" Perry

Photo by Joe F. Jordan

Arriving in Greenville, South Carolina

we'd have to wait for one more semester when the track and field season was to begin. We continued to work out on the indoor track in the Field House, and on the outdoor track, which was immediately east of the football stadium. But serious training wouldn't begin until after the Christmas break.

When we practiced in the Field House, Whitey and I had a favorite stunt. We would pick out our "sucker," usually a freshman track man, and tell him Whitey was the fastest man in the state. So fast, in fact, that Whitey would give anyone a ten-yard head start in a fifty-yard dash. We always had a taker.

We had a set of blocks on the starting line and another set ten yards behind the line. With starting gun in hand, I would call the runners to their marks, then say "Set," but before the gun was fired, Whitey would start running. Just before he reached the starting line, I fired the gun. Sometimes Whitey would have to keep running to stay ahead of the angry guy we had tricked.

In October, I was involved in the most publicized hitchhiking trip I ever took, and perhaps the most-publicized hitchhiking trip anyone has ever taken.

One evening, Whitey and I were discussing our travel experiences. I told him I had been in all of the forty-eight states—this was before Alaska and Hawaii joined the union—except Washington, Oregon, North Dakota, North Carolina, and South Carolina.

He asked me if I thought I could hitchhike to North and South Carolina over the Thanksgiving

break without missing any classes. That would be too easy, I told him. I could do it over a weekend.

He bet me five dollars I couldn't and said he'd throw in a steak dinner at the nearby Amana Colonies if I could make the 2,000-mile trip the following weekend. Some other students wanted in on the bet, so the total bet was ten dollars and a steak dinner. One of the other betters was John "Sky" Marschall, whom I hadn't met before but who has since become a life-long friend.

My friend, L.W. Ward was a film cameraman at KCRG-TV in Cedar Rapids. In order to help publicize the upcoming trip, Ward introduced me to two KCRG newsmen, Tom Pettit and Joe Bartelme. The two newsmen thought the hitchhiking adventure would provide a weekend of great TV news stories. They wanted to help in any way they could.

(Both Tom Pettit and Joe Bartelme later became award-winning television reporters at NBC News. Pettit, who won three Emmys and a Peabody Award while a reporter with NBC, was most famous for holding the only live microphone when Jack Ruby killed Lee Harvey Oswald in Dallas in 1963. Bartelme, vice president of NBC News and also a Peabody Award winner, was best-known for his successful revamping of *The Today Show* format and staff in the 1970s.)

It was agreed that I would take only one dollar with me, to ensure I wouldn't take any buses or trains, and that I would send a postcard to Whitey Perry on my arrival in South Carolina. The card was to be proof that I'd made it.

As it turned out, there was no need for any kind of proof. The Associated Press followed the story for the entire weekend. I hadn't expected the trip to be so well-publicized. I later learned that the nation was watching "the hitchhiker's" progress in newspapers and on radio and television around the country.

Later, people I didn't know sent me dozens of newspaper clippings from all over the country, including one from Anchorage, Alaska. I even received a clipping from a Long Beach, California, newspaper. It was sent in an envelope addressed to "The Hitchhiker, SUI." There was no name, no address, no city, and no state, yet it got to me.

I left from the east edge of Iowa City after my last class, at 11:30 a.m. Friday, October 8. To win the bet, I had to be back for my first class on Monday, October

11, at 8:30 a.m. It's important to note there were no interstate highways in those days. Most of the travel would be on two-lane highways, often having to slow down in small towns along the way.

Newspaper reporters, photographers, and TV cameramen were there to cover the start of the adventure. Here is a sampling of the first day's headlines in newspapers from around the country: Carolina, Here I Come; A Fast Man: Ecker Plans 2,000 Mile Hitchhike on Weekend; Good Trick if He Can Swing It; Will Thumb 2,000 miles to Settle Wager; Trackman at SUI Plans 2,000-Mile Race with Time; I'll Do Anything on a Bet; SUI Student Plans 2,000 Mile Weekend Hitchhike; Iowa Student Starts Long Trek to Greenville, S.C.; Student Starts 2,000 Mile Trip to Win Bet.

My first ride, from Iowa City to Davenport, was in a 1954 Packard. The driver knew I was the well-publicized hitchhiker, so he decided to drive between 95 and 100 miles per hour to help my cause. There were no speed limits on the open highways in those days. The posted speed limit throughout the state was "Reasonable and Proper."

Along the way, almost everyone who gave me a ride knew who I was. Some people even drove out of their way to make sure I'd be in a good place to catch the next ride. A little after midnight I reached Louisville, Kentucky, and was walking through town. Three GIs came out of a bar across the street, and one yelled to me, "Are you the hitchhiker from Iowa?"

Photo by Joe F. Jordan

Being kissed on the cheek by Rankin Suber, Miss South Carolina

Photo by Joe F. Jordan

Chatting with Officer Tinsley
of the Greenville Police Department

From Louisville, I got rides that took me across Kentucky, Tennessee, a corner of North Carolina, and into South Carolina. When I arrived in Greenville, it was 10:45 Saturday morning. I had averaged about a hundred miles a ride at a speed of almost 43 mph.

I was met at the edge of Greenville by a police officer, newspaper reporters and photographers, and a TV cameraman. After being interviewed and having many pictures taken, Jim Burns, the TV cameraman, gave me a ride to his station, WFBC-TV, for a live interview.

When the interview was finished, two photographers from the *Greenville News* drove me to Sirrine Stadium, where Furman University was hosting the South Carolina football team at 2:30 that afternoon. At the stadium, they wanted to take me down on the sidelines before the game started. I didn't need a ticket since everyone seemed to know who I was.

The reason they were so eager to get me down on the field became obvious once I got there. They wanted me to pose with Rankin Suber, a South Carolina cheerleader who had finished third in the Miss America contest earlier that year. They took pictures of Ms. Suber kissing me on the cheek, welcoming me to South Carolina. The picture, which became an AP wire photo, appeared in newspapers throughout the country. In the accompanying AP story, I was quoted as saying, "The kiss was the highlight of my brief stay in South Carolina."

Then the newsmen gave me a ride to the edge of town, one of them gave me $3 and said "Eat well," and I was back on the road. The Greenville newspaper wrote: "With a comfortable forty-three hours remaining on his schedule, he thumbed out of Greenville at 2:30 p.m., with confidence that he would be in class at 8:30 Monday morning to win his bet."

The trip back was considerably slower than the trip out. The first nine rides averaged only seventeen miles a ride, averaging barely fifteen miles per hour.

The car that picked me up in Greeneville took me only nine miles to a place called Traveler's Rest. It was my shortest ride of the entire trip, and appropriately, I was a traveler resting there for the next hour-and-a-half, waiting for the next ride.

From Traveler's Rest to Henderson, a distance of forty-one miles, the ride was in an old Chevrolet. There I was picked up by a new car that the owner was breaking in. We traveled a steady thirty-five miles per hour for the next twenty-one miles as he broke in the new car's engine. As we approached the city of Asheville, N. C., the car was involved in a minor collision with a truck. Then, the following driver, in a 1947 Kaiser, took a wrong turn, got lost in the hills of North Carolina, and we had to backtrack. Things were not going well.

The next driver took me into Tennessee but dropped me off at midnight at a lonely country spot, where I waited two hours for a ride.

Then my luck changed. A soldier stopped and gave me a ride in his 1952 Plymouth, all the way to Highway 6, just south of Chicago. It was a five-hundred-fifty-mile ride, and I slept for six hours and even drove part of the way for him while he slept.

The area south of Chicago was experiencing a great deal of flooding when we arrived there, so we had to follow a number of road detours. There was one more short, three-mile ride before I was picked up by the superintendent of schools in Cresco, Iowa, Abner Hendrickson, who drove me all the way to Iowa City. Abner and his wife bought me a meal on the way, took many pictures, and asked if they could keep my hitch-hiking signs as souvenirs.

At the meal stop, I called ahead to my roommate, "Whitey" Perry, and told him to meet me at the Dean Jones Texaco gas station on Burlington Street. He notified the press, and there were several reporters and photographers waiting when we pulled in. It was only

5:57 p.m. Sunday. My trip back to Iowa had averaged only 22 mph, but the arrival in Iowa City was still more than twelve hours ahead of schedule. I arrived back in Iowa City with ninety-four cents in my pocket.

We posed for photographs as Whitey paid off the bet. Then I decided to walk the few blocks across the river to Hillcrest Dormitory, where Whitey and I lived. As I was walking on the Burlington Street Bridge, a city bus stopped next to me, the driver opened the door, and he said, "I might as well get in on the act, too. Get in." So my final ride was on a city bus, all the way to Hillcrest Dormitory.

As I slept that night, some of the fellows at Hillcrest were listening to a late night disc jockey on KDKA in Pittsburgh. The disc jockey wondered aloud if that hitchhiker from Michigan had made it back. One of the guys called the disc jockey to set him straight, and the DJ apologized on the air and corrected his error.

A few days later, the following editorial appeared in the Greenville, South Carolina, newspaper:

A Lad with a Will

Where there's a will, there's a way.

That's what Tom Ecker, University of Iowa sophomore found to be true as he successfully hitchhiked from the university campus to Greenville and back the past weekend on a small wager.

Young Ecker evidently had a way to get a way. His phenomenal success at catching automobile or truck rides over the 2,000-mile course he set for the episode stamps him as a young man of exceptional initiative, plus a personality that surely must have served him in good stead.

The fact that he got around in Greenville long enough Saturday before starting his 1,000-mile return trip to get a buss on the cheek from Miss South Carolina bespeaks his evident ability to get along in life to his express advantage.

The heaviest cost to the young man seemed to have been sleep, but what's sleep to a healthy young man of 19, out to show the world he can win a $10 bet and a steak dinner!

The country probably needs some more Tom Eckers, young men who are a bit brash and find life enticing enough to challenge their paces under untried circumstances.

If they are as well contained and balanced in handling themselves as was the Iowa University lad in his impromptu swing south and back, they will serve as a tonic for the rest of us.

13

On Blueberry Hill

On Thanksgiving Day 1954, the Iowa cross country team sponsored a special race on the Finkbine golf course. The four-mile race was called the "Turkey Trot." Any student could enter. The prizes were a turkey for first, a goose for second, and a chicken for third.

I wasn't a cross country runner and had not trained for such a long run, but Coach Cretzmeyer encouraged me to enter. He told me to stay with a black freshman runner named Deacon Jones. (No one had bothered to tell me that Deacon Jones was one of the best distance runners in America. He ended up representing the United States in the Olympics in 1956 and 1960.)

For the first part of the race, I kept up with Deacon, but as the race progressed, I realized I couldn't keep up the pace. I faded and finished dead last. I didn't win a turkey, a goose, or a chicken. After the race, I was presented with a goose egg.

There was another experience that fall that was unusual. During my radio days in high school, I tried to do impressions of many actors and singers. But my best impersonation, by far, was of gravelly-voiced Louis Armstrong singing "Blueberry Hill." Usually, I would just sing the last line, "…on Blueberry Hill," followed by Louis' signature finish. I was told I sounded just like him.

In 1954, Louis Armstrong's band was playing the Riviera Ballroom in Janesville, Iowa, a little town about seven miles from Waverly. In those days, bands performed for dances, not concerts. It was rare for anyone at the dance to pay much attention to the band, except to listen.

My friend from college, "Sky" Marschall, and I, along with two high school girls we were dating, attended the dance that night. Between songs, Sky got the attention of the band's trombone player, Trummy Young. Sky told him that there was a guy in the audience who sounded exactly like Louis when he sang "Blueberry Hill." Trummy invited us to join the band backstage when they took their next break.

So, Sky and I went backstage where Trummy Young introduced us to Louis Armstrong. Louis was very friendly and gracious. He said he would call me out of the audience during the next set, to sing "Blueberry Hill." We noticed that Louis had large round scars on his lips, in the shape of a trumpet's mouthpiece. Obviously, there had been times in his career when he had played the trumpet until his lips bled.

The band members were all smoking and were pouring themselves large shots from a bottle of whiskey. It was definitely a time for them to relax.

During the next set, Louis called me up out of the audience. When I got to the microphone, the band began playing the familiar opening notes of "Blueberry Hill." As I began singing, the people on the dance floor stopped dancing and became an audience.

At one point, I pulled a white handkerchief out of my pocket and wiped my brow, as Louis always did. When we reached the place in the song when Louis would stop singing and play his trumpet, he was laughing so hard he couldn't play. We all had a great time.

One night, years later, long after Louis had died, I was in a hotel in Honolulu and saw that Trummy Young and his band were playing in the hotel's rooftop ballroom. I went up to the ballroom and immediately recognized Trummy on the bandstand. When that number was finished, I walked up to Trummy. He said, "I remember you. You're the guy who sang with Louis Armstrong." Trummy Young had a good memory.

One of my pet peeves when I was a student at Iowa was the expression "Giving 110 percent." Anyone who understands basic math knows you can't possibly give more than 100 percent, and the actual percentage is probably much lower. So one weekend that winter, after I had driven back to Iowa City from Waverly in a blinding snowstorm, I announced to the guys in the dorm that the roads were 110 percent snow-packed. No one questioned me.

The indoor track season began in March with an intrasquad meet on the Field House 220-yard track, pitting the freshmen-juniors against the sophomore-seniors. I won the 440-yard run in 51.1 seconds, but the sophomore-seniors lost the meet.

We were heavily favored in our next indoor meet against Marquette. It was during this meet that I was introduced to the "hip-bath recovery." Candidates for master's degrees in physical education were often looking for athletes to be the subjects of their master's theses experiments. Often, I participated in these experiments for the sake of academia, but none was stranger than the "hip-bath recovery."

It was explained to me that German pilots, near the end of World War II, had to fly repeated missions

Photo by University of Iowa Sports Information Service

Running the Open 440 on the indoor track in the Field House.

without any rest. Germany simply didn't have enough pilots. So they devised a method of recovery between missions by having the pilots sit in tubs of ice water. The secret, I was told, is freezing the area of the body's lower abdomen.

Normally, I would be in the open 440-yard run and then run a leg of the mile relay. The amount of rest between the two races was fifty-five minutes, plenty of time to recover completely. But in the meet against Marquette, I was told I was going to be in the open 880-yard run and then be the leadoff runner in the mile relay. There was only one short race between the 880 and the relay, giving me less than twenty minutes of rest, not nearly enough recovery time.

In the meet, I won the 880. As soon as I crossed the finish line, gasping for air, I was led quickly to the adjoining training room. There, a team of researchers had me lie down on a training table. They pulled down by running shorts and placed two bags of ice water on my lower abdomen. It was a very uncomfortable experience, especially when one of the ice bags sprang a leak with ice water running into the small of my back.

After fifteen minutes of "recovering," I was back on the track, warming up for the leadoff leg of the mile relay. When the starter had us take our marks, I jumped the gun deliberately, to give myself another few seconds of recovery time. I don't remember the race at all. All I know is that I ran the fastest relay lead-off leg of my life. I do remember that my vision was distorted immediately after the race, but that soon corrected itself. The hip-bath recovery worked, but I wouldn't recommend it to others.

The next meet was an indoor triangular competition at Illinois. We finished second to the host Illinois team, but we beat Ohio State. In the 440, I finished second to Ralph Fessenden of Illinois, one of the top quarter-milers in America. Fessenden came from behind on the final leg of the mile relay to beat me, too, running a blistering 47 flat quarter-mile.

After the meet, Coach Cretzmeyer told us to hurry and shower so the bus wouldn't be too late getting back to Iowa City. Whitey Perry, who had finished fourth in the sixty-yard dash, and I showered hurriedly and went to a nearby store to buy a case of Coca-Colas. Then we put the Cokes on the bus. As soon as we were on the road, we offered the Cokes for sale to anyone who was thirsty (which was everybody) at a

—47

considerable profit.

Next on the schedule was the Big Ten Indoor Championships in East Lansing, Michigan. We traveled by train, my first experience in a sleeper car. In the meet I managed to qualify for the 440 finals, but the next day, I was squeezed into fourth place after breaking for the pole and couldn't improve my position.

The next week we traveled to Milwaukee, Wisconsin, for the *Milwaukee Journal* Games, a competition on a banked, board track in a large arena. In the mile relay, we were matched against Wisconsin and Minnesota. Our leadoff runner came in well behind his opponents, so we had to run from behind for the rest of the race. I ran the anchor leg and was close to pulling it out, but not close enough. Wisconsin won.

The following week we hosted a dual meet with Minnesota. It was a special reunion for Bill Garner, running for Minnesota, and me. Bill was three years ahead of me at Waverly High School and was a track star when I was just beginning to get serious about track. Iowa won the meet, 83-21. Minnesota won only two events, both of them by Bill Garner. He won the seventy-yard dash in 7.2 seconds and the long jump at twenty-three feet, three-and-three-fourths inches. I won the 440 in 50.9 seconds.

Finally, the outdoor season started, but it didn't start well for us. We ran a dual meet at the University of Missouri in Columbia and lost, 87-35. In that morning's Columbia newspaper, they ran a picture of me and a headline: "Tigers, Hawkeyes Promise Topflight Track Competition." At the bottom of the article I wrote, "Hawkeyes Break Promise." I don't even remember how I finished, but I know it wasn't pretty.

The following Monday, Coach Cretzmeyer posted that day's track workout in the Field House. At the top he wrote, "After some of our brilliant performances Saturday, it should be quite obvious to you that some of you need more work. This schedule is to give you a general idea of what you need. If you are not sure whether you need more work be sure and check with us—we can straighten your problem out in a hurry."

While re-reading that day's workout, more than sixty years later, I am amazed at how easy a workout it was. It couldn't compare with some of the workouts my athletes had to endure at Western Kentucky and in Sweden. For 440 men, the workout was: "Work on sprints. Run 100 yards. Repeat in ten minutes. Run

660 at full effort. Baton passes." No wonder we weren't very good.

Our next meet was the Drake Relays in Des Moines, the highlight of the season for me. We entered a race called the 480-yard shuttle hurdle relay. Each runner runs a flight of 120-yard high hurdles and tags his teammate, who runs a flight of hurdles in the opposite direction. This is done four times, with the race ending where it had started.

I was selected to be the leadoff man. When the gun was fired, adrenaline must have taken over for me. I ran well and finished slightly ahead of the other leadoff runners. I tagged "Ockie" Peterson, who tagged Les Stevens, who tagged Jack Mathews. It was never close during the last half of the race. We finished first in 58.2 seconds, a new American record.

Because of the win, we were each presented with a Drake Relays wristwatch. I gave my watch to my father, who gave it back to me many years later.

That year, the Big Ten outdoor track meet was held at Ohio State University in Columbus. In those days, we usually took a bus or a train to get to competitions. But that year we flew in a twin-engine DC-3. The plan was to fly the Iowa team to Madison, Wisconsin, to pick up the Wisconsin team. Then we would fly straight to Columbus.

As we were boarding the plane in Iowa City, I said to my roommate, Whitey Perry, "I told Orville. I told Wilbur. Now I'm telling you. This thing will never get off the ground."

To promote my entertainment world, I continued to pull off publicity stunts whenever I could. But there was one stunt that failed that spring. This is the way Gus Schrader, sports editor of the Cedar Rapids *Gazette,* wrote about it in his column:

Not all of Tom's stunts have worked to perfection. He reluctantly reveals one that didn't come off.

Remember last May when a group of Iowa Falls residents came down the Iowa River to Iowa City in canoes to advertise their centennial? The trip took several days and was well-photographed by newspapers.

As a climax, it was arranged to have Governor Hoegh and other dignitaries meet the band of bearded Iowa Falls men when they climbed out of their canoes in Iowa City.

Tom was talking about this venture with Joe Bartelme and L.W. Ward, Iowa students who now work

for KCRG in Cedar Rapids, when an idea struck him. He put on bedraggled old clothes, let his beard grow a few days, smeared himself with dirt, and rented a canoe.

Tom paddled up around the first bend in the Iowa River and parked. He aimed to wait until he saw the Iowa Falls delegation approach. Then he would shoot out ahead of them and lead the group up to the shore where Governor Hoegh and the reception committee were waiting.

News photographers would snap his picture shaking hands with the big shots. The photos would be in all the papers and on TV.

Newsmen of the state can be happy the great hoax failed.

"The Iowa Falls people were delayed by bad weather," Tom recalls, "and stayed overnight up the river a ways. I waited all day in the canoe and finally had to come in. I couldn't go out the next day because we had to take off for the Big Ten track meet. Too bad, huh?"

Tom declares that he's done with all such foolishness now.

Those who know Tom best believe he means it, at least until another inspiration arrives.

14

North to Alaska

During the spring of 1955, some of the guys at Hillcrest Dormitory were sitting around one evening, talking about their plans for the coming summer. When I joined the group, I suggested we all go to Alaska and get summer jobs. At the time, Alaska was "the great frontier" and was still a U.S. territory, not a state. It would be a real adventure, plus there were many high-paying jobs in Alaska.

So we all decided we would go. But as the summer neared, more and more people backed out of the adventure. When school let out in June, I was only one who was still planning to go.

I borrowed $100 from my father and hitched a ride to Seattle with two college friends. During the ride west, we went through North Dakota, Oregon, and Washington, completing my goal of traveling through all forty-eight states before reaching the age of twenty-one. I sent my parents a postcard from Seattle that read, "46, 47, 48 and out!"

(In 1959, Alaska and Hawaii became states, which meant that I had been in only forty-nine of the fifty states. I finally got to Hawaii in 1972, completing my "collection" of all fifty states. I sent my parents a postcard from Honolulu that read, "Finally.")

When we arrived at Sea-Tac airport, between Seattle and Tacoma, my friends dropped me off and drove on to their destination. At Sea-Tac, I bought a one-way ticket to Anchorage. The cost was $82.50.

I flew to Anchorage and then took the daily train to the Port of Whittier, a military base that was hiring people for the summer. The ride to Whittier was sixty-two miles long, which took two hours and fifteen minutes. The final twelve miles, the train went over several bridges and through two tunnels, one was more than three miles long. I saw six moose along the way.

The Port of Whittier was a beautiful place, a small, flat settlement on an arm of the Prince William Sound, entirely surrounded by mountains, with many waterfalls and two bluish-white glaciers in sight, one across the harbor and one hanging over the mountainside above the town. Directly across the bay was a mile-high mountain rising out of the sea.

Whittier was the only deep-water port between Seattle and the Far East that didn't freeze over in the wintertime. That's why the military had big plans for the port, expecting it to be an important stopover for ships sailing to and from Asia. The original plan called for 3,000 troops to be stationed there.

When I arrived, I was immediately impressed by the nearly twenty-four hours of daylight during the summertime, and the huge piles of snow around the town. The snow, which would not be gone by the end of the summer, was the result of the previous winter's record snowfall, more than seventy feet.

Whittier was a unique community in 1955. The 1,200 residents, mostly Army personnel, could travel to and from the port either by train or boat. There were no roads. The joke at the time was that there were three ways to get to Whittier: by train, by ship, or by parachute, but there were only two ways to leave. Nowadays, an additional way in and out is by

The train that ran from Anchorage to Whittier, Alaska

The seagoing tugboat, the LT452, that was my "home" in the summer of 1955.

Posing in my raingear in the tugboat's galley

automobile, but to go through the tunnels, the cars have to take turns with the trains.

In Whittier, I interviewed for two jobs. One was in construction, which seemed like a lot of unnecessary work. The other was as a cook's assistant on a tugboat. I took the tugboat job. My assignment was to be on a boat that was already on its way to the Bering Strait. The LT-130 was scheduled to spend the summer patrolling the western coast of Alaska, getting within two miles of Russia at times.

I was to take the train to Anchorage the next morning and then fly to Kodiak Island to meet the tugboat. But there was some sort of mix-up, and the

trip was canceled. So, instead of cruising the rough waters of the Bering Strait, I was reassigned to a 126-foot seagoing tugboat, the LT-452, or, as it was named, Sergeant Raymond M. Baser. (Tugboats were named for non-commissioned war heroes who lost their lives in combat.) The tug was equipped to handle a crew of eighteen, but we never had more than eleven on board.

The tugboat's jobs were to tow barges from place to place, to help in the docking of troop ships on their way to or from the Far East, and to guard the military equipment anchored at Shotgun Cove. Shotgun Cove was an inlet two miles toward the sea from Whittier. We were moored there every other weekend, alternating with the port's other tugboat.

My job was to assist the cook with breakfast, lunch, and dinner, to serve the meals to the crew, and to clean up after every meal. The best part of the job was that I learned how to cook. In fact, there were many times, later in the summer, when I served as the boat's cook. Then the real cook could take some time off.

During the summer, the tugboat's skipper, Captain Paul Phillips, said he would recommend me to become a seaman, should I want to leave college and make life on the sea my career. I was flattered and actually considered the move. But later, when the tugboat actually left the Prince William Sound and went to sea, I changed my mind.

We went to sea three times during my two-and-a-half months on the tug. The seas in the Gulf of Alaska can be really rough, and I had regular bouts with seasickness, which didn't go well with kitchen work. Later, I told people that we went to sea three days and I was sick only three times—all day the first day, all day the second day, and all day the third day. During the difficult times, I just stayed below in my bunk.

Our first sea trip was to Chatham, a village to the southeast, on the Alaskan panhandle, not far from Juneau. Our second trip was to Kodiak Island, where I was told Kodiak bears can be as big as three feet. Then they explained that they measure Kodiak bears between their eyes.

Our final sea journey was around the Kenai Peninsula to Anchorage. Anchorage is not far from Whittier as the crow flies, but it's a long way by boat. Whittier is on the Prince William Sound; Anchorage is on Cook Inlet. There is no easy connection between the two bodies of water.

The daily tides in Whittier were noticeable, but they were nothing like the thirty-five-foot tides in Anchorage. After I finished work one evening in Anchorage, I stepped off the boat to explore the city. When I came back a few hours later, I had to climb down a slimy ladder to the tug, which was thirty feet below. Because of the tide changes, a seaman had to be on the deck at all times, untying and retying the ropes that secured the tug to the dock.

Our departure from Anchorage had to be delayed because of that day's tidal bore, a wall of water that rushes up Cook Inlet toward Anchorage every day. Bores, which sound like oncoming trains, measure up to six feet high and travel ten to fifteen miles per hour. We had to wait until the bore had passed and then took advantage of the outgoing tide as we sailed out of Cook Inlet.

The most important structure in Whittier was the Buckner Building. It was called "a city under one roof." With only ninety-seven acres of buildable land in all of Whittier, it was decided to concentrate everything in one big building, rather than in several smaller ones. And was it big. It had eight stories, with six above ground and two below. It contained 273,660 square feet of space. It was 525 feet long (nearly two football fields) and 160 feet wide.

The Buckner Building was not only the biggest building in Whittier, it was the biggest building in the Territory of Alaska. It provided comfortable housing for 1,000, a 540-seat cafeteria, offices, classrooms, a rifle range, a 350-seat theater (for both movies and live performances), a radio station, a photo darkroom, a bowling alley, a library, a hobby shop, a post office, a barber shop, a snack bar, a massive kitchen, a bake shop, a church, a six-cell jail, day rooms, lounges, and a large infirmary, made up of an operating room, X-ray clinic, seven examination rooms, and a four-bed ward. Also in the building was a huge post exchange (PX) where you could buy almost anything imaginable at very low prices.

The Buckner Building still stands in Whittier, but it has been long abandoned. It was seriously damaged in the 1964 9.2 Alaska earthquake and would have been torn down at that time except for the potentially dangerous levels of asbestos in the building. It now stands as Whittier's largest eyesore.

In my spare time, I could go to a movie or the PX while in port, and, thanks to the constant daylight, could go fishing or exploring while at Shotgun Cove. There was a sixteen-foot skiff aboard the tug, available to anyone who wanted to row ashore or go fishing while at the Cove.

The movie theater in the Buckner Building ran all of the latest movies. My favorite that summer was a low-budget film, *Marty*, starring Ernest Borgnine. For his performance in that romantic comedy, Borgnine won the Academy Award for best actor. Little did I know that I would get to meet and chat with Ernest Borgnine forty-six years later, when we were both speakers on a Holland-America cruise ship.

Showing my motion picture ignorance, I asked Ernest Borgnine if *Marty* was his first movie. "Oh, no," he said, "I made several earlier pictures where I was the 'heavy.' " Later, I learned that he was the "heavy" who beat Frank Sinatra to death in the 1953 Oscar-

The Buckner Building

winning film, *From Here to Eternity.*

In early July, an Army photographer who had heard I was a runner asked if he could shoot a picture of me running, with the harbor and mountain as the background. He wanted to try to sell the photo to newspapers in Iowa. Apparently the newspapers were buying. The picture ran in the *Des Moines Register,* the *Waterloo Courier,* and the Cedar Rapids *Gazette,* with the headlines "Hawk Trains in Alaska," "Iowa Track-man Finds Cool Spot," and "Track Practice in Alaska."

One night when the tug was moored at Shotgun Cove, a young Southerner, Ernest Pettis, nicknamed "Rebel," and I took the skiff to shore. Rebel was one of the tug's seamen (deck workers). When we reached shore, we decided to try to climb the small mountain there. It really wasn't much of a mountain, and we made it to the top easily. When we got back to the tug, Rebel announced, "Me and Tom, we clumb a mountain." None of the other crew members believed we had done it, so we had to wait a few days for our pictures to be developed to prove it.

Because we kept spotting black bears around Shot-gun Cove, Rebel, who said he was a great hunter, decided to buy a .30-06 Magnum rifle at the PX. We never saw any bears after that, but he did allow me to fire the rifle one time. It was my first and last shot with a .30-06. It kicked like a mule.

One day in June, we witnessed what had to be one of the most dramatic avalanches ever. It certainly was easy to watch. We were returning to the port from Shotgun Cove when the entire snow-packed, mile-high mountainside across the harbor began to slide into the sea. Everyone on deck scrambled to get a camera, but I just watched. It rumbled and roared for at least five minutes. For weeks after, we saw dead seagulls floating in the water, victims of the avalanche.

On my last visit to the PX, in mid-August, I bought a footlocker. Everything I had with me that I would not need for the trip home was packed in that trunk. I took it to the post office and mailed it home. The cost was $5.92. Then it was back to Shotgun Cove for one last time.

While we were moored at the Cove, the captain received a call for immediate assistance from a ship

The picture that appeared in three Iowa newspapers

that was sinking in the open sea beyond Montague Island. Bob, one of the seamen, was ready to start his vacation, so he had his small outboard motorboat tied to the tug. He invited me to join him for the ride back to Whittier. It was an easy decision. The rough open sea was not for me. I grabbed the belongings that were still on board, stuffed them into a small bag, and jumped into Bob's boat, just as the tug was pulling out for the rescue mission.

After two-and-a-half months on the tug, working at least ten-and-a-half hours a day, seven days a week, I was ready to go back to the lower forty-eight, I was, as the military people say, "short in the port." Because of all the overtime, I had made a lot of money during the summer and hadn't spent much.

I retraced my way back to Seattle, by train, bus, and airplane. Then I flew a "milk run" overnight flight to Minneapolis, making several stops along the way.

From there I hitchhiked south to Hampton, Iowa, where my friend Sky Marschall lived. It was a nice day, so I knew Sky would be on the golf course.

When my final ride reached Hampton, I asked the driver to drop me off near the golf course, which wasn't far from the highway. Between the highway and the golf course was a cornfield. I climbed the fence, walked through the cornfield, and by luck, came upon Sky and his friend, John Gutz, who were on the second fairway.

Running toward the two, I yelled at Sky, who immediately fell to the ground in shock. It was one huge surprise for him. Sky and John didn't bother to finish their golf game. We walked to Sky's car, and he drove the three of us the forty miles to Waverly.

My arrival in Waverly was on August 31, my father's fifty-third birthday. I had bought him a card that read "Happy Birthday Little 5-Year-Old." I penciled in a 3 after the 5 and gave it to him.

54—

15

The Loss of a Dear Friend

After returning from Alaska, I went to the West Side Sales & Service in Waverly to buy a used car. I picked out a 1949 Plymouth that had "Dee and Chubb" painted on the dashboard. Apparently Dee and Chubb were the car's previous owners. The cost of the car was $375.

It was time for me to go back to college. After loading the car, I drove it to Oelwein, thirty-one miles to the east, to pick up my friend, Al Baker, to drive to Iowa City.

Al's mother, Veronica, was there to see us off. A frail woman, she had suffered through a bout of tuberculosis earlier and had spent some time recovering at the Oakdale State Tuberculosis Sanatorium near Iowa City. As we were leaving, I joked with her it was too bad she wasn't still at Oakdale. That was one of my favorite places to entertain the patients. (None of us knew at the time that Mrs. Baker was going to be moving back to Oakdale within a few weeks.)

Al was beginning his sophomore year at Iowa. He had enrolled the previous year and had become a member of the gymnastics team, specializing in the trampoline. Because he was on the gymnastics team and I was on the track team, we didn't spend as much time together as we had in high school. But he seemed to fit in well with the other gymnasts, who were all daredevils.

On the first day of classes, I met Judy Koch, who looked to be too young to be in college. We were seated next to each other in a classroom in the Television Center, enrolled in History and Appreciation of the Cinema.

There weren't enough seats for all who had enrolled, so the instructor, John Winnie, announced that freshmen and sophomores would have to leave. You had to be at least a junior to stay, he said. So I turned to Judy and said, "Too bad you have to leave."

And she answered, "I'm a graduate student." That was the beginning of a whirlwind romance that led to our marriage the following February.

That year, my balancing, magic, and escape act almost always included a singer named Dixie Davenport. Dixie was a freshman at Iowa, and she had a beautiful singing voice, even accompanied by my ukulele playing. We always included "Someone, Someday" as one of Dixie's signature songs.

In the early fall, I decided to promote my Houdini-type escape act by adding an underwater escape to the repertoire. It was to be a monumental publicity stunt. I decided to have myself locked in handcuffs, padlocked inside a U.S. mail sack, nailed in a wooden box, and dropped into the Iowa River off the Iowa Avenue Bridge.

The box was sturdy, made of a frame of two-by-fours, covered with one-by-twelve boards. It was built by a local lumberyard and was put on display in front of Whetstone's Drug Store, on the corner of Clinton and Washington streets. A sign on the box, lettered by a student, Stanley Bye, read: "Iowa student Tom Ecker will be handcuffed, locked in a mail bag, and nailed in this box before being thrown off the Iowa Avenue Bridge. Bye." In front of the word "Bye," some wag had written the word "Good."

Helping me with the underwater escape trick was a student named Jerry Torrence. Jerry's job was to be the pitchman, explaining to the crowd what was happening during the event. He was to put the handcuffs on me, lock the mail bag, and nail the lid onto the box, while explaining each step. Then the box was to be lowered into the river below.

The night before the escape stunt, I got a phone call from Douglas Edwards' office in New York. Edwards was the anchor on the *CBS Evening News* at that time. If I was serious about the stunt, CBS would send a film crew to Iowa City to cover it.

On the day the stunt was to occur, I received a call from the dean's office. He wanted Jerry and me to meet with him at his office as soon as possible. When we went to the office, we were faced with the dean of student affairs, L. Dale Faunce, and William Tucker, the Johnson County attorney. Dean Faunce first asked me if I was serious about pulling the escape stunt. When I said I was, the county attorney told me if I went ahead with the plan, I would be charged with disturbing the peace, endangering public health and safety, and littering the river. I didn't really want to be pushed into the river anyway, so I canceled the stunt and was off the hook. Articles in the local papers wrote stories about the canceling of the stunt, emphasizing the "littering the river" charge.

Shortly after that, John Bogert, president of the university's Dolphin Club, asked me if I would do the underwater escape trick in the Dolphin Show, scheduled for homecoming weekend. The Dolphin Club, made up mostly of members of the university's gymnastics and swimming teams, sponsored the annual Dolphin Show, performed at the Field House swimming pool. There would be four shows with an African theme, "Congo Capers," one on Thursday night, one on Friday night, and two on Saturday night.

There were some amazing performers in the show, primarily gymnasts, swimmers, and divers. There were even trapeze performers, using a rig that hung forty feet above the pool. And between the acts, a full orchestra played original jungle music. I've seen many top level circuses in my time, but none could compare with that year's Dolphin Show.

To publicize the show, we had a rally on Tuesday night behind Currier Hall, the largest women's dormitory on campus. I was strapped into my straitjacket, they tied a rope around my leg, threw the other end of the rope over a tree limb, and pulled me up into the air. Hanging upside down, I struggled to free myself, but finally did so, to mild applause.

There was a dress rehearsal scheduled for the Wednesday night before the show, but tragedy struck that afternoon. My friend Al Baker was playing a game of "horse" on the trampoline with several other trampolinists, when he made a wrong move, came down in the middle of the trampoline bed on his head, and broke his neck. He was immediately taken to the nearby University of Iowa Hospitals, where they drilled small holes in the sides of his head and put him in traction.

Adjustments were made in the show, and the dress rehearsal went on as planned. For my part, I was to do the lawnmower routine, escape from a straitjacket, and finally do the underwater escape from the box. The three appearances were separated by other Dolphin Show acts.

Dressed in only a loincloth, I appeared at the edge of the pool, across from the audience. First, I balanced the lawnmower on my chin. Then I lowered it to the floor and began screaming, "Chargoggagoggman-chauggagoggchaubunagungamaugg." (I was told by a coed friend that this is the Indian name of an obscure lake in Massachusetts. She taught me how to spell it and how to pronounce it.) After I had screamed the name of the lake twice, a group of angry Africans appeared and chased me out of the room.

After a few more acts, I appeared forty feet above the swimming pool, hanging upside down with a rope tied around my left leg. I was dressed in a straitjacket

Posing for the audience after escaping from a straight jacket while hanging forty feet above the Iowa swimming pool.

and, of course, the loincloth. The idea was that the angry Africans had put me in this terrible position. With all the drama that could be mustered, I strained and writhed, trying to get out of the jacket. When the drama was milked to the limit, I managed to make my escape.

The final trick was the underwater escape from the box, which was sitting at the edge of the pool. A team of stagehands in jumpsuits helped perform this stunt. First, I was handcuffed and then was put into a large canvas mail sack. By the time I was in the sack, I was out of the cuffs (a secret). Then the sack was placed in the box. By the time I was in the box, I was out of the sack (another secret).

In the box, I was sitting on top of 270 pounds of bricks, placed there to ensure the box would go down quickly. Also in the box I had a metal pail. My plan was to put the pail over my head to catch air when going under so I could stay down longer. But during the dress rehearsal, the sharp sideways movement of the box when it hit the water knocked the pail off my head. The pail was no longer part of the act. I was out of the box quickly (another secret), probably too quickly for good drama, but I found it difficult to hold my breath for very long when excited.

Before every show, while audience members were finding their seats in the stands, a young woman would get bumped and would fall in the pool. It always got a big laugh, because no one knew it was a planned fall. The young female who was dunked four different times was Kay Halloran, who became a state legislator and then mayor of Cedar Rapids more than fifty years later.

On Friday evening, before our second show, I was walking from Hillcrest dormitory to the swimming pool when a classmate, "Clipper" Clizbe from Marshalltown, approached me. He wanted me to meet a young woman who had driven from Marshalltown to see the Dolphin Show and to meet me. I had several friends from Marshalltown in those days, including my roommate, Whitey Perry, so I figured she had heard about me from them.

Her name was Jean Seberg. She was a high school senior in Marshalltown at the time, and planned to enroll at Iowa the next year. Little did I know that Jean Seberg would come to Iowa, would be discovered by film legend Otto Preminger, and would leave Iowa to star in the movie, *Saint Joan,* the story of Joan of Arc. Jean went on to appear in more than thirty films in both Europe and the United States. I never saw her again after meeting her that Friday night.

The Dolphin Show that year broke all previous attendance records. We drew more than 10,000 people, including the governor of the state and the president of the university. Another attendee was Tommy Bartlett of Wisconsin Dells' water show fame. Tommy wanted to hire me to do the underwater escape act in his water show at the Dells, but I turned it down. Doing two escapes a day in a lake for an entire summer seemed a bit risky.

Beginning the day after Al's trampoline accident, I made daily visits to see him. Those visits were particularly unpleasant when Al asked others to leave the room when I was there. He did that so he could vent his anger by blaming me for convincing him to go to school at Iowa, instead of Upper Iowa University in Fayette. Of course, I was consumed with guilt.

Throughout the week, I watched as Al's health continued to fail. The following Saturday, I walked to the hospital with Frank LaDue, one of the all-time great trampoline performers. That morning, Al's breathing failed, and he had to be put into an iron lung. Frank and I went into Al's room, but Al didn't say much.

Late that night, actually it was early Sunday morning, I was talking on the phone to a friend from Waverly, Mary Lou Carver, who knew Al well. After we hung up, I couldn't sleep, so I walked back to the hospital.

I arrived in time to watch as Al took his last breath. He had held on for eleven days. The nurses opened the side of his iron lung. He had a large tear running down his cheek. It was a scene I'll never forget. He was only nineteen-years-old.

They called Al's mother, who was staying with friends in Iowa City, and I said I would stay until she got there. Veronica Baker was a frail woman. As a single mother with very little income, she had raised Al, living in a very small house in Oelwein. He was all she had.

Finally, Mrs. Baker arrived at the hospital. I could see her coming down the hall, walking slowly, with a Catholic priest by her side. When they arrived at the room, the priest did some praying, or whatever priests do, and then he said he had to leave. I needed the priest to stay there to help me get through this, but he refused. I followed him into the hallway and pleaded with him to stay. He said he couldn't. Then he turned and walked away. From that day, I've never been fond of priests.

There were no medical people in the room at that time. It was just Al, his mother, and me. Mrs. Baker, sobbing, asked me if it was OK to kiss Al. I said it was. Then she asked if she could kiss him one more time. It was my first experience with death up close. I've never been in a more uncomfortable situation. Finally, a nurse came in and suggested we leave. I walked with Mrs. Baker as we left the hospital. On the way she told me she wanted me to have Al's baritone ukulele.

The following Wednesday, Al's funeral was at his Catholic church in Oelwein. The church was filled to capacity, mostly with students and staff from the university. It was the sad ending of a very happy chapter in my life.

In November, I received a letter from Mrs. Baker, who had returned to the Oakdale Sanatorium. She wrote, "Remember the day you and Al left Oelwein for Iowa City and you said to me, 'Too bad you're not in Oakdale this fall as you might put on a show here again?' Well, here I am. A lot has changed our lives since then."

On December 15, we did a big show for Mrs. Baker and her friends at Oakdale. There were five performers. Marsh Lovrien narrated, Carolyn Moran did a comedy reading of "Mary Had a Little Lamb," Dixie Davenport sang, and I did my balancing act. Then I told the story of hitchhiking to South Carolina, which everyone knew, and Sky Marschall, dressed up like a South Carolina cheerleader, came out and kissed me on the cheek.

Mrs. Baker seemed to really enjoy the show, especially when I played Al's ukulele and Dixie sang "Someone, Someday." It was our final show for Mrs. Baker. She died soon after that.

At the time of Al's death, I thought that death was the beginning of a new life, something like you hear from a commencement speaker during a graduation exercise. But after extensive reading about religions and experiencing death close up so many times since then, I am now convinced that death is the end of everything. You live your life, do your best to enjoy it, and that's it. For some people, it is a wonderful, happy experience. For others, it is pure hell. Your life is a very

Sky Marschall, dressed as Miss South Carolina, came on stage and kissed me on the cheek.

short period of time separating two eternities.

When you die, you leave everything behind, including your relatives, your friends, and your property. My father used to say, "I've never seen a hearse pulling a U-Haul." But you also leave behind something even more important—other people's memories of you. Hopefully, they are fond ones. But even those memories fade and eventually disappear.

There are ways to be remembered for a longer time, such as with a tombstone, photographs, books or letters you've written, and, of course, your children. But for most people, those memories disappear after two or three generations and are pretty much gone forever.

Early in my youth, I attended the Episcopal Church. (My father always said an Episcopalian is simply a Catholic who flunked his Latin.) I left the Episcopal Church when I was in high school, when it went "high church," and I was told I could no longer eat meat on Friday.

I've studied both the Bible and *The Lost Books of*

the Bible. When I was a student at the University of Iowa, I took a college course called Greeks and the Bible and one called Religion in Human Culture. I now realize that I learned much more from those experiences than I thought at the time.

It is no secret that many ecclesiastical writings of early Christian authorities were not included in the New Testament. In the fourth century, some of the writings were accepted by Christian councils as being inspired by God. Others were rejected.

It is interesting to note that no one who wrote about Jesus of Nazareth ever met him. And there is no mention of Jesus in the Bible from his infancy to his life as a thirty-year-old. Apparently, the covering of his youth, which exists in other works, had not been inspired by God.

When King James oversaw the translation of his version of the Bible in the early 1600s, he left out more than 500 pages that he didn't agree with and added many more that supported his beliefs. It is obvious that humans, actually male humans, manipulated the "word of God" to suit themselves.

For me, becoming an atheist was a gradual process. The more I looked at various religions, the more inconsistencies I could see. And, because I was working in the school district for twenty-six of my adult years, I kept my beliefs private most of the time.

There are now more than 4,000 religions in the world, many espousing their particular beliefs to be correct, and all the others to be incorrect. With that many "incorrect" religions, it is easy to understand why it is easy to become a non-believer.

In recent years, I've discovered that many atheists prefer to be called humanists. I'm not sure what the difference is. Perhaps they think a humanist sounds a little more human than an atheist. After reading through a large reference book titled *Who's Who in Hell,* I've learned there are other synonyms for atheists, including freethinkers, naturalists, rationalists, and non-theists.

One of my favorite cartoons from my college days showed two gold fish in a fishbowl. One of the fish says to the other, "All right, smartass, if there's no God, who changes the water?"

Sometime in the 1980s, one of my friends, Tom Moran, asked me to deliver a speech to his Catholic study group, which met on Sunday evenings. He wanted my topic to be atheism. I said there isn't really much to talk about. But he was insistent, so I agreed to do it.

At the beginning, I told the small group that my presentation would be answering any questions they might have. The final question was "How do you live your life?" I responded, "I try to do as much good as possible, as little evil as possible, and I always try to respect others for their beliefs." The chairman of the group stood up and said, "Obviously, Tom is a Christian, and he just doesn't know it."

Over the years, several of my friends have confided in me that they were atheists. In some cases, even their families didn't know. One of them told me he became an atheist while he was taking logic courses in college. And, as you can imagine, all of my atheist friends who later died were given "Christian funerals" by their survivors.

My father probably said it best when he gave his description of a dead atheist's funeral. He said, "All dressed up and no place to go."

16

The Bad Luck Boys

To help promote my stage shows in 1955, I went to an Iowa City printer and had nine-by-twelve advertising placards printed that said "TOMFOOL-ERY with Tom Ecker (the versatile entertainer), a variety of acts featuring the nation's most talked-about college stunt man."

Under a picture of me in an Iowa letter sweater balancing a lawn mower on my chin are the words, "Tom Ecker combines a sense of balance with a sense of humor." Then there was this list: "Balancer, Magician, Comedian, Escape Artist, Hitchhiker and World Traveler." (The world traveler part might have been a bit of an exaggeration.)

The Thanksgiving vacation that year was spent staying in Waverly and commuting to Waterloo daily to work as a cameraman at KWWL-TV. My camera work improved so much at that time that I was selected to be a cameraman on a thirteen-part television series produced by "The Educational TV and radio center of the State University of Iowa."

The series, which was titled *The Secret of Flight*, featured Dr. Alexander Lippisch, a noted German aeronautical engineer. Dr. Lippisch was one of many German scientists brought to America at the conclusion of World War II. Dr. Lippisch, sixty-one at the time, was the director of the aeronautical research laboratories of the Collins Radio Company in Cedar Rapids.

The series featured a wind tunnel, which demonstrated the effects of wing placement and wing curvature on the lifting of an airplane as it moved through the air. (More than sixty years later, *The Secret of Flight* can be seen on YouTube.)

When we had breaks during the filming, I sat with Dr. Lippisch, discussing his life in Germany and his knowledge of and his acquaintance with Adolf Hitler. I had long been interested in Hitler's life and his psychotic behaviors. (Years later, Dr. Lippisch's son,

George, the owner of a design firm in Cedar Rapids, told me stories about going to school in Nazi Germany in the 1940s. And, because I was interested in Adolf Hitler, he gave me a copy of Hitler's signature, which he had gotten from his sister.)

The first week of the Christmas break was spent working at KWWL. That week I logged forty hours of regular time and forty-three hours of overtime. Then I went to Louisville, Kentucky, to meet Judy's parents.

While in Louisville, Judy and I were invited to a New Year's Eve party at the home of Tim Stivers, who was a good friend of Judy's. Tim was an outgoing, life-of-the-party storyteller, who was studying to be a podiatrist in Chicago. Judy and I decided we would turn the tables on Tim, so I loaded the pockets of my sports jacket with various props, and we went to the party.

When we arrived, Judy introduced me to everyone as her friend from Iowa, Charlie Johnson. For the early part of the evening, Charlie Johnson was the life of the party. Instead of alcohol, he drank milk from a small bottle he had in his pocket. He would pull various props out of his pockets and do tricks while telling jokes non-stop. When something went over really well, Charlie would pull his sport jacket open so everyone could see medals pinned to the inside of the jacket.

Finally, we thought we had taken the charade as far as we could. We confessed, telling everyone the truth. Tim was overwhelmed. He laughed, and continued laughing every time he came up to me to chat.

Tim and I have been friends now for more than sixty years. He became a very successful podiatrist, but his first love was comedy. He became a standup comedian and, until recently, he continued to entertain audiences in nightclubs and comedy clubs around the country. At Judy's invitation, Tim came to Cedar Rapids in 1974 to do his comedy act for the Rotary

Club's wine-tasting party. He was hilarious.

When Judy and I got back to the Iowa campus, we were pretty much inseparable for the next month-and-a-half. We had some classes together, and she even came to watch some of our track workouts in the Field House.

The 1956 indoor track season began with a home meet against Missouri on the night of February 9. That afternoon, at a team meeting, Coach Cretzmeyer announced that one of our two Olympic distance runners, Deacon Jones, had just been declared academically ineligible for the entire 1956 season. That was the year we had planned to dominate the Big Ten, so losing Deacon was quite a blow to the program.

Since Deacon was no longer on the team, Cretz said we needed someone to run the mile that evening, along with our other Olympian, Ted Wheeler. We knew that Ted would win the race, but we needed someone to get second place and score some valuable points. It turned out that someone was me.

I had trudged through an uninspiring cross country race before, but I had never run a mile race, even in practice. My training was for shorter, faster races. When I asked Cretz how I should run the mile, he said, "Keep to the left and hurry back." I managed to get the second-place points, but my teammates described my appearance as "light green" as I finished the race. We won the meet, 65-49.

Our next competition was also a home meet,

against Marquette. Judy and I had decided we wanted to get married, but the only day I didn't have to be on the track was the day before a meet, which was always a day of rest. The day before the Marquette meet, Judy and I drove to Galesburg, Illinois, to get married in the chapel of the Presbyterian church. My roommate, Sky Marschall, and Judy's roommate, Joan Bailey, also drove to Galesburg, so they could stand up for us. Fearing I might lose my scholarship if I did something foolish, we decided to keep the wedding a secret.

After the ceremony, both cars headed back to Iowa City. I took Judy to her apartment where we each ate a cinnamon roll, and then I drove back to Hillcrest dormitory. When I walked in the door to our room, Sky said, "What in the hell are you doing here?" I explained that I had a big track meet the next night, and I needed my rest.

The next day, I needed enough money to go on a one-day honeymoon, so I told a friend, Phil Hess, that I was secretly married. He bet me ten dollars I wasn't. When I showed him the marriage certificate, he paid up, and we had enough money to go to Boone, Iowa, after the track meet for our honeymoon. I thought "Honeymoon in Boone" sounded funny. Too bad it wasn't in June.

A dead heat finish in the 440, breaking an 18-year Field House record.

I was the leadoff runner on the Iowa mile relay team that became known as the "Bad Luck Boys."

We won the Marquette dual meet, 86-28. In my race, the 440-yard dash, I was running in second place, behind teammate Caesar Smith. Coming out of the final turn, I pulled up even with Caesar, and we crossed the finish line in a dead heat. Our time was 49.7, which broke an 18-year Field House record and was the fastest indoor 440 in the Big Ten.

After the meet, Judy and I drove to Boone, about 130 miles to the west. As soon as we checked into a motel there, Judy's jaw began to ache. She had an impacted tooth, so we checked back out of the motel and drove back to Iowa City, where she was in the university infirmary for the next few days.

As the indoor track season progressed, it became obvious that Iowa's mile relay team was one of the best in the nation. But a local journalist wrote: "Iowa's famous 'Klutch Kids' of recent basketball fame have lost the sports spotlight to their new track counterparts, the 'Bad Luck Boys.'" The bad luck began at the Big Ten indoor meet, where the mile relay was run in two heats. We won our heat easily, but Indiana, running in the faster heat, beat us by two-tenths of a second.

On the next three successive Saturdays, we ran in indoor "board" track meets, meets run on board tracks in large arenas. The first was in Milwaukee, the second in Chicago, and the third in Cleveland.

My father decided to attend the Milwaukee meet, as did Judy and a few Iowa friends from our television classes. That night, our anchor man, Caesar Smith, was far ahead, running relaxed, when suddenly he was surprised by Notre Dame's anchor man, Bill Squires, who finished fast. There was disagreement at the finish line as to which team had won, but the judges picked Notre Dame.

In Chicago, Notre Dame was ahead by three yards when Caesar got the baton, and he couldn't quite make it up.

In Cleveland, we were ready. We built up a huge lead over Notre Dame during the first three legs of the mile relay. Caesar, anchoring again, ran well and was seven yards in front coming into the short home stretch. There was no chance that the Bill Squires could catch him this time. Crash! A Notre Dame high jumper, Bernie Allard, standing beside the track and waving his arms frantically, encouraging Squires, knocked the baton out of Caesar's hand. You can't win a relay race without a baton. Notre Dame won again.

During spring break, the last week in March, we were scheduled to run at the University of Arizona on Thursday and Arizona State on Saturday. Because of the daytime heat, both meets were scheduled to be run at night.

Seventeen track and field athletes took a train to get from Iowa City to Arizona, a trip of about twenty-four hours. We didn't have sleeping car reservations, so we had to try to sleep on the uncomfortable coach seats. We won both meets handily. Against Arizona, I led off the mile relay team. We won in a record time of 3:16.6, which the local newspaper called the night's outstanding performance.

On Saturday afternoon, our team was in Tempe preparing to run against Arizona State. Instead of sitting around with nothing to do, I convinced Whitey Perry that he and I should go to Arizona Downs to see some horse racing. I had stayed in the home of the Arizona Downs veterinarian, William Kemp, when I was visiting Phoenix over the Christmas break in 1953. That's when I had been hired by his mother and sister to drive them from Iowa City to Phoenix and back.

We located Dr. Kemp and asked him if he could advise us how to bet. He explained that, because he was the track's veterinarian, he was not allowed to bet on races. However, he took our program and checked the horses he thought had the best chance in each race. We made only two two-dollar bets. We bet on Waste Basket in the third race and Gleebar in the fifth race. Waste Basket finished third, paying $2.40, and Gleebar won, paying $10.80.

That night, against Arizona State, I won the 880-yard run in 1:56.7. Because of the altitude, I had trouble catching my breath after the race. Teammate Ted Wheeler, who probably had better things to do, walked with me along the backstretch with his hand on my forehead until I was breathing normally again.

Although we had some very good performances for the rest of the season, and we almost won the Big Ten Outdoor title, the season's low point was the Kansas Relays in Lawrence. First, our housing for the weekend was in bunk beds in a large room under the stadium. We had black athletes on our team, and black athletes could not stay in hotels or motels in the south at that time. (Yes, Kansas was part of the segregated South.)

We had an outstanding two-mile relay team. I was the fourth best half-miler, so I was the leadoff runner.

We won the race handily, breaking the old meet record. After taking a victory lap, we stood on the victory stand and received wrist watches for winning the race. A few minutes later, I was lying on my bunk bed under the stadium, listening to the meet on a portable radio when I heard that the Iowa team had been disqualified. Meet officials were looking for us so we could give back our watches.

A judge from Texas disqualified our team, saying that our anchor man, Ted Wheeler, had run out of his lane. There are no lanes in races that long. Ted was well ahead of the opposition, so he ran in the second lane of the cinder track because it wasn't as chewed up as the pole lane. We thought it was more than a coincidence that Ted Wheeler was black and the team that moved from second to first was the University of Texas.

We had one brighter moment that afternoon. Our distance medley relay team appeared to be the best at the Kansas Relays. Leading off with the quarter mile (one lap) was Gastonia Finch. Running the half-mile (two laps) was Murray Keatinge. Running three-quarters (three laps) was Caesar Smith. Running the mile (four laps) was Ted Wheeler. I was not the best quarter-miler or half-miler, so I was not selected for the team.

When the race was about to start, I was standing by the track, holding Murray Keatinge's sweat clothes. He would be running the second leg. When the gun was fired and Gas Finch was racing down the track, Murray stepped off the track, took his sweat clothes from me, and said, "I can't do it." Quickly, I stripped off my sweat clothes, put on my spiked shoes, and stood on the track to take the baton from Gas Finch. I'm sure Gas was surprised to see me taking the baton, but probably not nearly as surprised as Coach Cretzmeyer was. We won the race, and I got my wrist watch.

17

Of Mice and Mental Challenges

The University of Iowa has long been known as a mecca for writers. Many well-known authors, including playwright Tennessee Williams, studied at Iowa. So, the second semester of my junior year, I decided to enroll in a course called fiction writing. I managed to get through it, but it wasn't easy.

I hadn't heard of the instructor, Marguerite Young, but I was the only member of the class who hadn't. Apparently, I also was the one student who had never been in any of her other classes, nor had I read any of her books.

Marguerite Young was an instructor in the Iowa Writers' Workshop, a graduate program leading to a master's degree of fine arts. I have no idea why I was accepted in the class since I wasn't a graduate student and hadn't written anything of note.

On the first day, Ms. Young said we were each going to write a short story during the semester, and asked each of us to tell the class what our topic was going to be. She said the story had to include some sort of conflict.

A young woman immediately volunteered that she wanted to write about incest. Ms. Young seemed pleased with the choice. A young man said he would write about target fascination, and then proceeded to explain to the class what target fascination was. I knew I was way out of my element.

I racked my brain, trying to think of some kind of problem that I could write about. When it was my turn, I said, "Alcoholism." I would base the story on experiences I had while working on the tugboat in Alaska. She didn't seem impressed, but she accepted the topic.

My favorite authors at that time were Damon Runyon, O. Henry, and Erskine Caldwell, so the literature I knew best wasn't very "deep." At the end of the semester, I submitted my short story, which I'm sure was the "shallowest" produced by anyone in the class. It was called "The Bottle," and the setting was a tugboat in Alaska.

I knew a lot about tugboats and Alaska, so that part was easy. It was the drinking I didn't really understand. I had never had a drink of alcohol at that time and remained a tee-totaler for another four years. Somehow, I got a B in the course.

One of my favorite classes my junior year at Iowa was Cinematography Techniques. Each week we would film a project. When the developed film came back from the lab, we would edit the film into a short movie. For our final project, the class was divided into teams of five, with two weeks to script, shoot, and edit a movie of about fifteen minutes.

My team titled our movie *The Stranger In Between*, a romantic comedy that the other class members thought was both touching and funny. The assignment was to make a film, using all of the techniques we had learned during the semester—establishing shot, close-ups, cut-ins, cut-aways, and reverse angles. I served as writer, director, and film editor. When the semester was over, the instructor, John Mercer, asked if he could keep a copy of the film to show future classes. I still have a copy of the movie, which has since been transferred to a DVD.

Another class I took that year was Elective Physical Education, which was a one-hour track and field course taught by my coach, F. X. Cretzmeyer. One of our assignments during the semester was to write a theme. A week after I had finished my paper and handed it in, the following item appeared in Gordon Gammack's column in the *Des Moines Register*:

The students in one of the physical education classes taught at the State University of Iowa by Francis Cretzmeyer were directed recently to write 300-word themes on a subject covered during the preceding weeks.

One youth, a member of Cretzmeyer's track squad, started his theme: In distance running, the runner gets set in the blocks and when the gun goes off, he runs and runs and runs and runs, etc.

When he reached 300 words (with two extra "runs" for good measure), he turned in his paper.

Cretzmeyer's comment to him: "Any more of this and you'll run clear out of eligibility."

There were about 100 students enrolled in the television department at that time. We got together as a group and decided to organize a new club, Student Organization for Television Study, or SOTS, designed to give TV students the chance to be involved in a series of new television productions. (How we got away with naming the club SOTS is beyond me, but the university recognized us and the name.) Dr. Sam Becker was our advisor.

The group decided to produce four shows during the year. From a list of thirteen candidates, I was selected to produce and direct the second show, a live, fifteen-minute drama titled *Huggins' Woods*. The play was a condensed version of a one-act play my brother Don had written. We held rehearsals and did the show in March, with the show captured on a kinescope recording.

The Big Ten outdoor meet was held at the University of Minnesota in Minneapolis. The morning of the second day, I was walking down a street near our hotel and noticed a pet shop with a display of two mice in an aquarium in the window. One of the mice was the color of a regular house mouse. The other was brown with white markings. As I watched them running on a treadmill, climbing a ladder, and generally cavorting in the cedar shavings, I could see how entertaining mice can be. I had to have those two mice, so I went into the store and bought them. The two mice were placed in a sturdy cardboard box, complete with cedar shavings, for the bus trip back to Iowa.

After the meet that afternoon, the team boarded the bus and we returned to Iowa City, arriving late at night. I woke Judy up and showed her the two mice. She thought they were really cute, and we decided to name the gray mouse Mickey and the brown and white mouse Minnie. Not terribly original, but it was late at night. We placed the box, complete with cedar shavings, food, and water in the bathtub.

When the track season was over, I did my final variety show. I didn't know it was my final show at the time, but it was. Sponsored by the West Liberty boys' and girls' basketball uniform fund, the show was held in the West Liberty High School auditorium.

West Liberty's weekly newspaper, *The Index*, carried information about the show on page one for three weeks before the show. The major headline in the last issue before the show was "Tomfoolery at High School, Monday, July 9." The article includes this teaser: "The feature acts of the show will be his escapes from padlocks furnished from stocks at the Brown Lynch Scott store, and the escape from a wooden box built at the A.L. Dice Lumber Yard after being put in a straitjacket before being nailed in the box."

The show was an artistic success but a financial failure. There was a decent crowd, but there wasn't enough income generated to make it worthwhile. That's when wife Judy told me it was time for me to get out of vaudeville and find a career without footlights. At the age of twenty-one, I was retiring from show business. There was still the senior year ahead, and plenty of time to better prepare myself for a career in television.

In the meantime, our two pet mice, Mickey and Minnie seemed to be enjoying each other's company, but they weren't producing any children. We bought a colorful booklet, *Mice As Pets, A Guide to Taming, Training and Caring for Mice*, which taught us a little about mouse anatomy. We did a cursory examination and determined we had two females.

On July 20, I went to a local pet store and bought a large, white male mouse that we named Mighty. We put Mighty Mouse in the box with the two females, and all we could see was rejection. Every time Mighty would approach one of the other mice, he would be angrily pushed away by the female.

The next morning we decided to separate the mice. There was so much animosity between the male and two females, we gave Mighty his own cardboard box. A few days later, Mighty gnawed through his cardboard box and escaped. We never saw him again.

It wasn't long after that when we could see that Mighty had lived up to his name while we weren't looking. It was obvious that Mickey and Minnie were pregnant. Apparently, they weren't rejecting Mighty as much as we thought. We put them in two separate boxes in the bathtub. Exactly twenty days after they had met

Mighty Mouse, they gave birth to nineteen baby mice.

Besides being very entertaining to watch, the mice were about to add to our income. There were researchers, both at Iowa and at Iowa State, who were anxious to buy any mice we could produce, as soon as they were a few weeks old.

A photographer for the Cedar Rapids *Gazette,* Jerry Mosey, decided he wanted to get a picture of a cat and mouse together. The picture of Mickey and a calico cat ran in the *Gazette* with the following caption: "The photographic excellence of this cat-and-mouse play speaks for itself. Here is a cat, owned by Mrs. Louis Oehler of Iowa City, intently watching a mouse named Mickey, reared with other mice by Tom Ecker of Iowa City for sale to researchers. In all probability, the cat had never before seen a mouse; the mouse had never before seen a cat. Neither seemed to be more than curious about the other."

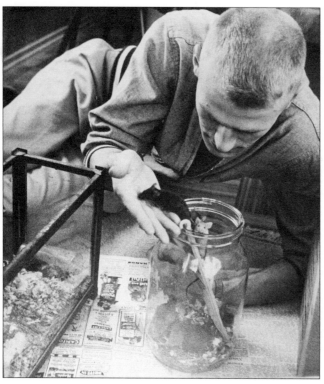

Pet mice of various colors were a source of income at the Ecker home.

The photo of the cat and mouse that appeared in the Gazette.

18

With a Song in My Head

The wrestling coach at Iowa, Dave McCuskey, was the head coach of the U.S. Olympic wrestling team in the Melbourne Olympics in 1956. And one of his wrestlers, Terry McCann, won an Olympic gold medal.

As soon as they returned from Melbourne, I contacted them to appear on a special TV program that I was to produce at the television center. It turned out to be an entertaining interview show, with local radio man Bob Zenner asking the questions. The only problem we had was with the set decorator, who had hung large Olympic rings at the back of the set. Halfway through the show, the rings came tumbling down. But we went on as if nothing had happened. Even with that minor flub, the show was considered an artistic success.

A vocal group called The Hilltoppers, former students at Western Kentucky State College, performed in Iowa City in the fall of 1956. My wife, Judy, who had attended Western Kentucky as an undergraduate, knew Jimmy Sacca, the group's lead singer. She was teaching fifth grade at Hoover Elementary School at the time, and she talked Jimmy into coming to speak to her students.

That's when I got the idea for forming a vocal group. If students from Western Kentucky could record and sell records as the Hilltoppers, why couldn't students from the University of Iowa perform as the Hawkeyes? The difference was that I would have a female lead singer—Dixie Davenport—instead of a male voice. All I had to do was find three male voices to back her up.

I found two of the voices, Derk Simonson and Don Roeder, on campus at the Sigma Alpha Epsilon fraternity house. They had been part of a vocal quartet there, and both had excellent voices for blending.

When I first got Dixie, Derk, and Don together for a rehearsal, I was supposed to sing the third male part. But it wasn't long before we all realized we needed a tenor, not another baritone. So the next task was to locate a tenor. Another student, Jim Williams, was recommended to us, and he was a perfect choice. The Hawkeyes were officially formed.

The next hurdle was to find two "original" songs to record. Using other people's songs was a complicated and costly process at that time, so we had to write our own songs. We already had "Someone, Someday," the song I had written in the eighth grade, but we needed one more. I had written "Full Moon Above" my freshman year at Iowa, but the chords were too complicated for our new singing group. So we had to come up with a new song—one that would be easy for the group to learn. Using the same ukulele chords as were used in "Someone, Someday," I created

The Hawkeyes in an early rehearsal. Here I'm making a point to the group, Bob Arvin on bass, Derk Simonson, Dixie Davenport, Jim Williams, and Don Roeder.

a completely different song, "Who Is He?"

Then came the biggest challenge of all, writing the musical arrangements. Since I couldn't write music and the three background singers couldn't read music, we had to create our own system. I had each singer sing one of the top three strings of each ukulele chord. Since any basic ukulele chord can be played using only the first three frets, no one had to sing more than four different notes on any song.

Using blank music paper, I wrote the words of a song below the musical staff, and then above each word, used colored pencil dots to indicate what each singer should do. Derk's dots were red, Don's dots were black, and Jim's dots were blue. As long as the first chord was established, they could "read music" by going up when the dots went up and down when the dots went down. They were simply singing ukulele chords. And it worked perfectly.

The only instrumental accompaniment the group had was a string bass, played by another student, Bob Arvin. Bob and the four singers began to get together to rehearse the two songs, spending more time on "Who Is He?," which we designated as the "A" side, and less time on the "B" side, "Someone, Someday."

Since it was nearly impossible to find a company to record original songs, we decided to form our own recording corporation, Sky Records, Inc. With the slogan "Sky's the Limit," the record company was incorporated in March 1957. I was "elected" president, Judy was the vice president, and my father, who had put up the money to press the records, was secretary-treasurer.

The next step was to find a place to record. We had a student friend, Arnie Gore, who worked at the campus radio station, WSUI. He told us he had a key and would let us in to record, but it would have to be after the station went off the air at 10 p.m. That created an additional problem for us. Dixie lived in a dormitory and was required to be back in the dorm by 10:30 p.m.

Somehow, Dixie got permission to stay out late that one night, and we were set to record. It was well after 10 when the radio station's door was unlocked for us. The group had been singing together for less than two weeks.

With Arnie Gore engineering the session, we recorded "Who Is He?" seven times before we got a

take that we thought was good enough. It was getting very late, but we still had one more song to record. We recorded "Someone, Someday" only twice, and we didn't think either take was very good. But, it was the "B" side, so it didn't really matter that much. The next day, I mailed the tape to a record-pressing company in Chicago to have 1,000 45 rpm records pressed. We had decided on a blue label with silver printing.

There were still some 78 rpm records being sold at that time, but only the big stars, like Elvis Presley, were featured on both 45 and 78 rpm records. The LP (33 1/3 rpm) albums were just beginning to be seen in record stores at that time.

In the meantime, the Iowa indoor track season was getting underway. We had home meets against the University of Missouri and the University of Minnesota. We were clobbered by Missouri, 80-34, but managed to beat Minnesota, 59-55. My daughter, Wendy, was born two days before the Minnesota meet.

When the 1,000 records arrived, the work really began. I sent copies of the record to every radio station in the area. Then we placed records in all of the area record stores, offering discounts for boxes of fifty records. Suddenly, "Who Is He?" was a big hit throughout Iowa, and the Hawkeyes were in big demand. They made personal appearances whenever they could squeeze them in.

One of the appearances was at a campus dance featuring the music of the Les Brown Band. The event was the Celestial Ball, held in the Iowa Memorial Union. The group's appearance was very brief. They still knew only two songs.

One of the biggest of their personal appearances was in Des Moines. This was the story that appeared in the *Daily Iowan*, the university newspaper:

The five "Hawkeyes," the SUI singing group still green in the record business, had their first taste of the 'big time' when they spent a day plugging their disc here Thursday.

From a furniture store display window, the singers appeared with disc jockey Don Bell on his afternoon KIOA radio show.

Bell, billed as Des Moines' Dean of Disc Jockeys, interviewed the Hawkeyes and played both sides of their record, "Who Is He?" and "Someone, Someday."

The group appeared as special guests of Bell's Thursday

night Teen Hop at the Val Air Ballroom on Des Moines' west side. They sang their two recorded songs.

Then Bell gave twenty-five copies of the record and 100 pictures of the Hawkeyes to some of the more than 1,500 teenagers that were jammed into the ballroom.

Following the performance, the singing group was swamped by teenagers anxious to get autographs.

Earlier in the day, Tom Ecker of Waverly, president of Sky Records, composer, and arranger of the two songs, manager of the Hawkeyes, and distributor for the record company, went on a tour of Des Moines record stores peddling some of the platters. Ecker, laughing, says he is also the top record salesman.

The Hawkeyes also visited the headquarters of a Des Moines distributor who sells their records to drug and grocery store record racks.

"Who Is He?" is now the top selling record in Iowa City and is fast approaching the top in Cedar Rapids. It is also in the top ten in several other Eastern Iowa cities.

On March 1, the Iowa track team flew to Columbus, Ohio, for the Big Ten Indoor Championships. On the first day of competition, I managed to qualify for the finals of the 600-yard run, which would be held the next day.

That evening, I decided to get a haircut. Our best runner, Deacon Jones, was a world class distance runner and an accomplished barber. He had learned the trade at Father Flanagan's Boys Town, where he was brought up. Deacon wasn't allowed to take money, but he had a plate by his hotel room door for "tips."

I sat in the chair, Deacon placed a towel over my shoulders, and he proceeded to cut my hair. There was no mirror, so I couldn't see that he was cutting me nearly bald. (I felt I had to leave him a tip anyway.)

The next day, in the 600-yard final, I finished second to Dave Lean, an Australian Olympian attending Michigan State. But the judges ruled that Lean had cut in front of another runner during the race, and he was disqualified. That moved me up to first place.

As I was standing on the victory stand to receive the gold medal, my brother Don walked into the arena. He lived in Columbus and had meant to be there for the race, but something had delayed him. After I received the medal, he walked over to me and said, "What the hell were you doing up there?"

Then I walked across the arena to see Coach Cretzmeyer. I said to him that was an awful way to become a Big Ten champion. He said, "A year from now no one will know the difference."

He was right.

The next day, there was a picture on the sports page of the Chicago Tribune showing the runners in the 600-yard run on the first curve. Leading the pack was a runner who looked a little like a skinny Yul Brynner.

My time of 1:13.7 wasn't considered a very fast time then, but it seems really fast now. The 600-yard run has now become the 600-meter run. It's still called the 600, but the modern-day race is fifty-six yards longer.

After the Big Ten indoor track meet, I was selected to run the anchor leg on relay teams in the *Milwaukee Journal* Games and *Chicago Daily News* Relays. In Milwaukee, we finished third. After the meet, I wrote my father, "Our lead-off man ran a 55.8 quarter—thus the third place. We should really be tough in Chicago. We were close enough to first place that we feel a decent lead-off man can get us in there. Hope you can make it to Chicago."

My father did come to Chicago for the meet. We went to the Erlanger Theatre for an afternoon performance of No Time for Sergeants and then to the meet that night, where we finished a close second. The next day, the *Des Moines Register* wrote:

In a mile relay featuring Wisconsin, Iowa, Illinois and Minnesota, the Hawkeyes finished second despite a brilliant anchor leg by Tom Ecker. Ecker picked up eight yards of a 12-yard deficit but couldn't overtake the front-running Wisconsin anchor man.

The "brilliant" anchor leg was one of the few brilliant things I did while I was a student at Iowa.

The next weekend, a few of Iowa's trackmen were invited to participate in an indoor meet in Cleveland, Ohio. One of the meet's big races was the 600-yard run, featuring the 600-yard champions from the Southwest Conference, the ICAAA Conference, the Big Eight Conference, and the Big Ten Conference. Two Ohio State runners, Al Roberts and Mead Burnett, both friends of mine, were added to the race to complete the field. The ICAAAA champion, Charley Jenkins, had won the Olympic 400-meter title the year before, so he was a shoo-in to win the race. I finished second.

Over spring break, the track team went to Arizona

by train, with meets scheduled in Tucson and Tempe. The train trip took twenty-four hours each way. We lost to both the University of Arizona and Arizona State. In the Arizona meet, I won the 880-yard-run in 1:57.6, but the rarified air was my enemy after the race. I couldn't get my breath and became quite ill for a short time.

Right after that trip, I noticed my wisdom teeth were coming in, so I went to the university's dental college for a checkup. The dentists there found there was not enough room in my mouth for the four new teeth. They advised me to have all of the wisdom teeth pulled. The cost would be only $5 per tooth, so it appeared to me to be a real bargain. If I had waited until after graduation, the cost would have been considerably higher.

All four pulled teeth produced dry sockets, exposing bare bone, so I had to return to the dental school every day to have them fill the dry sockets with gauze strips coated with eugenol. It turned out that one of the teeth had four roots, a rarity which left an especially large dry socket. I was advised not to exert myself for the next few weeks.

The holes in my mouth had a detrimental effect on my training. I didn't know it at the time, but my tooth problems were going to be the end of my track career at Iowa. I did run in the Drake Relays and in two more dual meets, but my results were not impressive.

The rest of the spring was spent alternating track meets on weekends with sessions with the singing Hawkeyes whenever we could get together. (I was also carrying sixteen semester hours of classwork.)

Much of my track career at Iowa was as a relay runner. Until my senior year, I was always the lead-off man. Many times I've told people that the coach always gave me the same advice before every race: "Don't lose so much ground that the other three guys can't make it up." (The other three guys won me a lot of wrist watches, gold medals, and other prizes.)

At Iowa, I was called a "utility man." I filled in wherever I was needed, competing in the 440-yard dash, the 600-yard run, the 880-yard run, the mile run, the 120-yard high hurdles, the 220-yard low hurdles, the 440-yard intermediate hurdles, the 4x220-yard relay, the 4x440-yard relay, the 4x880-yard relay, the sprint medley relay, the distance medley relay, the shuttle high hurdle relay, the high jump, the long jump, and the decathlon.

In later years, when I was delivering banquet and commencement addresses, I told my audiences that I had a unique distinction: I was the biggest loser in intercollegiate track and field. I had lost in sixteen different events.

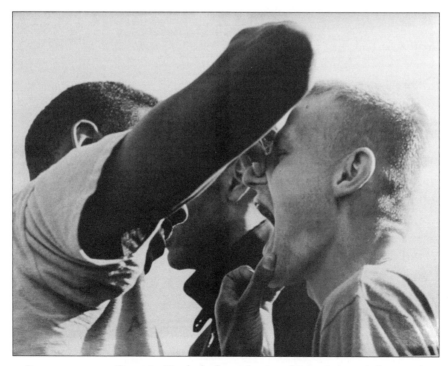

Iowa teammate, Gastonia Finch, looks at the site of my missing wisdom teeth.

19

The Old Walrus Goes to Hollywood

On the music front, the Hawkeyes' records were selling so fast we had to order another 1,000 copies from the company in Chicago. (My father got his investment back, and more.) With a new baby at home and final exams and graduation closing in on both Judy and me, plus trying to promote the Hawkeyes on radio stations and record stores, it was an extremely busy time.

We heard from a few fly-by-night music publishers and record companies that showed interest in our record. But then we heard from one of the biggest music publishers in the country, Bregman, Vocco and Conn in New York. They wanted to publish both songs.

Then we got the biggest break of all. Warren "Jorgy" Jorgensen was a regional salesman for Capitol Records and he lived in nearby Mount Vernon. Ford Roberts, a disc jockey on WMT in Cedar Rapids, had become a big Hawkeyes' promoter. Ford suggested that Jorgy send a copy of the record to the A&R (artists and repertoire) people at Capitol. He did send it, and after a few phone calls, Capitol put us under contract.

The Hawkeyes publicity photo

At the time, I was quoted as saying, "The whole record idea was a one-in-a-million shot. It isn't every day that new people in the business get a break like this."

We signed a four-month contract with Capitol. If the record was a big seller for them, the contract would be extended to one-year options for a total of seven years. Should there be a contract extension, half of any songs recorded by the group would be written by me. Plus I would do all of the group's vocal arrangements.

Capitol decided to re-master our original recordings and release the same two songs nationally on the Capitol label. But they decided to make our B side, "Someone, Someday," the A side. Tom Morgan, A&R man for Capitol, set the release date for July 1, 1957.

In the meantime, I had to get a job. My goal throughout college had been to become a television director. I had taken all of the television courses that were offered at Iowa and had held part-time jobs at local TV stations as a cameraman and floor director. However, there was a federal freeze on building and licensing new television stations at that time. Plus, it was an industry made up largely of young people. Almost no one was dying or retiring. TV stations that already had broadcast licenses were hiring inexperienced people right out of high school for $1 per hour.

The country was suffering from a mild recession that year, so jobs were difficult to find in any field. Desperate for jobs, Sky Marschall and I became traveling salesmen for a small drug company in Hampton, Iowa. The company was co-owned by Sky's father, "Smoke" Marschall. The products were Teen Clear, an acne treatment, and Odor Gone, a foot deodorizer. The secret ingredient in both products was the chemical hexachlorophene. I was able to commute to the job during the week and be back in Iowa City on weekends.

At the time, my wife, Judy, our six-month-old daughter, Wendy, and I were living in a thirty-five-by-eight-foot house trailer near the University of Iowa campus. It was a common housing option for married students. Our plan was simple. If I got a good, steady job somewhere, we would pull the trailer to wherever the job was.

I quit the sales job after six weeks when I was offered a job at radio station KVFD in Fort Dodge, Iowa, as a night disc jockey. Driving our 1953 Pontiac, we pulled the trailer the 185 miles from Iowa City to Fort Dodge.

The owner of the station, Ed Breen, wanted me to spin records and be funny, which was right up my alley, but he wanted me to call myself "the Old Walrus," which I didn't think really fit me. But he was the boss, so I became the Old Walrus as I spun records and tried to sound happy. One of the canned recordings I used during the show was a station promo with a musical group singing, "This is the greatest radio station in town." Then I would say, "That's because it's the *only* radio station in town." Ed Breen didn't think it was funny.

Breen was on the air in the afternoons, interviewing people on the street. I began to do parodies of his show as part of my comedy each night. Ed Breen wasn't amused. He called me into his office one day and suggested we part company. That was fine with me. I didn't like the job, or Ed Breen, so the house trailer was back on the road. I had been the Old Walrus for exactly one week.

This time the destination was KWWL-TV in Waterloo, Iowa, only 100 miles from Fort Dodge. I had worked there as a cameraman during the Christmas break the year before, so they knew me. They had a position for a "sound engineer," with very low pay. After two weeks on the job, I decided to quit. But the station's owner, R.J. McElroy, asked me if I would be interested in taking a promotion job that would start in two weeks. That was fine with me. I could spend the two weeks promoting the Hawkeyes and their new record.

About the same time, I received word that Bregman, Vocco and Conn had printed sheet music for "Someone, Someday" with the Hawkeyes' picture on it, to be distributed to music stores throughout the country. Its British counterpart, Chappell & Co., Ltd., printed sheet music for both "Someone, Someday" and "Who Is He?" for distribution in Great Britain.

After the Capitol Records version of "Someone, Someday" was released nationally, it was on the national charts for three weeks before dropping off the list. But it was a huge hit in a few places around the country, especially in Los Angeles, where a disc jockey named Earl McDaniel was playing it non-stop.

Within a few days, I received word from Capitol that they wanted to exercise the contract option, signing us to a new yearlong contract. Then they asked me if the group could come to Hollywood to record four more sides over the Labor Day weekend. At the same time, they said they had made arrangements for the group to appear in Earl McDaniel's stage show, *Recording Stars of 1957,* at the United Artists Theatre in Los Angeles. Income from the stage show and the recording session would be $1,500—a huge sum for us.

I called the four singers, who had taken summer jobs in different parts of the country, and told them they should be back in Iowa by August 27. I explained the reason: "We're going to Hollywood!"

Everyone was excited about the trip. We started by driving to Des Moines, where we were interviewed by the *Des Moines Register* for a front-page story, and then on to Omaha, where we caught our flights to Denver and Los Angeles.

Our A&R man from Capitol, Tom Morgan, met us at the airport with a Cadillac limousine and a driver. We were first driven to the Vine Lodge, a motel that was a block-and-a-half from the Capitol Tower, and we checked in and dropped off our luggage.

Then we were driven to the famous Brown Derby restaurant, where we were treated to a large, upscale dinner. At the table across from us were Gale Gordon and Bob Sweeney, who were starring at that time in a sit-com, *The Brothers.* Previously they had starred with Eve Arden in *Our Miss Brooks.* During the dinner, a number of people came to our table to meet the Hawkeyes. After dinner, we went to the Vine Lodge and slept.

The next morning we met Earl McDaniel, the DJ who was starring in the stage show, and Mike Casino, the show's promoter. We were to be third-billed in a stage show of seven musical acts. Eddie Beal and his orchestra would be on stage, providing backup music for all of the acts. We were scheduled to do twenty-one shows in five days—four each afternoon and night, and a special midnight show on Saturday. We would do two songs, "Full Moon Above," and finish with "Someone,

Someday." Between the live shows, there was a sixty-three-minute movie, *Rock all Night,* starring the Platters, a vocal group on its way to stardom.

The lineup for each live show was The Kip Tyler Trio, Young Jesse, Don & Dewey, Richard Berry, The Hawkeyes, Frankie Lymon and the Teenagers, and LaVern Baker. In my notes, I wrote, "Frankie Lymon is polite and more than friendly. LaVern Baker is crude and obnoxious."

Richard Berry's short act included a song he had written titled "Louie, Louie." He had recorded the song that year on a little-known record label, Flip Records, but the song was not popular enough to make the charts. Six years later, Berry became a wealthy man when "Louie, Louie" was recorded by the Kingsmen and became one of the biggest hits of that era. As the songwriter, Berry collected a nice royalty on every record sale.

We went to the theater for a rehearsal later that morning. As we had expected, it was not a smooth rehearsal. We had to get used to the orchestra, and they had to get used to us. That afternoon we had our first live show.

Tom Morgan had told us the opening show on a Thursday afternoon wouldn't bring much of a crowd, but he was wrong about that. Youngsters, mostly teenagers, were crowded on the sidewalk for two blocks down Broadway from the theater. The police and the ushers weren't sure the theater doors were going to hold with all the pushing and shoving that was going on. There were many newspaper photographers around the scene, getting pictures of the mob.

The first show for the Hawkeyes went very well. I noted that they "were flashy and on the notes. The kids looked like they had been singing together for years and years. When Dixie made the spiel that she was going to sing 'Someone, Someday' (while the boys vamped), there were many screams from the crowd." Between shows, DJ Earl McDaniel told us, "As far as the kids in the audience know, you've got one of the top records in the country."

The Hawkeyes continued to get better with every show, and the crowds seemed to be more and more appreciative. When we finished the final show on that first day, we were driven back to our motel. It was after midnight when we arrived there.

The next day, Tom Morgan and Milt Raskin drove us to the theater. Tom would be the A&R man for our recording session on the following Tuesday night, and Milt would be conducting the band.

Milt Raskin was a noted musician, songwriter, arranger, and accompanist, well-known to everyone in

The Hawkeyes listening to a playback of one of their recordings at Capitol records in Hollywood.

The Hawkeyes at Capitol Records in Hollywood

Hollywood. When he learned he would be the conductor for our recording session, he wrote a song especially for our group's sound. It was called, "I'll Be There."

According to our recording agreement, Capitol would select two songs to be recorded, and I would pick two of my own. Capitol picked Milt's song and a song titled, "Don't Play Games with Me." My two were "Full Moon Above" and "Waiting in the Dark."

With shows taking up every afternoon and evening, the only time Milt and I could work on arrangements was during the mornings. We would meet at the motel early each morning and work out the arrangements. My part was easy. All I had to do was write the parts for the three background voices. Milt had to write parts for piano, rhythm guitar, fill guitar, bass, and drums.

During one of our morning meetings, Milt said he would nominate me to be a member of ASCAP, the prestigious American Society of Composers, Authors and Publishers. For a songwriter to be a member of ASCAP, he has to have a song recorded by a major

recording company and sheet music printed by a major music publisher. Milt said he would have his partner in the music publishing business, the well-known Johnny Mercer, second the nomination.

After Monday night's final show, I went backstage to meet with the group. I told them how proud I was of their performances. Then I showed them a tall ladder than was leaning against a wall. "Look at the bottom rung," I said. "That's where you are. Now look at the top of the ladder." They all looked up, but no one could see the top because it was so dark up there.

The next night we were to begin our recording session at 8 p.m. During the day, the group went to a barbecue at a friend's home, but I didn't go. I met with Milt at Coffee Dan's, a regular hangout for Hollywood musicians, and we put the finishing touches on the arrangements. After dinner that evening, we walked to the Capitol Tower for the recording session. When we arrived, we heard that Judy Garland was recording in the next studio, but Tom Morgan told us we weren't allowed to go there. "She swears," was the explanation.

The recording session was quite an experience. I sat in the control booth with Tom Morgan and a few recording engineers. The session lasted until midnight, but the kids' voices held up pretty well. During the final song of the night, "Don't Play Games with Me," Jim had to hit some high notes at the end of the song. His voice went out, but one of the engineers said he'd fix it. He took the final notes from a previous take, spliced it into the last take, and the problem was solved.

As we were walking back to the motel, after midnight, we were waiting to cross a street when an MG pulled up next to us. In the passenger seat, wearing a fur coat, was Judy Garland, one of the biggest stars in the world. Her recording session must have lasted as long as ours.

Ukulele chords became the source of the harmony for the Hawkeyes

20

My New Kentucky Home

We flew back to Iowa the next day to begin another school year. Two of the singers were seniors at the university; two were juniors. And I was ready to report for my new job at KWWL-TV in Waterloo.

The job in Waterloo was as a promoter of television "westerns" that would be in the fall lineup on NBC. Debuting that fall were *Tales of Wells Fargo, The Restless Gun,* and *Wagon Train.* KWWL had a solid market in Waterloo, but the station wanted me to sell these programs to the viewers in Cedar Rapids, some sixty miles south.

The Asian flu pandemic of 1957 was at its height, so all TV employees, including me, received flu shots. That was a lucky break. It kept me well all year when so many others became ill.

I drove from Waterloo to Cedar Rapids every day, pulling a variety of stunts with western themes. The best stunt, and the one that got the most publicity, was pulled off one night in downtown Cedar Rapids. My longtime friend, Ocie Trimble, borrowed a pair of draft horses and a hay wagon from his brother, Bruce, and he drove the team to Coe College on the east side of the city.

At Coe, I hired a few coeds to ride on the wagon, sitting on bales of hay. We had signs on the sides and the back of the wagon advertising the upcoming *Wagon Train* television series. We paraded up and down the streets of downtown Cedar Rapids, with the students throwing candy to gathering onlookers. The downtown was crowded and busy in those days.

After we had made several passes on the downtown streets, a police officer pulled us over and asked to see our permit to parade. Of course, we didn't have one. He wrote Ocie a ticket and told us to get the wagon off the streets. That's when Ocie "got lost" and couldn't find his way home. We went up and down several more streets, trying to find our way, and we finally

arrived back at Coe College to drop off the coeds. We removed the signs from the wagon, and Ocie rode off for home.

A few days later, the ratings came out, and the three NBC westerns took a large share of the Cedar Rapids market. I was very proud of myself. The station's owner, R.J. McElroy, called me into his office, congratulated me on my success, and told me my job was done. He didn't need me anymore. As it turned out, my brief career in television was over.

The Hawkeyes' new record was released October 7, so I thought money would be rolling in. But in the meantime I had three mouths to feed and no prospects for work. That's when the phone call came that changed our lives.

The call was from my mother-in-law, Helen Koch, who was a school secretary in an elementary school in Louisville, Kentucky. She suggested I give up my television plans and music aspirations for a time and become a school teacher. There was a shortage of teachers in Kentucky, and she said I could get a provisional teaching certificate if I would agree to take the required seventeen education hours.

Even though I knew how important it was to stay close to the singing group, we had reached a critical "fork in the road." I thought the move would be temporary, so we decided to leave Iowa behind and pull our trailer the almost 600 miles to Kentucky.

I didn't know very much about Kentucky, except I had heard it was "the land of beautiful horses and fast women." And I knew that the state's economy was based on three basic evils—whiskey, tobacco, and betting on horses.

After getting settled in Louisville in late October, I began substitute teaching during the day, attending classes on Saturdays, and working behind the counter of a drugstore at night.

All of the classes were at Catherine Spalding College—a school for Catholic women. (My father told me I didn't seem to fit into either category.) In some of my classes, I was the only student who was not a Catholic nun.

The drugstore job was from 7 to 10 p.m. weeknights. There were busy times, but there were also long periods of inactivity, so I had plenty of time to think and be creative.

One of my ideas was to start an organization called the Louisville Track Club, designed to encourage young athletes to continue training and competing in the "off-season." I even designed the club's uniform—red, black, and white with LTC on a shield in the front of the shirt. (I still have the original sketches.)

My plan was to have the club operate much like a semi-pro baseball team, with athletes recruited from local high schools, colleges, and post-graduates. The club would sponsor one indoor and one outdoor meet each year and would send the club's top performers to the big meets, including national championships and Olympic trials.

But before I could get my idea off the ground, I heard of a new organization that had just been formed in Louisville, the Kentuckiana Cinder Club. It was a non-profit organization dedicated to promoting track and field in Kentucky and southern Indiana. I dropped my plans for the Louisville Track Club and became a charter member of the Kentuckiana Cinder Club.

The club's founder was George Gibson, a soft-spoken insurance man who had been on the track team at Yale in the 1920s. The club's weekly meetings were held in George's home in Louisville. For the next three years, I drove to George's home on many Sunday evenings to attend meetings of the Cinder Club.

We were planning to raise enough money to have a portable 220-yard banked board track installed in Freedom Hall in Louisville. It would be the largest banked indoor track in the world and would be certain to produce many world records.

It was agreed that once a year the Cinder Club would host a large invitational indoor meet that would attract outstanding athletes from throughout the world. At my suggestion, the name "Mason-Dixon Games" was chosen for the meet.

Because Louisville sits on the Mason-Dixon Line, I thought the name would be ideal. I could see

matched relay races featuring teams from Northern and Southern colleges. I even suggested having crossed flags—an American flag and a Confederate flag—as the meet's logo.

The club decided the first Mason-Dixon Games would be held in February 1961. That gave us more than three years to raise the money, have the track built, and make all of the necessary preparations. Eddie Weber, the athletic director at Bellarmine College, was named meet director, or "Meet Head," as we called him. I was named as coordinator of special events. I was the one who had to bring in the big-name athletes so we could guarantee a big-time audience.

I worked as a substitute teacher almost every day I was in Louisville that school year. Many teachers were affected by the Asian flu pandemic of 1957-58, so subbing jobs were plentiful.

I did leave Louisville several times to hitchhike back to Iowa to be with the singers. Every time I was with them, I arranged new songs, so they had a variety of music to perform. However, when I was with them, I was spending money and not making any.

Times were tough for the Eckers that year. Our second child was born in April, so suddenly there were four mouths to feed and not very much income. Louisville's school lunch program helped me out at noon each day I was subbing. I was able to buy a peanut butter bun and a glass of reconstituted milk for a total of six cents. That was my lunch every day that I subbed.

The new record, "Full Moon Above," backed by "I'll Be There," had brisk sales in Iowa and the Hawkeyes were in demand for personal appearances. I had booked them into the Surf Ballroom in Clear Lake, Iowa, before I left for Kentucky, but in my absence the singers were doing their own bookings. Since they were all in school, they were doing shows only on weekends. That spring they performed in Oxford Junction, Cedar Rapids, Mount Vernon, Cedar Falls, and Ottumwa.

I hitchhiked back to Iowa for the Ottumwa performance. The group's concert was scheduled for a Saturday evening, but in the afternoon they appeared with the traveling Aunt Jemima on an outdoor stage in the center of town. Aunt Jemima, who was in town promoting pancake syrup, asked the group if they would back her up as she sang the McGuire Sisters' big hit, "Sugartime." I was nervous because they had never done that song before. But, fortunately, the chords were the same as from our first two songs, and they sang it perfectly.

The group had hired three student-musicians, the Dave Lanning trio, to provide backup instrumental music. The shows were getting to be very professional sounding and very professional looking. When *Billboard* magazine voted the Hawkeyes as one of the ten most promising vocal groups in America, I was convinced we were going straight to the top.

In March, during one of my trips back to Iowa, the four singers and I signed an agreement outlining our obligations and duties. We all thought we were going to be successful in the music business, so we felt we needed the agreement, which called for each of us to receive 20 percent of any net proceeds.

Shortly after that, Dixie hit me with a bombshell. She wanted out of the agreement. She said she was quitting the group to get married. I knew she really wanted out because she thought she would become a singing star on her own, making much more than 20 percent. That meant we had to find a replacement singer soon since we had a big audition in Chicago on May 23. However, we weren't really worried. There were lots of female singers around.

We advertised for a new singer in several newspapers, and we received many responses. After holding more than 200 auditions, we finally selected Barb Bywater, a freshman from Des Moines, to be the new Dixie Davenport. But Barb was having trouble adjusting to the group's style. The sound wasn't right, and we had the big Chicago audition coming up. So we asked Dixie if she would sing with the group one more time. Then we would find the replacement singer. She agreed to do it if we would pay all of her travel and lodging expenses, which we agreed to do.

We went to Chicago and auditioned for MCA (Music Corporation of America), the world's largest booking agency. Also present was the woman who booked acts into Chicago's Conrad Hilton Hotel. The audition was a huge success. MCA offered us a three-year contract. Their plan was to have the Hawkeyes sing in resorts during the summer and on college campuses during the school year. We signed the contract.

But the representative from the Conrad Hilton Hotel said she would first like the group to perform at the Conrad Hilton for six months, beginning in the fall. We signed that contract, too. Everyone was happy.

For the first half of the summer, we struggled to keep the Hawkeyes together without Dixie, but it was impossible. We continued to look for a possible replacement singer, with no luck. Derk and I even drove to Kansas City when we heard another Capitol recording artist, Ann Leonardo, was singing in a nightclub there. We talked with Ann and her father, who was also her manager, but they weren't interested in joining the Hawkeyes.

Then, suddenly, we also needed a replacement for Don Roeder, who was drafted into the Army. I sang Don's part as we continued to look for a new lead singer. Reluctantly, we decided to give up on the music career.

It was painful, but I had to cancel the contracts with Capitol Records, MCA, and the Conrad Hilton Hotel. Then I headed back to Kentucky to try to find a real job. The final two sides that we recorded in Hollywood, "Waiting in the Dark" and "Don't Play Games with Me," were never released by Capitol.

21

On to E-town

After completing the seventeen required education hours at Catherine Spalding College and getting my teaching certificate, I began looking for a teaching job for the 1958-59 school year. I learned there were two jobs open in the Elizabethtown, Kentucky, school system—high school English, for which I was qualified, and eighth-grade math and science, for which Judy was qualified.

So we applied for the two jobs and were interviewed by Talton K. Stone, the superintendent of schools. After talking with us, and checking our credentials, he offered us the jobs, but he reversed the assignments. Judy would be the high school English teacher, and I would be the eighth-grade math and science teacher. (I had never had a math or science course in college.) He also wanted me to coach the eighth-grade football and basketball teams.

The eighth grade was part of Morningside Elementary School, with a very strong, opinionated, vocal principal, Henry Pilkenton. I really liked him. Elizabethtown High School was attached to Morningside, but the only facilities that were shared by the two schools were the office area, the gymnasium, and the cafeteria. The high school principal, Paul Kerrick, was not nearly as forceful as Mr. Pilkenton. The two principals shared the same office area, but it was no secret that the two didn't like each other.

There were ninety eighth-graders, divided into three rooms of thirty students. The three teachers, Mrs. Alvey, Mrs. Jones, and I, each had a primary classroom, with a teacher's desk and thirty-two student desks. When the bell rang, signaling the end of a class, the students would stay in their seats, and the three teachers would change classrooms. I taught three math classes before lunch and three science classes after lunch. Often I had to scramble to keep ahead of the brighter kids in the classes.

My math students used a book that was published and copyrighted by the American Book Company in 1956. Although some of the information in the text might have been a little outdated during the four years my classes used it, I don't recall the information was inaccurate enough so that anyone noticed.

Recently, when I dusted off a copy of the book and glanced through its pages, I realized how soon we forget. The following story problems illustrate dramatically what's happened during the past sixty years:

Posing with my principal, Henry Pilkenton.

- *Mr. Porter has an annual income of $4,000. Find the amount the Porter family should plan to save each year.*

- *The price of an adult ticket to the movies is 60 cents. This includes a tax of 20 percent on the actual price of the ticket. How much is the tax?*
- *About one-fourth of the price of a gallon of gasoline is taxes, which means that if a gallon of gasoline costs 22 cents, then 5 1/2 cents of it goes for taxes. Find the cost of gasoline in your city and also the state tax on gasoline in your state.*
- *Jane is saving to buy a new bicycle that costs $27.50. If she has saved $9.50 already, how much more must she save?*
- *When the price of a quart of milk increases from 16 cents to 19 cents, find, to the nearest whole percent, the percent of increase in the price.*
- *Find the profit on a new stove selling for $60 if the profit is 12 1/2 percent of the selling price.*
- *Mr. Dodd is building a house that will cost $9,000. He has $3,000 in cash and has borrowed the balance of $6,000 from a savings and loan association at 4 percent. He will make monthly payments of $60 each, which will be as convenient as paying rent. Make a table showing the monthly unpaid balance, monthly payment, interest, and the amount used to reduce the debt.*

My classroom was on the second floor of the school and faced west. The school's flagpole was right outside my window. One afternoon we could see a thunderstorm coming toward us from the west. Since the speed of light is far faster than the speed of sound, I quickly taught my students how to compute the distance to each lightning strike by recording the time between the lightning strike and the thunder. It was both a math and a science experiment.

Looking at my stopwatch, I computed the distance to the lightning strike by noting when we saw the lightning and then noting when we heard the thunder. I would call out the time between the two and the students would record their answers.

When the time between the flash and the thunder was fifteen seconds, we knew the strike was about three miles away. As the storm moved toward us, and the time interval was only four seconds, we knew the lightning strike was less than a mile away. The final strike was a great flash of light and a huge bang right outside the window. The lightning bolt had struck the flagpole, right in front of our eyes. It was a valuable lesson.

My favorite activity while teaching eighth-grade

math was a unique way to teach students how the stock market works. In our math book was a chapter entitled Investments and Savings. Sub-headings in that chapter were Ways of Investing Money, Forming a Corporation, Stock Quotations, Buying and Selling Stocks, and Profits and Losses.

In February 1959, my students, after learning about the stock market, began producing a mimeographed six-page monthly newspaper called *The Inkblob*. In the paper was news about students in grades five though eight, plus honor rolls, other interesting tidbits, cartoons, puzzles, and jokes. We even ran ads for some students' "businesses," such as Snead's Worm Ranch. All of the newspaper's copy was gathered and written by fifty-three eighth-grade students.

We formed a corporation, selling each eighth grade student and five faculty members one share of stock in *The Inkblob*. The cost was one cent per share. That gave us 95 cents, enough money to purchase the paper we would need to produce the first newspaper.

There were four issues of The Inkblob, sold by the students during the first week of each month during lunchtime. We charged five cents per copy and were able to sell about 250 copies per issue.

There was a lot of stock trading during the four months. The seventy who bought and sold shares had a variety of experiences. One student earned $2.20, I earned $1.13, and one student (Jimmy Snead of Snead's Worm Ranch) lost $3.20. Of the ninety-five shareholders who invested one cent, twenty-one students and four faculty members held their shares, without any trading, and received fifty cents each when the corporation was dissolved in May.

The superintendent, Talton Stone, sent *The Inkblob* staff an open letter, which appeared in our final publication.

I believe the best financial investment I ever made was when I bought one share of stock in The Inkblob. *It cost a penny, and I have been offered as much as 50 cents for that one share. Even the oil magnates who are striking oil aren't making that kind of return on their investments.*

And, in addition, it has afforded me during the year several hours of pleasant and enjoyable reading. I learned things about people I wouldn't have known before, and it has helped me to "keep up" with our Junior High group—and that's a big job.

But more important, it gave me the feeling of satisfaction over being a part of an institution that makes it possible for boys and girls to grow and develop and learn to 'do things.' This Inkblob *was an accomplishment—a real project in which all who had any part can be really proud.*

Congratulations, again, to the sponsor, the staff and all who in any way contributed to the success of this fine little publication. No—siree! I don't want to sell my share of stock. If nothing more, I want to keep it to remind me of what eighth-grade boys and girls can do when they put their minds to it. I'm proud of you.

Earlier in that school year, I was faced with a major fork in the road. I was approached by the high school basketball and track coach, Charlie "Spud" Rawlings with a proposition. He asked me if I would like to be the high school track coach. It didn't pay anything, he said, but it would be a lot of fun. Actually, he wanted to give up the track job so he could be the golf coach and play nine holes every afternoon. I accepted. Later, I found out there was no track, just an unmeasured path around the football field.

As long as I would be coaching track in the spring, I decided to start a cross country program in the fall. So, I was coaching eighth-grade football and high school cross country in the fall, eighth-grade basketball in the winter, and high school track and field in the spring. It was quite a load, considering I had never wanted to be a coach of any kind.

As soon as it was announced that I would be the eighth grade football coach, the high school coach, Bill Hogg, met with me. He told me to pressure the kids in my eighth-grade classes to stay away from band and to go into football where they belonged. That didn't seem reasonable to me, so I met with the high school band director to see what the problem was.

The band director was Ken Neidig, a soft-spoken, dedicated musician. Immediately, Ken and I became friends and are still good friends more than sixty years later. The year after we first met, we even wrote the E-town school fight song together.

It seemed that Ken Neidig and Bill Hogg were vying for some of the same students. Ken was willing to share, but Bill Hogg was not really interested in the welfare of students. His interest was in winning football games—nothing else. He got his high school football players to harass members of the band, and they even began to harass my cross country runners.

To illustrate the kind of person Bill Hogg was, all you had to do was hear the story of the remarks he made after one of his football banquets. At the end of every football season, it had been a tradition for the boosters to present the football coach with a check for $100 at the football banquet. One year the team was undefeated, so the boosters decided they would raise extra money so they could present the coach with a check for $1,000. The following year, the boosters went back to presenting the coach with a $100 check. The team had lost one game that season. Coach Hogg remarked to a group of us after the banquet, "One loss cost me nine hundred bucks."

The eighth-grade football team was really good that year. We had six wins and no losses before I decided to resign from football coaching. During the seventh and final game, Bill Hogg showed up with some of his varsity players. He insisted on taking over the role of the coach, playing some of his varsity players in order to win the game. He was clearly cheating. I quit on the spot, retiring from football as one of the few undefeated football coaches in the country. Maybe the only one.

22

The Donald Hough Connection

One of my favorite instructors when I was a senior at the State University of Iowa was Donald Hough (pronounced Huff), a down-to-earth, folksy, freelance writer who had many literary successes but had never finished high school. He taught the course magazine article writing because of his 400 published magazine articles and eight published books. He told the class that he was working on a new book, *Cornstalk,* about his yearlong experience at Iowa.

Don Hough (he insisted we call him Don) was not your typical academician. For example, he was a heavy drinker and didn't hide it. Each afternoon, after class, he would head to the nearest bar. Often, some of his students would accompany him, but I never did. And he decorated his classroom by taping covers of old *New Yorker* magazines to the walls.

Don didn't mind that I would sometimes bring my favorite pet mouse, Mickey, to class. The gray mouse would stay in my shirt pocket, tearing up small pieces of tissue or eating Rice Krispies when I was walking, but would come out and sit on my shoulder when I was sitting in class.

In December of that year, Don Hough had an article published in *Esquire* magazine. The article explained methods bartenders use to cheat martini drinkers. I bought a copy of the magazine, and had Don sign the article for my father. When I told Don that my father's favorite drink was gin and Pepsi-Cola, he autographed the article: "To Bob, Get that Pepsi out of your gin. Don Hough"

Don once told us the secret for getting an article published in the New Yorker, which included articles that didn't make much sense to some of us. He said, tongue in cheek, you write the article, remove the first and last pages, and then submit it.

I learned a great deal from Don. He taught me that the three most important factors in writing are read a

lot, write a lot, and experience a lot. He said: Don't write what you want to write; write what they want to read. And never write about anything you don't know about.

When it came time to actually write an article, I was stuck. I didn't have any ideas. Don asked me if I knew anyone who had an unusual occupation. I told him that one of my good friends in nearby Cedar Rapids was George Nissen, whose company manufactured trampolines. Don said that was a natural for a fascinating magazine article.

So I drove to Cedar Rapids, armed with a notepad and camera, and interviewed George Nissen, the inventor of the folding trampoline. I took several pictures of George and of some of the manufacturing operations. When I submitted the article to Don Hough, he gave me an A for the article, and an A for the course.

At the end of the school year, Don Hough left Iowa City and returned to New York. After my graduation from Iowa, I continued to stay in touch with him. His book, Cornstalk, was still only in the planning stages. He wrote me, asking me to send him information about some of the places he had visited during the year he was in Iowa City.

In November 1958, he wrote me a letter explaining why I hadn't heard from him for a while. He wrote, "I have the best excuse I ever heard of for not replying: I have been in an insane asylum. Okay, Tom, try to top that one, man. I was an honored guest of the New York State Department of Mental Hygiene until three weeks ago. I was on an extended vacation, that is to say, from the bridge of the nose up. I now seem to be what they call normal, which is probably worse."

He closed the letter with this: "Tom, please send me all possible information, as we discussed. I want this not only for the book—which, frankly, still is a year away—but some possible magazine work. And because I do so like you and would hate to lose touch."

In the spring of 1959, in my first year as the track coach at E-town High, I was scrambling to learn everything I could about coaching. It didn't take me long to realize that there weren't any easy-to-read, comprehensive track and field coaching books on the market. I decided it was time to fill the void and create the ultimate track and field coaching book—one that young coaches would be certain to buy.

Since the best-known college coaches in America were too busy to write, or perhaps they didn't have the ability to write, my idea was to select twelve of the best-known track and field coaches in America, interview them, and write a twelve-chapter book. It would be their ideas in my words. Each of the coaches would be one who was well-known in a particular area of track and field.

I had never written a book. But I had written three magazine articles for *Athletic Journal* that would not be published until spring. The only published writing I had ever done was in the sixth grade, when I won a citywide essay contest, and in the eighth grade, when my two short stories about a man named White were published in the Waverly newspaper.

Armed with only an idea—one that I thought was really a good one—I decided to hitchhike to New York over the Christmas break to sell the idea to a publisher. Looking back now, I realize that took a lot of nerve.

My first stop in New York was at 2 Beekman Place, an upscale apartment building near the United Nations building, where Donald Hough lived. Don Hough had written several award-winning books about Jackson Hole, Wyoming.

My favorite Don Hough book is *The Cocktail Hour in Jackson Hole*. In the book, he explains that the cocktail hour in New York is generally a two-hour period, usually from 5 to 7 p.m. In Jackson Hole, the cocktail hour starts in mid-September and lasts until March, or jail, whichever comes first.

When I told Don about my book idea, he advised me to go to Prentice-Hall, Inc., on Fifth Avenue, one of the biggest book publishers in the world. So I went there, on foot.

The Prentice-Hall reception area was on the ground floor of a multistoried building. I walked up to the receptionist and asked if I could I could meet with an editor of sports books. "Do you have an appointment?" she asked. Of course I didn't.

She told me she was sorry, but there wouldn't be any editors available for the rest of the week. I told her I was from Kentucky, and I had to leave later that day. She said all she could do was take my name and number, and she'd have an editor call me the following week. Of course, it was a big disappointment for me.

So I decided to leave my name and number, knowing that it is not nearly as effective explaining an idea over the telephone as it is in person.

"My name is Tom Ecker," I told her.

"Ecker?" she answered, "How do you spell that?"

"E-C-K-E-R," I replied.

She seemed very surprised. "That's my last name," she said. "I've never met anyone outside my family with the name Ecker."

"Neither have I," I responded.

That was my lucky break. Ms. Ecker (I never learned her first name) used her lunch hour to track down Prentice-Hall's top sports book editor, Alan Williams. She introduced us, and I showed Alan a rough outline for the book. I told him I wanted to call the book *Championship Track and Field by 12 Great Coaches*.

He liked the idea and said he'd be in touch with me the following week. Shortly after I arrived back in Kentucky, the contracts arrived. I was about to write a book about twelve great coaches, even though I had not yet selected or contacted any of the coaches. The publisher sent me $600, so I could pay each of the coaches a $50 stipend.

When my father found out I was going to write a book, he had one of his typical responses. He said, "Before you write a book, you should probably read one."

In January, after I had returned home from New York, I received a letter from Don Hough. He wrote: "It was wonderful having you stop in, if even for a few minutes, the other day. I do so hope you had good luck at Prentice-Hall." I wrote him back that I had had really good luck, thanks to him.

The next step was to write letters to the twelve coaches that I thought would be the best for the book. They all accepted. I told them I would pay each of them $50 for their contributions to the book, even though they probably would have done it just to be included as one of the great coaches.

Collecting the information for the book wasn't easy. As I wrote in the preface: "The material for this book was collected through a series of tape-recorded interviews with the twelve coaches. Traveling to and from these interviews carried me through one blizzard, one automobile accident, and twenty-six states. The first interview was held in a New York hotel. The final interview was held five months and 27,000 feet of tape later on a hillside terrace overlooking San Francisco Bay."

Championship Track and Field by 12 Great Coaches was published in 1961 and was a huge success. It was that month's featured book in Prentice-Hall's Coaches Book Club, which guaranteed its success. It went through several printings and was in print, both in English and Spanish, for more than twenty years, a Prentice-Hall record for a trade book. It was my first of seven books published by Prentice-Hall. Don Hough should be given much of the credit.

Beginning in 1960, I was writing magazine articles for several different publications. Most of the articles dealing with sports were published in *Athletic Journal* magazine—dozens of them over the years. Often I also would supply color photos for the magazine's covers.

Almost all of the articles were written with my byline, but there were times when the publisher, Jack Griffith, would ask me to ghost write articles for coaches in other sports.

I really liked Jack Griffith and the quality of his magazine. We became best of friends and were partners in many writing and travel projects over the years. When we were collaborating on various projects, he would often ask me to spend the night in his spacious, three-level home in Kenilworth, Illinois, an upscale neighborhood north of Chicago. I was always amused that Jack and his wife, Kay, kept a large number of goldfish in the bathtub of a spare bedroom. The fish spent the warmer months in an outdoor fishpond but were always brought inside for the winter.

Essentially, *Athletic Journal* was a one-man operation. Although Jack had a few employees, he selected and edited the articles, took the sequence photos that accompanied many of the articles, laid out the pages, sold advertising, and sold subscriptions. He was an amazing man.

My favorite non-sports articles appeared in the 1960s. The first was "Commuting Captain," which appeared in the *Louisville Courier-Journal Magazine* in

Looking at the track and field manuscript with Prentice-Hall's top sports book editor, Alan Williams

1962. It was the story of the captain of a Mississippi River towboat who lived with his wife and five children in landlocked Elizabethtown, Kentucky. The captain, Allan Rickett, who was my next-door neighbor, had to commute the more than 200 miles between his home and his job every fifteen days. To get the story, I rode with Captain Rickett on the towboat, Gilda McCool, from Cairo, Illinois, downriver to drop off a barge in Arkansas, and back up to Memphis, Tennessee.

In 1963, an article titled "Absentminded Profs? Nope! Athletic" appeared in *The Courier-Journal Magazine.* It was a cute piece about Western Kentucky professors who had formed a very successful fast-pitch softball team called The Pedagogues. On one occasion, the team's pitcher, economics professor Clyde Bates, told the manager, mathematics professor Allan Anderson, that he couldn't pitch that night because he had a "psychosomatic pain" in his arm. He pitched anyway, and the Pedagogues won the game.

I played second base for the Pedagogues and was a reasonable fielder, but my hitting wasn't very good. If I drew a walk, I would steal second and third base on the next two pitches. Bert Barrone, the sports editor for the local newspaper, wrote, "Ecker is really fast. If he could steal first base, he'd be on every time."

One of my favorite articles was "P.T. Barnum's Ocean Trial," which appeared in Yankee magazine in 1964. I had long been a follower of Barnum's exploits, so it was fitting for me to do the research for an article about him. Along with the article, the magazine ran the following teaser: "P.T. Barnum loved a good joke but, on an ocean voyage in 1857, the joke was on him. Yet he had the last laugh!"

The final article was "The Pill that Could Kill Sport," which I wrote in 1966 while living in Sweden. It was the first-ever article offered to a U.S. publication about the use of steroids in sports and their effects on athletes. It was originally accepted by *The Saturday Evening Post,* a very prestigious magazine at that time.

But then I got word from the Post's editors that they had been told by a U.S. Olympic team doctor that such drugs didn't exist. It was later learned that the same Olympic team doctor had administered steroids to many U.S. athletes at the 1964 Olympic Games in Tokyo. When *The Saturday Evening Post* rejected the article, it was sold to *True* magazine and was published in their April 1967 issue.

When the steroids article first appeared, I was criticized by some of the U.S. coaching community. There were coaches who didn't believe such drugs existed. And those who did know about steroids didn't want their secret to be known. It wasn't clear to me whether they wanted their athletes to have an advantage over others, or whether the use of drugs in sports might appear to be a form of cheating.

Anyway, the article was soon forgotten, and it was many years later before anabolic steroids became a hot topic of conversation again.

23

Progressive Interval Training

Three runners came out for the Elizabethtown cross country team in the fall of 1958—a freshman and two sophomores. One of the sophomores, Russell Banks, showed a great deal of promise. He finished first in four races and was tenth in the state meet.

The regional meet, which qualified individual runners for the state meet, was run at Beech Bend Park in Bowling Green. Beech Bend was an outdoor amusement park, complete with a large campground, various rides, an automobile race track, and a small zoo.

Since we had only three runners on our team, I drove my car to the meet, with the three runners as passengers. When we arrived, early on a Saturday morning, it was so foggy at the park that I could barely see to drive. Very slowly, I drove up and down some grassy hills that we thought would be the cross country course. Suddenly, I stopped the car. Right in front of us was a very large, live elephant. Naturally, we didn't get out of the car. Later we learned that the zoo animals at the park were allowed to roam freely—even the elephants.

The fog cleared before the race started, and the elephants were not around to see Russell Banks win the first regional championship, in any sport, in Elizabethtown High School's history. We didn't know it at the time, but because of Russell, cross country was about to become a very successful sport at Elizabethtown High School. And track and field was going to be even more successful.

The primary reason for the success of the track and cross country programs was a new training program I developed called progressive interval training. Actually, it was a combination of two training programs that already existed—progressive weight training and interval training.

The basic principle behind interval training is quite simple: Repeated speed develops both speed and endurance. The four factors in progressive interval training are:

1) DISTANCE—The distance to be run repeatedly. It is always shorter than the runner's racing distance.

2) INTERVAL—The interval of easy jogging between runs. The jogging continues until the athlete's heart rate lowers to 120 beats per minute.

3) SPEED—Slightly faster than the runner's racing speed.

4) NUMBER—The number of times the distance can be repeated. This is the progressive part of the training program, which I called N +1 (Number + 1).

Each runner would run repeats to near-exhaustion. When he felt he could not do any more, he would run one more at top speed. The final run was always faster than any of the preceding runs.

As soon as the cross country season began, I realized that public relations play a large role in the success of any sports program. I met and became friends with the sportswriters and columnists at the *Louisville Courier-Journal,* the *Louisville Times,* and the two semi-weekly newspapers in Elizabethtown. Whenever one of my high school athletes did anything of mention, I called the newspapers.

Every year, during the fall, my cross country team was getting headlines in the papers, while the football team rarely got a mention. It was clear to me that newspapers can't report what they don't know. One of the sportswriters at the *Courier-Journal* told me he received an angry phone call from Bill Hogg, the E-town football coach, asking, "What's all this cross country crap you're putting in your newspaper?"

I also learned that the two local newspapers filled most of their pages early, but saved page one until last. As soon as I found out what the deadlines were for page one news, I filed the stories just before the deadline. Our results were usually on page one.

As a publicity stunt, we had the slowest of our three cross country runners challenge the fastest running back on the football team to a 100-yard race. The football player accepted the challenge, and the race was set for the following afternoon, immediately after school. Word got around school about the race, and the students poured out of the building to watch.

Everyone thought the running back would win easily, but I knew enough about training to know what was about to happen. When the gun was fired, the football player sprinted to a commanding lead. But at about fifty yards, he began to fade. The cross country runner passed him well before the finish line as the football player was struggling to stay on his feet.

Coaching the junior-varsity basketball team that winter was a lot of fun, but I was definitely out of my element. At the end of the season, I convinced the superintendent that I should concentrate on coaching track and cross country, abandoning basketball forever.

My first year as the track coach was a pretty good one. There were ten runners, mostly sophomores, who came out for the team. Russell Banks was the conference, regional, and Junior Olympics mile champion. Four other runners won titles in the Junior Olympics as well.

I had been running pretty regularly during the season, so I decided—at the age of twenty-three--to do some serious training and get back into shape. My goal was to run for the Kentuckiana Cinder Club. Competition wasn't very keen, and I made the team easily.

Our first track meet was an Olympic development meet in Lexington, Kentucky. The winner of the 440-yard hurdles and runner-up in the triple jump was a fellow listed in the Louisville newspaper as Tom Acker. Acker's time for the hurdles was listed as 46.9, probably a misprint since 46.9 was well under the world record.

Our second meet was the AAU Regional Championships in Dayton, Ohio. I was supposed to be running the 400-meter hurdles against the two-time Olympic champion, Glenn Davis. But Davis missed his plane from Dallas, and I had to run without him. I won the hurdle race that night and finished second in the triple jump, scoring eight of our team's fifteen points. Not bad for someone who was two years out of shape.

Winning the 400-meter hurdles in Dayton quali-fied me for the National Track and Field Championships in Boulder, Colorado. The Cinder Club voted to send me to Boulder, but they had only enough money for a one-way plane ticket. I agreed that, after the race, I would hitchhike back to Kentucky.

After my race (I didn't qualify for the final), I met Vice President Richard Nixon, who was giving out ballpoint pens and chatting with athletes beside the track. By the time I got to him, he had run out of pens, but he gave me his business card instead, which said "Richard M. Nixon, Vice President of the United States of America." He autographed the back of the card. The signed card was a lot better than a ballpoint pen.

I showered, packed my bag, and then began the long journey back to Kentucky. Two years out of college, with a wife, two children, and a full-time job, I was about to embark on the most unusual hitchhiking experience of my life.

I managed to hitch a ride to Highway 36 on the eastern side of Denver. But then I was stuck. There were no rides, and it was getting dark. Finally, a car stopped and offered me a ride. Eager to move on, I didn't even ask where he was going.

He drove for a few miles and then took a side road to the left. Hitchhikers never want to get off the main roads, so I asked him where we were headed. "To a small, private airfield," he responded. He turned into an open area, and I could see a two-passenger single-engine plane in the car's headlights. He drove to the plane, parked the car, put my bag behind the airplane's seat, and told me to hop in.

After I got into the plane, the pilot explained that he had to deliver the plane to a service station about twenty miles east, along Highway 36. When we closed the airplane's doors and the pilot started the engine, he told me that the plane had no lights—no landing lights and no running lights. I asked the pilot how other planes could see us if we didn't have running lights. He told me they can't see us, but we can see them.

We taxied to the end of the grass strip, and he prepared for takeoff. He revved the engine, and we were rolling down the runway. When we got into the air, I could see the lights of many other airplanes in the area. But, of course, the other airplanes couldn't see us.

It didn't take us long to get to the service station. It had bright lights around the station, but the field in back, where we were supposed to land, was totally dark. And we didn't have landing lights.

On the pilot's first landing attempt, we hit the ground hard and bounced. The pilot gunned the engine, and we circled the field to try again. By now the people in the station knew what we were doing, and two cars came racing out to the field so we could see their lights. With help from the cars' lights, we made it on our second attempt, but we bounced pretty hard again before the pilot brought the plane to a halt.

I grabbed my bag, thanked the pilot, and ran all the way to the highway. It was my second race of the day.

The rest of the trip was pretty routine. I arrived back in Kentucky the next day, eager to tell anyone who would listen that I had hitched a ride on an airplane.

By the fall of 1959, cross country was becoming very popular at Elizabethtown High. Eleven runners came out for the team, defeating twenty-four different teams during the season. Russell Banks was again the team leader, winning ten of his fifteen races.

One of our cross country meets, against Louisville's Valley High School, was staged at the halftime of a home football game. The band director, Ken Neidig,

E-town's Russell Banks poses with me after he won the Kentucky State Cross Country championship.

was kind enough to give up his band's halftime performance so we could show off our cross country team to the 2,000 people who attended the football game against Bardstown St. Joe.

Elizabethtown won the meet, 19-40. In cross country, the winner receives one point, the second place finisher receives two points, etc. The lowest total score of the first five runners wins the meet. (I had one runner that year who bragged to his classmates that he was the high point man on the cross country team.)

During the winter, I took a Saturday night job as a disc jockey on the local radio station, WIEL. I would spin 45 rpm records, read commercials, and tell jokes between 6 p.m. and midnight every Saturday. There was a teen center in town where the kids all congregated. My show was broadcast into the teen center for the final two hours of the show, when I would spin the top records of that week. The show was very popular with the local high school kids.

A record twenty-three students came out for the 1960 track and field team. Dominated by juniors, the team won the Mid-Kentucky Conference championship and became the first athletic team in the school's history to bring home a regional championship. In the regional meet, Elizabethtown outscored the second place team, 68-26.

One of the meets held that year was against two Louisville high schools—Shawnee and Central. Shawnee's track coach, Wayne Cooper, who was a fellow member of the Kentuckiana Cinder Club, made the arrangements. The meet was held at Louisville Central, an all-black high school at that time.

Even though E-town finished a distant third, there was one event worth remembering. After the 440-yard run was completed, a Central runner was writhing on the ground, yelling that he had never done anything so difficult in his life. The runner was Cassius Clay, an eighteen-year-old boxer turned trackman, who won six Golden Gloves' titles in his six years as an amateur fighter.

A few months later, he won the light-heavyweight gold medal in the 1960 Olympic Games. Later that year, he became a professional boxer. In 1964, Cassius Clay changed his name to Muhammad Ali, and the rest is sports history.

The 1960 cross country team was truly outstanding, winning four dual meets, plus the conference and regional championships. The season was climaxed

*I am seated at the banquet's head table with the speaker,
Larry Snyder, and Pete Bowen, the master of ceremonies.*

sell Banks and his teammates. The school was famous
for its football and basketball banquets, but cross
country had never gotten that kind of recognition.
Since it was a first, I knew we had to have an outstanding
after-dinner speaker.

I had met the track coach at Ohio State, Larry
Snyder, the previous spring when I interviewed him
for a chapter in my book *Championship Track and
Field By 12 Great Coaches.* Larry was very well-known
in track and field. Not only had he been the coach of
four-time Olympic gold medalist Jesse Owens in the
1930s, he had been the head coach of the 1960 U. S.
Olympic team the previous summer.

I called Larry and told him we'd like him to be the
speaker at our banquet, but I also said we didn't have
any money—even for expenses. He said he'd do it at
no charge, and he'd pay his own way.

On a cold December day, Larry drove all the way
from Columbus, Ohio, to Elizabethtown, Kentucky,
on roads that were not up to today's standards. He
arrived in time for the evening banquet, and, after he
was introduced, he told stories and related incidents
about the 1960 Olympics in Rome.

The master of ceremonies for the event was the
president of the AAU and former national track champion,
Pete Bowen. Also at the head table that night
was the Cinder Club's chairman, George Gibson, who
took time to tell Larry Snyder about the club's plans
for the Mason-Dixon Games, which would be held
less than three months later.

About 125 people attended the banquet, including
Board of Education members, faculty members,
parents, and fans. It was a wonderful evening.

when Russell Banks won the state cross country title,
the first state championship in any sport in the school's
sixty-year history.

Besides bringing home the championship trophy,
I was presented a key to the city by the mayor of
Elizabethtown.

When the season was over, we decided to stage the
school's first-ever, cross country banquet to honor Rus-

24

The Mason-Dixon Games

One of the first things we had to do to prepare for the initial Mason-Dixon Games in February 1961 was to produce an entry form. We printed 1,000 single-sheet entry forms, with red ink on white paper. When the forms arrived, I entered my two-year-old son, Kerry, in the 600-yard run. I wanted him to be the first entry in the first-ever Mason-Dixon Games.

There were nineteen indoor board meets around the country at that time. Most of the biggest of these, called Track and Field "Carnivals" by the press, were located in the East and Midwest, although a few board meets were beginning to spring up in Canada and on the West Coast.

The size of each of the indoor board tracks was limited, depending upon the size of the arena floor. All but one of the tracks in existence at that time were eleven laps to the mile, or 160 yards per lap. That meant that some relay exchanges had to be made on curves, difficult to maneuver on a track where the curves are banked. At the Knights of Columbus meet in Cleveland, the arena floor was even smaller, allowing twelve laps to the mile, or almost 147 yards per lap.

The size of the floor at Louisville's Freedom Hall was large enough to have a 220-yard oval, or eight laps to the mile, with all relay exchanges on straightaways. We knew the size of the track would be a big attraction for athletes. The four-lane oval was going to have flat straightaways on both sides, with curves banked up to two-and-one-half feet at the middle of the turns. Made of 176 numbered portable sections before being installed, it was to be the largest banked board track in the world—an ideal place to set records.

The five-lane flat board track down the middle, for running the seventy-yard dashes and hurdles, was to be 90 yards long. No other board facility could accommodate more than sixty-yard races.

Other facilities that would certainly draw top athletes were the field event runways. The pole vault and long jump runways would be 144 feet long, the longest runways of any board tracks in the world. The track and runways, which cost $25,000, were made of Sitka spruce.

Not only would the wooden pieces have to be joined together, the club also had to bring in eighty bags of cedar shavings for the high jump landing area and eight tons of sand for the long jump area. For the pole vault, the necessary foam rubber was borrowed from the University of Louisville track program.

Because of my work with the promotion of the Elizabethtown track and cross country programs, I already knew some of the writers for the *Louisville Courier-Journal*, a morning paper, and the *Louisville Times*, an evening paper. I decided it was time to get to know all of the writers for both papers so the Mason-Dixon Games would get the best possible coverage.

On a trip to Louisville, I spent part of the day talking with the writers who would be covering the Mason-Dixon Games. In the morning, I met with the sports editor for the *Times*, Dean Eagle. He told me that he and writer Bob Weston would be my contacts.

In the afternoon, I met with Larry Boeck of the *Courier-Journal*. He told me that he, sports columnist Earl Ruby, and writer Bill Endicott would be my contacts. I already knew Larry Boeck well, and, because he was a track enthusiast, I knew he would be writing most of the stories publicizing the Mason-Dixon Games.

On a daily basis, I began feeding the two Louisville newspapers announcements of the athletes who would be competing in the Mason-Dixon Games, along with biographical information and photos.

I had an opportunity to meet with top track stars that year at the Sugar Bowl Invitational, an outdoor track meet held in conjunction with the Sugar Bowl football game in New Orleans. I drove to New Orleans and got a single hotel room in an old downtown hotel. The prices had been raised for the Sugar Bowl events, so I had to pay much more than I had expected—$18 a night.

After one night there, I found I could stay with the athletes free in a dormitory at Tulane University. That was not only the cheaper way to go, I had the opportunity to talk with athletes and coaches one on one, to try and convince them to come to the Mason-Dixon Games the following February 18.

I recruited several athletes from the Sugar Bowl meet, including Olympian Ernie Cunliffe, who would run the mile in the Mason-Dixon Games. At the time, Ernie was the world indoor and the outdoor record-holder for 1,000 yards and was one of America's fastest milers. I spent a lot of time with Ernie, who became a lifelong friend.

Another "catch" at the Sugar Bowl meet was fiberglass pole-vaulter Aubrey Dooley from Oklahoma State University. At that time, almost all pole-vaulters were using aluminum poles, which did not bend. Dooley was producing bends of almost 45 degrees. I knew he would be a big crowd-pleaser.

Both the *Courier-Journal* and the *Times* ran advance stories about Dooley. One of them had a picture of him pole-vaulting, showing the extreme bend of the pole. The other had a mugshot of Dooley and the lead, "Sure and 'tis an Irishman's privilege to get high if he pleases. But will you look at the way Aubrey Dooley does it."

Also recruited at the Sugar Bowl meet were some outstanding athletes from the University of Houston and Southern Illinois University.

One of the coaches I met in New Orleans was Lew Hartzog of Northeast Louisiana University. He turned out to be an invaluable source of track and field talent. Two of his athletes, twins Don and Dave Styron, could do just about anything. Don was outstanding in any sprint or hurdle race. Dave was a sprinter, long jumper, high jumper, and pole-vaulter. Between them, they held many national titles and records. (They laughed that Don won their very first race on March 8, 1940, when he was born twenty minutes ahead of Dave.)

Hartzog also coached pole-vaulter John Pennel at Northeast Louisiana. Pennel didn't enter the 1961 Mason-Dixon Games, but he did come to Louisville the next year. Pennel went on to set eight world records in the pole vault in the 1960s and was the first to vault over seventeen feet.

The Sugar Bowl meet was held on December 31. When it was over, I said my goodbyes and climbed into my car for the 700-mile drive back to Kentucky. I drove all night, spending New Year's Eve in my 1959 Chevrolet.

When I returned to Kentucky, I heard from the track coach at Tennessee State, Ed Temple. He wanted to enter two Olympic champions in the Mason-Dixon Games—sprinter Wilma Rudolph and long-jumper Ralph Boston, both students at the Tennessee school. Temple said he would also like to bring his "Tiger-belles" women's team to try to break the indoor world record in the 440-yard relay.

To save money, I asked Ernie Cunliffe if he would stay at my home in Elizabethtown. That was perfect for him since he was a graduate student at Stanford University in California and needed to study on weekends. He went to the high school on Thursday and Friday to sit in on classes.

On Saturday, the day of the meet, a column by Earl Ruby featuring Ernie appeared in the *Courier-Journal.* Cunliffe said, "I have been in track meets seven consecutive weekends, and you know what that has done to my studies. I caught up with a little classroom work the past two days in Elizabethtown. Visiting with Tom Ecker, I sat in on two high school classes as part of my practice teacher work. That's how I've managed to keep up my grades. Have to study as I go."

The first-ever Mason-Dixon Games were held on Saturday evening, February 18, 1961. We had an outstanding meet, with spectators filling 8,129 of the 14,501 seats in Freedom Hall. Sitting in a box seat in the middle of the stands was former Governor A.B. "Happy" Chandler, who had done so much to make that evening a reality.

A young photographer from *Sports Illustrated* introduced himself to me that night. He was Neil Leifer, an eighteen-year-old with bright red hair. As he took photos during the evening, he stopped often to ask me questions or just to chat. He was a very likable young man. I had no idea at the time, of course, but Neil Leifer was to become known as the greatest sports photographer of all time. His 1965 photo of Muhammad Ali standing over a defeated Sonny Liston is one of his most famous photographs.

There were many exciting events during that inaugural meet, but there were only three world records set. The Tennessee State 440-yard relay team, anchored by Wilma Rudolf, was almost assured a world record in that event. This is what Bob Weston wrote later in the *Louisville Times:* "Remember the lead-off runner who fell on her face in the women's 440-yard relay at the Mason-Dixon Games and cost Tennessee State an almost certain victory in the event? As if that weren't enough humiliation for one meet, she also jumped the gun twice in the women's seventy-yard dash and was automatically disqualified. They could have dubbed Jean Holmes 'Miss Fortune of the 1961 Mason-Dixon Games.' No one had worse luck."

We were very pleased with the enthusiasm of the crowd and with the meet results. The meet director, Eddie Weber, summed it up when he said, "I was amazed at the enthusiasm of the fans, especially the women seeing their first track meet."

My biggest challenge in the operation of the first Mason-Dixon Games was having enough expense money to attract top athletes. We had to rely on the size of the track and the length of the runways to attract athletes since the club had allowed me only $3,700 for expenses. We were counting on colleges, universities, and high schools to pick up the tabs for their athletes. It was the superstars who did not have a school to sponsor them that we would have to pay for. And even though some athletes were receiving large payments "under the table," for competing in other indoor meets, we vowed not to go that route. We offered the top performers only coach air fare, a hotel room, and $15 a day living expenses.

As it turned out, I was in contact with some athletes who wanted "under the table" payments, but I always refused. One athlete wanted money for a first-class air ticket so he could pocket the extra money by flying coach. Another said he needed money for two air tickets, even though he would be using only one.

Track and field old-timers still enjoy telling a "money-under-the-table" story from the early 1950s. It seems that two-time Olympic 800-meter champion, Mal Whitfield, was scheduled to run the 600-yard race at a well-known Midwestern indoor meet. He demanded $1 per yard, or $600 to run the race. He was paid the $600, and he won easily.

At the same meet the next year, the promoters wanted him to run the 1,000-yard race. Whitfield demanded $1 per yard, or $1,000, but the promoters said they would only pay him $600, as they had done the year before. Whitfield was not happy. He collected the $600 and ran the 1,000-yard race, but when he reached the 600-yard mark, he dropped out.

25

Mumps and Bruises

In early March 1961, with the first Mason-Dixon Games completed, I decided to attend the *Milwaukee Journal* Indoor Games in Milwaukee, Wisconsin. I had run in that meet three times while I was a student at Iowa, and I knew many of the athletes and coaches who would be there. It was a great opportunity to talk up the next Mason-Dixon Games. My hitchhiking days were over, so I decided to drive the 450 miles to Milwaukee.

I asked one of my senior runners, Russell Banks, the state cross country champion, if he would like to go along and help me drive. That way we could make it a "day trip," and we wouldn't have to get a hotel room. We would leave very early Saturday morning, drive to Milwaukee, attend the meet that night, and then drive straight back, arriving in E-town Sunday morning.

Several days before the trip, I visited the home of one of my athletes, David Olson. He had not been in school that week because he was suffering from a case of the mumps. There was no mumps vaccine at that time, and, because I was twenty-six years old, I thought I was immune.

The trip to Milwaukee went as planned. We left early the morning of March 11, and arrived in plenty of time to attend the meet. But after the meet, we had a brief interruption in our plans. Some of the coaches I knew invited us to a post-meet party that was hosted by the meet's sponsor, the *Milwaukee Journal.* They were eager to meet Russell Banks, who was a hot college prospect.

At the party, we were chatting with some of my coaching friends when I decided to sample the relish tray. I bit into a pickle, and I felt a sudden, very sharp pain in my left jaw. I suspected it might be the beginning stages of mumps, so I told Russell we should probably leave. We said our goodbyes and left. I remember we ran quite a distance to where the car was

parked, which was probably not the best thing to do.

I drove for a while but had to give it up. I had a severe headache and was unusually weak. Russell had to take over the driving while I tried to rest in the back seat. He drove all the way to E-town, only stopping for refills at gas stations.

By the time we arrived in E-town, I was very ill. I went straight to bed, and Judy called our doctor, Fred Rainey, who came to our home. The diagnosis was a severe case of mumps, but only on the left side of the body. My left parotid gland (below the jaw) was very swollen, which was normal, but there were three dangerous complications—orchitis (inflammation of the testicle, again only the left side), pancreatitis (inflammation of the pancreas), and the most dangerous complication, encephalitis (inflammation of the brain), which gave me a severe headache.

The doctor gave me a shot of morphine and then fashioned a sling to support my left testicle, which had swollen to the size of a grapefruit and was hanging down to just above my knee. I was then put to bed and the doctor left. During the night, I crawled to the bathroom and began vomiting (the result of the pancreatitis).

Later in the night, when the morphine made me feel better, I stood beside the bed, stripped off the sling, woke Judy up, and said, "I'm cured." That was when she made the decision to put me in the hospital, where I spent the next three weeks in isolation. Only medical staff and Judy could enter the room.

After two-and-a-half weeks in isolation, the doctor came to visit me and told me we had a problem. He had just come from a Jaycees meeting where there had been a motion to start a fundraising campaign to help Judy with her expenses after my death. Because he was my physician, he couldn't say anything at the meeting, so he thought we should jointly write a press release to put a halt to the rumors.

My fellow teacher, Royce Speck, took over as track coach while I was hospitalized. He had a frightening experience on the track one day. He was racing against some of the high school runners, and he collapsed after finishing the race. I don't know what the diagnosis was, but he was rushed to the hospital. We were in the same hospital at the same time, but, because I was in isolation, we never saw each other. He recovered quickly.

Recovery for me was not as fast as I would have liked, but I did get back to my teaching and coaching after a few more days. I was really eager to get back to work. The 1961 track and field team promised to be our best ever.

One of the highlights of the season was participating against the best runners from seven states at the News-Piedmont Relays in Greenville, South Carolina. Our sprint medley relay team had received a special invitation to participate in the meet, which was held in mid-April.

I was still recovering from the side effects from the bout with mumps, so I couldn't drive yet. We were driven to Greenville by Kelly Vance, the local Volkswagen dealer, in a Volkswagen bus. Kelly's son, Kevin, who was also on the track team, made the trip with us. In the bus were Kelly and Kevin, the relay team of Richard Burnett, David Olson, Kenny Maffet, and Russell Banks, and me. Needless to say, with that load the bus had trouble negotiating some of the hills in eastern Tennessee and western South Carolina.

Our team won the race in 3:45.5, just one-tenth of a second off the meet record, on a slow, wet track. According to a newspaper article in the *Louisville Courier-Journal*:

When anchor man Russell Banks began the final leg—the 880—Elizabethtown was in last place, twenty-five yards behind the leader. However, despite the wet track, Banks ran the half mile in two minutes flat to put E-town in the winner's circle.

Besides winning the race in South Carolina, the E-town team dominated the area track and field scene. The team was undefeated and set five regional records, four conference records, and nine school records. The team brought home six trophies.

As it turned out, that was my last season coaching high school track or cross country. On September 4, 1961, after the cross country season had already begun, the high school football coach, who had always been an enemy of our program, announced there would not be room for any cross country runners in the locker rooms. I went to the school principal to complain, but he wouldn't take a stand. So I resigned as a coach but continued teaching my classes in mathematics and science. That would give me much more time to spend on the next Mason-Dixon Games.

I knew that Royce Speck, who had helped us out before, would step in as the new cross-country and track coach. And he was very successful. Years later, Royce said I had given him the coaching break of a lifetime—twenty years of winning championships at Elizabethtown High School.

When *Championship Track and Field* came out in the spring of 1961, I was making a reasonable living as a teacher and coach in Elizabethtown. But to me, this wasn't the time to quit writing. As soon as I realized there was money in a book about coaching track and field, I knew there would be even more money in a book about coaching football.

First I asked a friend, Paul Jones, who coached football at nearby Fort Knox, if he'd help me put together a football book. When he told me he would, I went to Prentice-Hall and suggested I do a second book for them, this time with twelve football coaches. As you might expect, we decided to call this book *Championship Football by 12 Great Coaches*. The

E'town's 1961 track team, sporting six trophies they had won during the season.

contracts were completed and signed, and I began to select the twelve coaches.

Most of the coaches I contacted were honored to be chosen to be in such an elite group, but I had considerable trouble getting the one coach I really wanted—Paul "Bear" Bryant of Alabama. Bryant had a book of his own on the market at the time, and he simply wasn't interested. I had Paul Jones, who had played for Bryant, contact him, but Paul was turned down abruptly.

So, in desperation, I called Bryant's office at the University of Alabama. When his secretary answered the phone, I told her I was calling from Prentice-Hall in New York to speak with Coach Bryant about an exciting book project. (I was actually calling from Kentucky.)

It turns out the Bear was vacationing in a beach house on the Gulf of Mexico in southern Alabama. His secretary promptly gave me the phone number.

So I called the beach house. When Bryant answered the phone, I told him I was from Prentice-Hall in New York, and we were putting together a book with ideas from the top twelve football coaches in America. He told me he wasn't interested.

My friend Paul Jones had told me that one of Bear Bryant's best friends was Bobby Dodd, the football coach at Georgia Tech. So I said to Bryant, "Bobby Dodd is one of the twelve coaches."

"Really," he answered. "If Bobby's on the book, put me down, too."

Then I called Bobby Dodd at Georgia Tech and got him to sign on, assuring him that Bear Bryant was in the book.

Getting the tape-recorded interviews was not always easy. I hired two of my high school students, Russell Banks and Larry Perry, to drive my station wagon to meet with many of the coaches. We had a mattress in the back of the station wagon. I would sleep at night while they drove. They would sleep during the day while I conducted interviews.

Our initial trek took us from Kentucky to the following universities: Penn State, Maryland, Georgia Tech, Tennessee, Alabama, Texas, Arkansas, and Missouri. The other four interviews were conducted later at the National Football League's coaches meetings in Chicago. In Chicago, one of the interviews was conducted while the coach, Murray Warmath of Minnesota, was taking a shower and dressing to go out for the evening.

Some of the coaches talked to me initially, but then assigned assistant coaches to be interviewed. One of those assistants was Hayden Fry (later to become the University of Iowa head coach for twenty years), who was an assistant to Frank Broyles of Arkansas at the time. Fry contributed the entire chapter on "Offensive Back Play."

Speaking of Hayden Fry, some twenty-two years later, when Fry was the football coach at Iowa, he was scheduled to be honored at a 1983 I-Club function. The emcee for the evening was Gus Schrader, the long-time sports editor of the Cedar Rapids *Gazette* and a longtime friend of mine. Gus told me he wanted to play his banjo during his time behind the microphone, and he asked me if I'd write a song about Hayden Fry that he could sing.

I had a lot to work with. Fry had come to Iowa from Texas. He helped design Iowa's Tigerhawk logo, which adorned all varieties of clothing. He had a saying about scratching where it itches. And the previous two years, Fry's Iowa teams had played in the prestigious Rose Bowl and in the lesser-known Peach Bowl. So I wrote four verses to the tune of "My Bonnie Lies over the Ocean."

When Fry headed north out of Texas,
Complete with a handful of maps,
He wanted a place to coach football,
And sell lots of T-shirts and caps.

The chorus followed each verse:
Bring back, bring back,
Oh, bring back that Rose Bowl to me, to me.
Bring back, bring back,
Oh, bring back that Rose Bowl to me.

The other verses:
Fry says that the schedule is awful,
That some of the tough games must go,
Just schedule Northwestern more often,
And add games with Cornell and Coe.

Oh, Hayden arose from the masses,
Arose to the heights he could reach,
He quickly arose to the knowledge,

He can't tell a rose from a peach.

Fry says you must scratch where it itches,
And that takes two very good hands,
Fry knows how to scratch where it itches,
He does it in front of the stands.

The audience loved the song, even though Gus wasn't a very good banjo player. Everyone in the room was laughing, no one more than Hayden Fry himself.

The most entertaining of the coaches I interviewed for the book was "Cactus Jack" Curtice of Stanford. Besides contributing the material for the chapter on "The Passing Game," Jack told me how he managed to keep his job, even though Stanford's record in football was not very good. (Jack's teams were 14-36 during the five years he coached at Stanford.) He said he always recruited the two biggest linemen in California, even if they weren't very good players. Their assignment was to carry Jack off the field after every loss. Then the alumni would look at each other and say, "Old Jack isn't much of a coach, but the kids love him. Let's keep him one more year."

Championship Football by 12 Great Coaches was published by Prentice-Hall in 1962 and was another big seller. The first printing of 5,000 copies sold out before the book was released. It went through several printings before it finally became an out-of-print book.

A gift from University of Iowa former football coach Hayden Fry

Coach Hayden Fry, enjoying one of the lighter moments at the 1983 I Club function

26

Sixteen Feet or Bust

Throughout the remainder of 1961, I drove the fifty miles from Elizabethtown to Louisville to attend Sunday evening meetings of the fourteen-member Mason-Dixon committee. The meetings were held at 7:30 p.m. around the dining room table in the home of George Gibson, at 2115 Village Drive.

The meetings usually lasted five to six hours. And, as Bill Endicott reported in the *Louisville Courier-Journal,* "when the meetings were over, the committee always left behind a conglomeration of stuffed ashtrays, half-full cups of cold coffee, and stacks and stacks of notes, letters, and diagrams."

"We've had 18 meetings, starting back in September of last year," Ecker told *the Courier-Journal.* "And we have to settle everything that is going to be part of the Games."

"For instance, budget is one of our big problems. We allotted $3,700 for athletes' expenses last year, and we've upped that to $6,500 this year. But, at last count, if we paid expenses for every athlete who wants to come here to compete, it would be more than $10,000."

"We'll have a great meet. That I promise you," said Ecker. "We've got world record-holders, Olympic performers, everybody."

Attending the Sugar Bowl Invitational had been so successful for me the previous year, I decided to drive my 1959 Chevrolet to New Orleans again the following year. As usual, the meet was held on December 31.

The surprise winner in the pole vault was a little-known twenty-four-year-old Marine corporal from Quantico, Virginia, John Uelses (pronounced YULE-sus). Jumping fifteen feet, six-and-a-half inches, he beat out several other fifteen-foot vaulters, including the outdoor world record-holder, George Davies of Phoenix, Arizona.

As soon as the competition was over, I talked with Uelses about coming to the Mason-Dixon Games on February 17. When he heard me tell about the 144-foot runway, he was enthusiastic and said he wouldn't miss it.

Others I talked into running in Louisville were Oregon miler Jim Grelle and his Oregon teammate, long distance runner Keith Forman. Keith told me he was hoping it would rain during his race in New Orleans, since he was an Oregon Duck, and ducks love rain. During the two-mile run, with Forman leading the pack, it began to rain. He smiled, waved to me in the stands, and held his hand out as if to catch some of the rain.

After returning from New Orleans, I was mentioned in an article in the *Louisville Courier-Journal.* "Tom Ecker, coordinator of the Mason-Dixon Games, describes John Uelses as a man who 'eats and sleeps and lives pole vaulting 24 hours a day—he loves it.' Ecker was with Uelses at the Sugar Bowl Meet in New Orleans."

To demonstrate how much pole vaulting engulfed his life, on the last day we were in New Orleans, I asked Uelses if he'd like to see some of New Orleans' sights. We got into my car and we drove through some of the upscale waterfront neighborhoods, which I had done the year before. I pointed out one of the mansions and said, "That's the home of Louis Prima." Uelses asked me, "Who does he pole vault for?" Obviously, he had never heard of the famous bandleader and singer or his talented wife, singer Keely Smith.

In early January, after Uelses had committed to come to Louisville, I contacted his longtime vaulting rival, Henry Wadsworth, to see if he would join the Mason-Dixon Games pole vault field. Those two were among the vaulting elite who had soared over fifteen feet. In fact, each would consider it a poor performance if he failed to clear fifteen feet.

Henry Wadsworth later enrolled at Western Kentucky and became our best-ever pole vaulter. I often referred to him as "two-thirds of a poet."

The friendly rivalry between Uelses and Wadsworth began when the two were in high school in Miami, Florida. Both said they would not be as good as they were if it hadn't been for the keen high school competition.

Unlike Wadsworth, John Uelses was not a native Floridian. He was born Hans Feigenbaum in Berlin, Germany, in 1937. Hans' father was killed on the Russian front during World War II, and his mother struggled to make ends meet after the war came to an end.

Hans' uncle, who lived in Miami, contacted a Florida state representative, George Smathers, to see if there was anything that could be done to help his nephew in Berlin. Smathers, a lawyer in Miami, sponsored legislation in 1950 that enabled young Feigenbaum to enter the United States and to become eligible to be a U.S. citizen. He was twelve at the time.

After he arrived in the United States, Hans Feigenbaum changed his first name to John, the anglicized version of Hans, and he took the Florida family name of Uelses. (Later, some of his detractors referred to him as John Useless.)

When John Uelses became a world-class pole vaulter years later, an ambitious young reporter asked him if he had escaped East Germany by pole vaulting over the Iron Curtain.

Early in the 1962 season, John Uelses had his personal best at the Sugar Bowl meet in New Orleans when he cleared fifteen feet, six-and-a-half inches. Wadsworth had cleared fifteen feet, five-and-one-quarter inches. Since both vaulters were young, either of them could have been the first to clear sixteen feet. At that time, the record was fifteen feet, ten-and-one-fourth inches, set by George Davies of Oklahoma State in the spring of 1961.

In the summer of 1961, Uelses and Wadsworth had traveled abroad to represent the United States in competitions against Russia, Great Britain, Poland, and West Germany. They finished first and second in all four meets, with Uelses winning against Russia and Poland and Wadsworth winning against Great Britain and West Germany.

The Uelses-Wadsworth matchup in Louisville would demonstrate the differences between vaulting with a fiberglass pole and metal pole. Uelses was converted to the fiberglass pole by Aubrey Dooley, the 1961 Mason-Dixon winner. Wadsworth, although impressed with the thrust Uelses was able to get from his fiberglass pole the past summer, continued to use a steel pole in 1961 and 1962. (Later, Wadsworth converted to using a fiberglass pole and used one in both the 1965 and 1966 Mason-Dixon Games.)

As it turned out, the 1962 indoor track season was filled with controversy and became a meet promoter's dream. On January 27, John Uelses tied the pole vault world record by vaulting fifteen feet, ten-and-one-fourth inches. He did it at the District of Columbia Invitational Track Meet in Washington, D.C., but not on boards. He was urged by meet officials to try for sixteen feet, one of the "four magic barriers" in track and field, but he declined, saying he was too tired to go on.

But he added, "When I go to Louisville for the Mason-Dixon Games, I'm going for the limit of my ability. I hope it will be sixteen feet or more."

The four magic barriers, originated by the 1948 Olympic track coach, Dean Cromwell, were the four-minute mile, the seven-foot high jump, the sixty-foot shot put, and the sixteen-foot pole vault. The mile and high jump barriers were broken in 1954; the shot put mark was bettered in 1956.

Then, on February 2, Uelses became the first vaulter to clear sixteen feet when he cleared sixteen feet, one-fourth inch, at the Millrose Games in New York. However, before the height of the crossbar could be re-measured to ensure the world record, some of Uelses' Marine buddies rushed to congratulate him, bumped the upright, and the bar fell down. (The height of the crossbar must be measured before and after a world record attempt in pole vaulting and high jumping.)

At the conclusion of the pole vault competition, Uelses predicted he would clear sixteen feet, five inches, but not that night. "I'm pooped," said the vaulter who has etched his name in the record books by breaking the final of the four magic barriers—the sixteen-foot pole vault. He joins Roger Bannister (the first four-minute mile), Charles Dumas (the first seven-foot high jump), and Parry O'Brien (the first sixty-foot shot put).

"I think I can reach 16-5 eventually, maybe even

this year," Uelses said. "I am more likely to do it outdoors than indoors. But 16-5 would be about my limit; I don't have enough speed to go higher."

Uelses, like astronaut John Glenn, whose orbit attempt has been delayed at Cape Canaveral, had trouble getting into space. He missed on his first two attempts at sixteen feet before making it on his final attempt.

"I reached the Garden (Madison Square Garden) late and didn't have time to warm up," he said. "So I had to warm up during the competition." He said he missed his first two attempts at sixteen feet because "I was rushing too much."

Almost immediately there came cries of "foul" from former Olympic pole vault champion and world record-holder, Don Bragg, who had done all of his vaulting on a metal pole.

Bragg, who called the new pole a "gimmick," said the fiberglass pole gave pole vaulters a decided advantage. Uelses, he said, "gets a slingshot effect from his pole that helps him attain higher heights. He is successful because of his fiberglass pole, not because he is a better pole vaulter."

"I always felt there were three major factors in pole vaulting—speed, strength, and coordination," Bragg said. "Now the fiberglass pole has removed the first two and left coordination or timing as the big factor."

Bragg was not only the Olympic champion and former indoor and outdoor world record holder in the pole vault, he was also the self-appointed heir apparent to the role of Tarzan in the movies. He even screamed out the Tarzan yell when he was on the victory stand at the 1960 Rome Olympics. "Bragg has an opinion and I have mine," Uelses said. "You have to go along with progress."

But Uelses' big weekend wasn't over. The next night, at the Boston A.A. Games, he vaulted sixteen feet, three-fourths inch. The height of the crossbar was quickly re-measured before anyone could dislodge it.

Uelses held a news conference and announced he could vault sixteen feet with either a fiberglass or a metal pole. He said he could clear sixteen feet with a metal pole if given two month's practice.

"Every time someone sets a record with a new device," Uelses said, "members of the old school always bring up some sort of argument."

Since the Mason-Dixon record was only fourteen feet, six inches, set the year before by Aubrey Dooley, and since pole vaulting is one of the more exciting of the track and field events, I decided that pole vaulters would be foremost on my recruiting list. Joining Uelses would be several fifteen-foot-plus vaulters, including John Pennel, Mel Schwarz, Henry Wadsworth, J.D. Martin, John Rose, and John Cramer. It was going to be a great field.

But the Mason-Dixon Games were still two weeks away. In the meantime, Uelses was scheduled to vault in two meets the following weekend—the Los Angeles Indoor Games on Friday and the Philadelphia Enquirer meet on Saturday. Uelses predicted he would set a new mark in one of the meets, possibly going as high as sixteen feet, two inches. However, he said he had developed a mild case of the flu, which he said might affect his vaulting.

The mild case of the flu became a severe case, and John Uelses was admitted to a Quantico, Virginia, hospital. The doctors there told him he shouldn't exert himself for at least two weeks. That meant he would have to drop out of the next weekend's meets in Los Angeles and Philadelphia, and the following weekend's Mason-Dixon Games.

The day after Uelses announced he'd have to miss the Mason-Dixon Games, I called George Davies of Arizona State, who held the world outdoor record of fifteen feet, ten-and-one-fourth inches. Davies agreed to fly to Louisville for the Games, and said he would try to go sixteen feet.

At the Philadelphia meet, Don "Tarzan" Bragg was disappointed Uelses wasn't there. "I'll give Uelses $10,000 if he jumps 16 feet with a metal pole within two months," Bragg said. "Who is he kidding anyway? I don't believe he could jump 15-6 with a metal pole in 200 years."

Bragg continued: "I came here to see Uelses jump 16-4. I also had another deal for him. I wanted him to offer me $10,000 if I jumped 16 feet with his fiberglass pole."

Another critic of the fiberglass pole was the Reverend Bob Richards, who set marks of fourteen feet, eleven inches and fourteen feet, eleven-and-one-half inches in winning the pole vault in the 1952 and 1956 Olympics. Richards, who used a metal pole, said, "These glass poles make it almost a different kind of event. I hate to see them used to ruin marks set by athletes who must try to come back or be penalized because they didn't have the same kind of equipment."

On the Tuesday before the Mason-Dixon Games, the *Louisville Times* ran a picture of Uelses in his hospital bed with a nurse taking his temperature. In the photo's cutline, it said Uelses announced he would not be able to vault in Louisville on Saturday night, although he was expected to be released from the hospital on Thursday.

Then, two days before the meet, I received a surprising phone call from John Uelses. He had just been released from the hospital and wanted to enter the Mason-Dixon Games. He said he felt great. I told him to book a flight to Louisville, call me back with his arrival time, and I'd meet his flight at Louisville.

Immediately, I called the Watterson Hotel in Louisville and reserved a room for a fictional "John Marshall." I knew Uelses would be bugged by journalists if they knew where he was, so I gave him the name Marshall so he could get some rest.

On Friday, the day before the meet, Uelses hitchhiked, with his fifteen-foot pole in hand, from Quantico, Virginia, to Washington, D.C., where he caught a flight to Louisville. For some, it may seem difficult to hitch rides while carrying a fifteen-foot pole, but not for John Uelses. He simply rolled down the window and held the fiberglass pole in his hand.

I met the flight at Louisville's Standiford Field and drove Uelses to the Watterson Hotel. I explained to him that he was registered as John Marshall to keep the press away. But Uelses would have none of that. As soon as he was checked in and went to his room, he returned to the lobby to let everybody know he was there.

When George Davies heard that Uelses would be in the meet, he said he welcomed the opportunity to vault against him. "I'm sure someone else is going to clear sixteen feet this season," he said. "And I hope it's me."

Davies was upset that his vault of fifteen feet, ten-and-one-fourth inches in the Big Eight championships the previous summer was still not recognized as an official world record. "The International Committee on records met recently," Davies said. "I guess they put off recognition of my record until a decision is made on the fiberglass pole."

"There wasn't such a hassle over the fiberglass pole when I set the record eight months ago," Davies continued. "It's only been since Uelses did sixteen feet."

Meanwhile, former world record-holder, Don Bragg, continued his vocal opposition to the fiberglass pole. He said the new pole operates as a catapult.

Davies, a soft-spoken twenty-one-year-old Arizonan, scoffed at Bragg's criticism. "Old Tarzan talks like he's been in the jungle for ten years," Davies said. "He says the fiberglass pole does 60 percent of the work and the vaulter 40. What a lot of hogwash! The vaulter does as much of the work with a fiberglass pole as he did with a metal pole.

"They talk about a catapult effect. There's no such thing that I know about. It's just a longer swing and requires different timing. Actually, vaulting with a glass pole is easier at the start of the vault and more difficult in the completion."

Beginning at 7:30 p.m., 8,129 people saw five world indoor records set and one tied at the second-annual Mason-Dixon Games. They also saw pole vaulter John Uelses miss all three of his attempts at the opening height—fourteen feet.

Uelses did not warm up before beginning the vaulting competition. He decided to save his strength and get his warm-up by vaulting at fourteen feet. He was well over the crossbar on his third attempt, but his timing was off and he hit the bar on the way down. Disconsolate because of the three misses, Uelses managed a smile and said, "Well, it proves one thing. It's the man, not the pole."

Because the long jumpers and pole vaulters used the same runway, with the long jump sandpit at one end and the foam pole vault landing pit at the other, the two events lasted much longer than we had planned. When the final running event was completed, the pole vault was still going on. In fact, it was midnight when the pole vault competition was finally over. In first place, tied at fifteen feet four inches were George Davies and John Rose, both of Arizona State University.

But the competition wasn't over for John Uelses. He came up to me and asked if he could take an exhibition vault at fifteen feet, eight inches. It wouldn't count, but at least it would help him save face if he could clear it. I checked with George Gibson, and he agreed it might be a crowd-pleaser, even though most of the crowd had gone home.

Not willing to concede that the eight days he spent in the Camp Lejeune infirmary had weakened him, he attempted a vault at fifteen feet, eight inches, and he didn't even come close. So he decided to try again. That time he landed short of the landing pit and appeared to be injured. I was the first to reach him. He looked up at me and said, "The goddam box is shallow."

Uelses measured the depth of the box, where the pole is planted at takeoff, and said it was three-quarters of an inch shallower than the required eight inches.

He added that the lack of depth in the box caused him to reach his peak too soon.

Ray Page, the head field judge, measured the box and found it was only one-eighth of an inch too shallow. The "shallow" box didn't seem to bother any of the other vaulters.

The meet announcer, Tom Conner, thanked everyone for coming, and the second Mason-Dixon Games were finally over.

27

Go Western, Young Man

While I was living in Elizabethtown, Kentucky, in the spring of 1962, I received a telephone call from Dean Raymond Cravens of Western Kentucky State College. He had heard about my coaching successes at Elizabethtown High School and wondered if I might be interested in becoming the Hilltopper track coach, beginning in the fall of 1962.

I arranged for an interview at Western, driving the fifty miles south to Bowling Green and meeting with Dr. Cravens and the assistant athletic director, Ted Hornback. I was told that Western's legendary basketball coach, Ed Diddle, was nearing retirement, and Western needed some new "excitement" on "the hill."

A photo of Coach Ed Diddle, taken by my five-year-old son, Kevin

Mr. Diddle, who was in his forty-second year as Western's basketball coach, was known as much for "Diddle-isms" (his muddling of the English language) as for his basketball coaching. I discovered this during my first conversation with the venerable (and often confused) coach. Mr. Diddle was telling me about a basketball player who had recently eloped with his campus sweetheart. "He had no more business getting married," Coach Diddle sputtered, "than a bull in a china shop."

Even though coach Diddle had been credited with many Diddle-isms during his long coaching career at Western Kentucky, that was the only one I heard from him personally. Here are a few that have been related to me by others:

Describing his son: "He's about as big as I was when I was his size."

At the beginning of a freshman physical education class: "All right now, I want you to line up here alphabetically according to your height."

Describing a campus tree to a basketball recruit: "That's called a pussyfootwillow."

Explaining to a basketball player the scientific reason for driving straight for the basket: "What's the straightest line between two points?"

Describing an outstanding basketball prospect he had seen: "The kid shoots with his right hand. He shoots with his left hand. He's amphibious."

Explaining how tall one of his prospective players was, Coach Diddle stretched his hand about two feet above his head and said, "He comes up to here on me."

Describing a player from an opposing team: "He is really tall. He must be six feet thirteen or fourteen, at least."

He once told his team that he wanted them to "act courtesy and be sportsmanship."

Old-timers at Western love to tell the story about

the day Coach Diddle was walking through the campus and began chasing a car that had run a campus stop sign. Mr. Diddle caught up with the car and asked the driver, obviously a student, "Where you from?" The student answered, "Chicago." "Don't give me that crap," Mr. Diddle answered, "I see your Illinois license plate."

One of Coach Diddle's best shooters, Curly Ellis, was at practice one afternoon, dropping in shot after shot from the corner. He just couldn't miss. A by-stander called to Mr. Diddle and said, "Coach, I think he could hit a million from there." Coach Diddle answered, "A million? Hell, he could hit a thousand."

After collecting a number of Diddle-isms, which were part of the campus lore at Western Kentucky in the 1960s, I began to include them in my banquet, service club, and commencement speeches. They always got big laughs.

Western's stadium, which served both football and track, was built into the side of the famous hilltop. It was thought that night track meets under the lights would bring large crowds of students into the stadium from the surrounding dormitories.

It was agreed that I would join the Western staff the next fall to become the head track coach and the first-ever cross country coach. I would teach two basic physical education courses and would take courses to get my master's degree from Western. By transferring two graduate level courses that I had taken at Nazareth College, I would be able to get the master's degree in one year. My salary as a graduate student would be $1,400 a year, plus the master's degree. It was a great deal for me.

To sweeten the deal, Dean Cravens asked Judy if she would join the Western staff as an English and journalism teacher for $4,600 a year. And they offered us a small house on the south edge of the campus, rent-free.

Western had never had a winning track season and had been last in the Ohio Valley Conference for several years running. They had lost thirty-eight of thirty-nine dual track meets. It was obvious they hired me to change that.

In his book, *Western Kentucky University*, Western history professor Lowell H. Harrison wrote:

The most dismal record of any of the spring sports belonged to track. In a six-year stretch, the Western squads won one dual meet (Austin Peay in 1960) and lost thirty-eight. Turner Elrod, the long-suffering track coach, could

have blamed the football recruiting, for most of his participants were off-season footballers.

The renaissance of track and field came with the 1962 appointment of Tom Ecker, the twenty-seven-year-old coach at Elizabethtown High School. Brash, energetic, unpredictable, and controversial, Ecker was a winner. He had already published a very successful book, Championship Track and Field, as well as a companion volume on football that he co-authored.

He was reported to have announced upon his arrival in 1962, "Within three years and with thirteen boys of my choosing, we will be able to win the OVC (Ohio Valley Conference)." He won the OVC championship in 1964, after taking the Kentucky Federation Championship in 1963. Ecker won two more OVC titles and was the conference track coach of the year in 1963, 1964, 1965, and 1966. When he left Western after four years to become one of Sweden's national track coaches, he left an 18-1 record in dual track meets and a 19-3 record in cross country, which he started in 1962. Ecker's major controversy was with the track coach and athletic director at Eastern (Kentucky), whom he accused of "extreme reluctance" in competing against Western in both track and cross country.

Western's biggest rival, Murray State College, had been undefeated in track and cross country for several years and had become the perennial conference champions in both sports. Murray State was the target.

I had ten half-scholarships to work with—each with tuition and room, but no meals. Everyone got free books since they were available directly from the athletic department for all sports.

From the first day, I divided those ten halves into twenty quarter-scholarships, ten with tuition and books, and ten with room and books. Since out-of-state tuition was much higher than in-state, scholarship athletes coming from outside Kentucky received tuition and books. Kentucky residents received room and books. Bert Barrone, the sports editor of the Bowling Green newspaper, joked in his sports column, "Ecker is the originator of the 'tuition and you eat every-other-day' scholarship."

During the spring of 1962, while I was still a teacher in Elizabethtown, I contacted every high school track coach I knew in the country, asking them to consider Western Kentucky for their top athletes. Because of my work with the Mason-Dixon Games, I knew many coaches from around the country. There were many positive responses, including one from Mead Burnett, whom I had run against when he ran for Ohio State and I ran for Iowa. Mead was the coach at East High School in Cleveland, Ohio.

He talked to one of his black runners, Frank Hemphill, about the possibility of attending Western. When Frank asked Mead what it might be like to attend a predominately white college in the South, Mead said, "It will be an adventure."

No black athletes had ever been recruited into any of Western's sports programs before. Frank was the first at Western, and perhaps the first in the entire South. He didn't receive any aid, so he was recruited but was not on a scholarship.

Frank wasn't a great runner, but he was a lot better than most of the track men who had attended Western previously. He ran with the team for part of the first year, but as better and better athletes were being recruited, the competition got to be too much for him. He dropped out of track to concentrate on his studies. And it paid off for him. Frank graduated from Western in 1967.

Throughout the spring and summer of 1962, I continued to "beat the bushes" to find outstanding high school runners, jumpers, and throwers. I drove to track meets in Illinois, Indiana, Ohio, and even to Long Island, New York. To save money, I slept in the car. Rarely was I interested in recruiting state champions. I was looking for those athletes who finished in second or third place, but who had the potential to be great. In many cases, tracksters who were already on campus contacted their high school track and field friends to sell them on the Western Kentucky experience.

We needed special young men, those who were willing to come to Western with small scholarships, or with none at all. As it turned out, many of the recruits just wanted a coach who cared; they didn't have to receive any kind of aid. By the time school started in the fall, we had assembled an outstanding nucleus of track and cross country athletes.

When the 1962–63 academic year began at Western Kentucky, the new cross country team, the first in the school's history, was running daily interval training workouts, either on the track or at a local golf course. But the distance runners weren't alone in their workouts. The other track and field athletes, mostly fresh-men, were on the track every afternoon, drawing crowds of student observers.

The most entertaining athletes, as far as the students were concerned, were the pole vaulters. We had three who could clear fourteen feet, a height that seemed out of reach for most college vaulters in those days. We had many other outstanding athletes, too, many whom I did not know until school started. They simply walked up to me on the track and asked if they could be on the team. Everyone was looking forward to spring and the coming track season.

But it was fall, and it was time for football and cross country. The football staff, headed by a delightful character, Nick Denes, was friendly and cooperative—unlike football coaches I had worked with previously. When I suggested we run a cross country meet at the halftime of Western's first home game, Nick thought it was a great idea.

The football game was against Morehead State, and the halftime cross country meet was a two-mile team race against Louisville's Bellarmine College. Pictures of three of Western's top three runners appeared both in the local newspaper and in the football program.

The meet was held on the oval track around the football field so the crowd in the stands could see the entire race. However, it wasn't much of a race. We placed all seven of our runners ahead of Bellarmine's first finisher, for a 15-50 victory.

Western won three dual meets during that first season, including one against rival Murray State, but we lost a dual meet to the University of Kentucky. We won the nine-team Union University Invitational winning the first trophy won by a Western sports team in twenty-three years. In the final meet, we were barely edged out by Murray for the Ohio Valley Conference crown. It was a very good first season, and we received a lot of good press from the local newspapers.

Later that fall, when the cross country season was over, I became a spelunker. My British friends said I was actually a potholer. My academic friends at Western said I was a Speleologist. In short, I became a cave explorer, or caver.

The state of Kentucky is "undermined" with caves, some of them dry, and others with small rivers running through them. The limestone bedrock in Kentucky is ideal for the formation of caves. However, because of the difficulty of getting into many of them, a great number of Kentucky's caves remain unexplored to this day.

The most famous attraction in the area, of course, is Mammoth Cave, with more than 500 miles of explored caverns. The influence of Mammoth Cave is obvious when you visit the area. There are the towns of Cave City and Horse Cave, Caverna High School, and Our Lady of the Caves Catholic Church.

Spelunkers always dream of discovering something new. Sometimes it is a second entrance to the cave they are exploring. Sometimes, but rarely, it is a cavern that has never been seen before. But the dream of every cave explorer near Mammoth Cave is to find a cave that leads into the Mammoth Cave complex. Anyone who owns a cave entrance becomes part-owner of any cave to which it connects—even Mammoth Cave.

One sunny fall day, two of my pole vaulters, Paul Woodall and Gary Imel, asked me if I'd like to become a spelunker. They were fearless, as pole vaulters tend to be, and they found spelunking to be an exciting pastime. They thought I would enjoy it. They had an extra carbide lamp (necessary for serious spelunking), and they introduced me to "Big Bertha," a nearby cave that was often frequented by college students with flashlights.

The carbide lamp had two chambers. The upper chamber held water; the lower chamber held calcium carbide. As the water dripped slowly into the lower chamber, flammable acetylene gas was created, which was released through a tiny orifice in the middle of a two-and-three-fourths-inch reflector. When the gas was ignited, a bright light was created, making it possible to see a great distance in total darkness.

As soon as we entered the cave, which was easy to access, I fired up my carbide lamp, and commented to Paul, "It's really dark in here. I can't see anything." He answered, "Try taking off your sunglasses."

When I looked at the walls of the cave, there were countless names of previous visitors and the dates they were there. That was when Paul taught me the first lesson of spelunking: Don't leave anything in a cave but footprints. Don't take anything out of a cave but photos. Bertha wasn't much of a challenge, so we graduated to more difficult caves. Paul and Gary seemed to know where many of them were.

Usually we did our caving late at night, sometimes coming back out around dawn. And as stories about our adventures spread, our spelunking group kept growing, even though the hours weren't very appealing.

We explored many caves during that time, but our biggest discovery was a long cave, a few miles south of Bowling Green, that we called Deep River Cave. We first entered it in 1963, and we made many more trips through it during the next three years. The cave had two entrances, one in which a small river ran into it, and a dry entrance beside it that provided easy access. But once inside, the two caves became one, and the only way to continue was by water.

The river was too deep to wade and too cold to swim. We devised two different ways to negotiate the descent into the cave. Our first few trips, we floated in inner tubes, pulling our sweatshirts up over our heads and holding our carbide lamps between our knees. Our rule about complaining was simple. Each person was allowed one scream when first sitting in the cold water but couldn't complain after that.

Then we got smarter. We took a sixteen-foot aluminum boat into the cave and floated through it. There was one large waterfall, but we managed to get the boat over that. From that time on, we only went by boat.

There were a few bats that hung out near the entrances, but the most interesting wildlife in deep

A carbide lamp. Water drips from the top chamber onto calcium carbide in the lower chamber, giving off flammable acetylene gas.

River Cave were the small fish and crayfish that lived in the river. Because both species lived in total darkness, they were pure white and blind. They were easy to catch, so I took a few of the fish and crayfish home and put them in an aquarium. Within a few days, all of them had returned to their natural colors, but they were still blind.

On one of our trips through Deep River Cave, we found a small opening in the cave's wall, with barely enough room to squeeze through. We managed to get through the opening and found ourselves in the largest room I've ever seen underground. We estimated it to be about the size of a football stadium. It was so big, the beam of my carbide lamp couldn't reach the opposite wall.

In the room were many beautiful stalactites and stalagmites. One combination of the two was so big around that two of us, one on either side, couldn't reach around it and touch the other person's hands.

But the most exciting discovery for us was that no human had been there before. Ours were the first footprints in the thick dust on the room's floor. We could see that the dust had been disturbed eons before by a large slab of limestone that had fallen from the cave's ceiling. On top of the slab of limestone was a six-foot stalagmite, which had taken thousands of years to create. Exploring that room was my biggest spelunking thrill.

My only commercial spelunking venture came during the summer of 1963. A new hotel complex, Park Mammoth Resort, was being constructed by Marco Development Corporation of Louisville on a high ridge overlooking the valley below. It was scheduled to open the following year.

Besides the hotel, a restaurant, and an eighteen-hole golf course, the property was undermined with caves. The two largest caves had been explored thoroughly over the years. The largest, Jesse James Cave, was fourteen-and-a-half miles long with seven entrances. Coach Cave was six-and-a-half miles long and had two entrances. Both caves were ideal for spelunkers but not good for tourists.

Someone at Marco Development contacted me and asked if I could bring my spelunking crew to the resort site to explore some of the smaller caves on the property. The thought was that small caves, with easy access, smooth footpaths, and electric lights, might become an additional attraction at the resort.

We explored some of the smaller caves, but we didn't find any that we thought could be commercialized. We were not successful, but it was nice to be asked.

I visited the resort fifty-three years later and everything was pretty much the same as before, except now the two larger caves are home to some 40,000 endangered gray bats that hibernate there every winter.

28

Where There's a Wilt, There's a Way

Since I had had two big-selling trade books in 1963, my publisher, Prentice-Hall, was eager for me to keep writing. The company had to produce one coaching book per month for its Coaches Book Club, and it knew I was a reliable contributor. So I teamed up with Fred Wilt, a two-time Olympian, a longtime FBI agent, and a big collector of technical track and field information. Fred was well known in the sport of track and field. I was not.

I first met Fred in 1962, when I was in my first year as the track and cross country coach at Western Kentucky in Bowling Green. While serving as the coach that year, I was also getting my master's degree. I knew that Fred would be the ideal person to copyedit the thesis I was writing, so I called him, and we arranged to meet at his home in West Lafayette, Indiana.

The inimitable Fred Wilt, during a track and field lecture.

I flew to West Lafayette on a Sunday morning. Fred met me at the airport dressed in sweat clothes. From the airport, he drove to a high school track where he wanted to practice throwing the hammer. (The hammer is a sixteen-pound iron ball on the end of four feet of wire and a handle.)

Hammer-throwing was one of the few track and field events Fred hadn't mastered in his forty-three years, so he was teaching himself. My job was to stand in the field and retrieve the hammer for him every time he threw it. After fifty throws, he ran two miles on the track. Then we went to his house, where he showered, we had a bite to eat, and I took out a copy of my master's thesis for Fred's perusal.

But Fred wasn't just going to let me sit by idly. He had a manuscript for a book he was writing titled *Run-Run-Run*. He asked me to copyedit his manuscript while he went over mine.

We finished our work late in the afternoon, Fred took me to the airport, and I flew back to Bowling Green. I didn't realize it at the time, but the meeting with Fred Wilt that Sunday was the beginning of a thirty-three-year friendship.

Throughout our friendship, he seemed to have one objective for me, and he mentioned it every time we were together. He wanted me to become an FBI agent. He told me that originally those applying to become agents had to be lawyers or accountants. But that rule had been relaxed so that anyone who passed the examinations could become an agent. But I always politely refused his requests. I had no interest in becoming an FBI agent.

But he was the ideal partner for writing books. He knew everyone of note in track and field, from all over the world. And he called on those people to provide ideas and photographs for our books.

Our first book together, which came out in 1966,

was *Illustrated Guide to Olympic Track and Field Techniques.* We always said that the book would never be on a best-seller list because the title was too long to fit on the list. For some reason, the Prentice-Hall editors wanted to come up with long and unusual titles for their coaching books. The book enjoyed good sales in the United States and was republished in London by Faber and Faber, Ltd., for British readers.

When we began work on *Illustrated Guide,* we decided that we needed someone who was well-known in track and field to write the foreword. In August 1965, a year before the book was published, Fred and I were instructors at a track and field clinic held at the University of Guelph in Canada. The keynote speaker for the clinic was Jesse Owens.

One night, during the time of the clinic, Fred and I were attending a cocktail party at the home of one of the university's professors. When Fred saw that Jesse Owens was also there, he backed him into a corner, as only Fred Wilt the FBI agent could do, and asked him if he would write the foreword for our new book. Jesse said we should write it for him, and he'd sign it.

So Fred and I left the room and hurriedly wrote the foreword. When we finished, we brought it back to Jesse, who signed the paper without reading it. The foreword was included in the book the following year. It's probably a good thing Jesse didn't read it. We called the book "a monumental effort on the part of two discerning track and field authorities."

Then, Fred decided we should have a further chat with Jesse. But the conversation was more of an interview than a simple chat. Fred Wilt became Agent Wilt, and he asked Jesse some difficult questions. Fred and Jesse did all of the talking. I took notes.

Fred got Jesse to admit that he had not been snubbed by Adolf Hitler at the 1936 Olympic Games. We already knew that, but it was good to hear it from the man himself. And Jesse also admitted that he and Luz Long, the German long jumper, had never talked with each other at the 1936 Games until after the long jump competition was completed. That quashed another longtime story about how Luz Long gave Jesse Owens the advice that allowed him to win the long jump. It's a story that will not die, no matter how many times we've tried to kill it.

It's a good thing I took notes. That interview turned out to be the first of many. I had made the decision to collect as much Olympic information from the past as possible, not realizing it would still be going on more than fifty years later. Eventually, the information formed the basis for a future book on the Olympics I wanted to write and for lectures I would be giving on cruise ships.

In 1970, we came out with our biggest book (7 ¼ -by-10 inches, 350 pages), *International Track and Field Coaching Encyclopedia.* Each of its twenty-two chapters covered an area of track and field, including nine chapters on teaching beginners. The contributing coaches were from all over the world, except we had no contributors from the Eastern Bloc nations. The Iron Curtain was the great separator at that time, and communicating with the east was usually impossible.

I contacted Fred and said we should try to get a coach from the Soviet Union or East Germany to contribute a chapter. "Impossible," he said. "There's no way their governments would let them cooperate with us."

So I came up with a solution. I invented an East German shot putting coach named Friedrich Hess. My favorite German first name was Friedrich, and I took the name Hess from Rudolf Hess, who was convicted of war crimes in the Nuremberg trials of 1945-46.

I wrote Friedrich Hess' chapter, "Teaching the Beginning Shot Putter," which took up only four-and-a-half pages of the book. The final paragraph was just two words, "Viel Gluck!" (My German was very limited.)

We needed a biographical sketch for Hess, so I wrote the following: "Friedrich Hess earned his diploma in physical education and sports at the Deutsche Hochschule Fur Korperkultur in Leipzig. Considered one of the outstanding authorities on the throwing events, he has contributed many articles to East Germany's sports publications."

There was no way anyone would ever know that Hess didn't exist, since the Eastern Bloc nations were so secretive at that time. And, of course, I wouldn't let Friedrich's memory die. I quoted him once in one of my articles in *Athletic Journal:* "It takes people of vision to discover the truth; it takes people of courage to share the truth with others." –Friedrich Hess. Hess was often the topic of conversation among the few coaches who knew the truth about him.

One coach who knew the Friedrich Hess story was my old friend, Bill Huyck, who coached at Carleton

College in Northfield, Minnesota. Bill was always sending me things to test my resolve and to challenge my sense of humor. One Christmas, he sent me a picture postcard of a bank robber named Miller who was gunned down in Northfield in September 1876. Miller's eyes were open, but there were visible bullet holes in Miller's head and shoulder. On the other side of the card, Bill wrote, "Thinking of you fondly at Christmastime."

Bill sent me a long letter in 1966. The last line was, "I hope the paternity suit in Newfoundland wasn't too troublesome." Later, he sent me a letter in a brown envelope. On the outside was a note: "This is the sex manual you ordered."

Under the name Willie Hess (exchange student from Rostock), Bill sent a letter to *Track and Field News,* complaining about the author of a high jump article, Tom Hecker. "If he is supposed to be an internationally recognized authority on the application of biomechanics to track, then I can assure you he is not. It is a matter of fact that several of Tom's articles contain verbatim passages stolen from the recent works of my father, Friedrich Hess."

In response to the letter from "Willie Hess," *Track and Field News* writer, Jon Hendershott wrote to me: "Thought I would forward this little gem to you we got from some weirdo at Carleton College. Well, as they say, have a nice day, Tommy! By the by, Willie and all his brown-shirted friends were very glad to get your home address. Just listen for the jack-boots in the middle of the night."

I wrote Jon Hendershott and told him the problem was solved. Willie Hess had been deported. That seemed to settle things for the moment, but then the game became more interesting. *Track and Field News* received a letter from an American coach, wanting to know how to contact Friedrich Hess. He wanted clarification on some of Hess' ideas. When we got the word, I thought it was hilarious, but Fred was panicked. He wrote me that we should never admit "the awful, awful truth." Fred said to tell anyone who asks about Hess that, as far as we know, he had been purged.

The book was one of Prentice-Hall's biggest trade book sellers and was in print for several years. Fortunately, it was out of print, and Friedrich Hess had long been forgotten by the time the Berlin Wall came down in 1991.

Fred Wilt was probably the greatest collector of track and field knowledge in history. He had a massive track and field library and received stacks of mail daily from people from all over the world, sharing information or asking for advice. He always answered every letter by the end of the day it was received. We used to love telling the story about two perfect strangers who were standing in Trafalgar Square in London. One of the men wanted to start a conversation, so he asked, "Have you heard from Fred Wilt lately?"

Fred and I did two more track and field books for Prentice-Hall, taking on our friend, Dr. Jim Hay, a native New Zealander, who was professor of biomechanics at the University of Iowa, as a third co-author. *Olympic Track and Field Techniques* came out in 1974. *Championship Track and Field for Women* came out in 1978. In 1978, the Prentice-Hall trade book editors told me I was their all-time best-selling sports author. I'm not sure if that was true or not, but it felt good to hear it.

Posing in Toledo, Spain, with co-authors Jim Hay and Fred Wilt

29

The John K. Meredith Caper

Fred Wilt was a great story-teller. He told long, involved stories about his experiences with the FBI, which he called "capers." When he told stories about his experiences with the coaching of athletes from the Soviet Union, he would mention his favorite Soviet coach, Yuri Sonovavich.

Fred often commented on the difficulty of heading up an FBI district in northeast Indiana. He explained that it was not uncommon for someone to steal a car in Chicago, begin driving it to Florida, and run out of gas in northeast Indiana.

Fred told me he was once called to testify in a trial in east Tennessee, where a local sheriff had pulled over a car and arrested the driver, who turned out to be a bank robber from Fred's FBI territory.

At the trial, the sheriff was on the witness stand being questioned by the prosecuting attorney. The attorney asked, "When did you realize you were following a dangerous criminal?" The sheriff responded, "When he crossed the double yeller."

One of Fred's best stories was called "The Parachute Caper," dating back to June 1972. It seems that a man named Martin J. McNally hijacked American Airlines Flight 119 on June 23 and demanded $502,500 and five parachutes from the airline. The plane landed in St. Louis, where the money and parachutes were delivered and all but one of the passengers released.

The plane took off again, heading for JFK airport in New York, but McNally never made it to New York. He strapped the forty-five-pound bag of money to his leg with a belt, strapped on a parachute, and jumped out of the back door of the Boeing 727. He landed in a farm field near Peru, Indiana, which was in Fred Wilt's territory. But the bag of money, which landed far from McNally, had been ripped away from him, leaving a severe bruise on his leg.

Fred managed to track McNally down and arrest him. Fred's comment: "If McNally had waited a couple of minutes more, he would have landed in someone else's territory."

Also in Fred's territory was a nudist colony called Naked City, near the town of Roselawn, Indiana. At the time, it was the largest nudist colony in the country and was best-known for hosting an annual Miss Nude Universe contest. As the local FBI agent, Fred told us he was required to make regular visits to Naked City. He said the most fun for him was watching the nude volleyball games.

Probably my best Fred Wilt story is about a man named John K. Meredith. In October 1964, the FBI was contacted by a Lafayette, Indiana, printer who had been asked by Mr. Meredith to print checks for several businesses in the area. Naturally, the FBI thought Mr. Meredith was up to no good, and they sent agent Wilt over to the print shop to investigate.

Fred drove to the print shop, located Meredith's car in front of the shop, took out his gun, and promptly shot holes in all four tires of the car. Obviously, he didn't want any quick escapes. (Fred told me that was the only time he ever fired a weapon in the line of duty.)

When Meredith came out of the print shop, Fred began questioning him.

"What's your name?"

"John K. Meredith," was the quick reply.

"What do you do for a living?" Agent Wilt asked.

Meredith responded, "I'm a scientist."

"If you're a scientist," Wilt continued, "what's the formula for determining angular momentum?"

Of course, Meredith couldn't answer that question. The formula for determining angular momentum is used by coaches when analyzing certain track and field techniques.

—109

Then Wilt asked Meredith to open the trunk of his car. Inside the trunk was a suitcase, which Wilt asked him to open. In the suitcase was clothing, so neatly packed that Wilt said it had to have been packed by an ex-con. And, sure enough, it was. Meredith had just been released from the federal penitentiary in Leavenworth, Kansas.

Wilt arrested him and drove him to the nearest jail. On the way, Meredith told him he had spent more than half his life in prisons. Then he asked Wilt if he would do him a big favor. For many years, he had been writing a book and needed a contact to try to get it published.

Wilt told him he had a friend, Professor Tom Ecker at Western Kentucky State College, who would be happy to help him out. On October 29, 1964, John K. Meredith mailed me the first of many letters. It read, in part, "Dear Professor: I am sending under separate cover a novel, fiction based on fact. Mr. Fred Wilt of the FBI suggested that I send the work to you. He suggested further that if it has merit, you might be willing to do something with it.

"So that you will understand the situation, I should tell you I am on my way to Atlanta Federal Prison. I expect to be there for between two and three years. What I am doing is possible because of the courtesy of a deputy sheriff, who furnished the paper and ballpoint pen. Thank you for any help you see fit to extend. Respectfully Yours, John K. Meredith."

The "book" arrived a few days later. It was a long, hand-written manuscript, alternating blue, black, and red inks. Whenever one of his pens ran out of ink, he would change to another.

On November 7, Meredith wrote to me again. He was still in the jail in Lafayette, Indiana. He finished by saying, "The rush of incoherency is because they are liable to come for me any hour."

Then I received a form from the U.S. Penitentiary in Leavenworth, Kansas. Meredith had been sent back to Leavenworth, rather than going to Atlanta. The form outlined all of the rules for communicating with an inmate. It turned out that Meredith had no friends or relatives. I was his only contact with the outside world.

He wrote me regularly over the next two years, and I made it a point to answer every letter he wrote.

In early 1965, Meredith developed pneumonia and was transferred to the federal medical center in Springfield, Missouri. In August 1965, Meredith wrote: "Your letter was the best therapy ever. Thanks! It is indeed encouraging to learn that you liked what you read in the book. Perhaps it is too much to hope that, as you proceed through it, you may become enthused beyond what you first expected."

In December, he sent me a Christmas card. The following March, he wrote, "A letter from you is something more than an event. Thanks!"

I didn't tell Meredith that Judy and I were divorcing and I would be leaving Western Kentucky in June to live in Sweden. Judy was still on the Western staff that year, and in July she was hit with a bombshell. She received a telegram that read: REGRET YOUR FRIEND, JOHN K. MEREDITH, DIED AT 7:00 AM TODAY. PLEASE ADVISE BY COLLECT WIRE WHETHER OR NOT YOU DESIRE TO CLAIM BODY AND GIVE PERMISSION FOR COMPLETE EXAMINATION OF BODY, INCLUDING HEAD, TO VERIFY CAUSE OF DEATH. IF CLAIMED, GOVERNMENT WILL FURNISH CASKET AND PAY SHIPPING EXPENSES BUT NOT COST OF FUNERAL. PLEASE FURNISH NAME AND ADDRESS OF FUNERAL HOME TO WHICH SHIPMENT IS TO BE MADE. IF NOT CLAIMED, BURIAL WILL BE MADE HERE AT NO COST TO YOU.

Obviously, Judy didn't want to claim the body. She asked the prison to donate Meredith's savings of $191.94 to the prison library to buy books for the inmates. And that was the end of Fred Wilt's John K. Meredith caper.

In the winter of 1962–63, Western's basketball team was struggling through a dismal 5-16 season, the worst record in Coach Ed Diddle's forty-one years as the coach. One of the losses was on a Saturday night at Bowling Green of Ohio. Western's team was humiliated by a very tall black Bowling Green player.

On Monday morning, Coach Diddle, who was also Western's athletic director, called me into his office. In his role as athletic director, he told me I should probably try to recruit a nice "colored boy" from "up north." I should be the first coach to do so, he said, because I was "a Yankee."

He said he was going to recruit black basketball players right away, but because of NCAA rules, they wouldn't be eligible to play on the varsity team until they were sophomores. Track and field participants were eligible as freshmen.

I had recruited a black runner earlier in the year, but he never became a member of our team. It was clear to me that Coach Diddle wanted me to find a really outstanding black runner this time, so I began making phone calls to my various contacts.

One of the calls was to my old friend Ernie Cunliffe, who was on the staff of the Air Force Academy in Colorado. He recommended I contact an outstanding quarter-miler he knew from Dallas, Texas, who was about to be discharged from the Air Force. The quarter-miler was Roy Turner, who enrolled at Western the following fall—the first black athlete to get a scholarship to Western.

When I knew that Roy would be attending Western, I approached our team captain, Tom Graham, and told him to look after Roy and help him get established on the track team. Not only did Tom help Roy get established, they became best friends. In fact, when Roy Turner got married two years later, Tom Graham flew to Dallas (his first airplane ride) and served as Roy's best man.

The following spring, Roy was the only black runner on our track and field team. He broke many school and conference records and usually scored the most points for our team. Roy was so successful on the track, he was inducted into the exclusive Western Kentucky Hall of Fame in 1992.

My first season as Western's track and field coach began with a trip to the Mason-Dixon Games in Louisville. We entered a mile relay team, a sprinter, a hurdler, three pole vaulters, and our crack freshman two-mile relay team. The two-mile team won in 7:51.7, the best time ever run in the United States by a freshman team. When I told one of the team members that they had just set a world record, he was visibly excited. Later, I explained to him that the race isn't run in any other country in the world.

After an easy 106-30 win at Austin Peay College, we traveled in four cars on a 2,800-mile spring break trip to the northern Midwest states. The group was made up of sixteen athletes, one manager, one journalist, and one coach. Our first stop was at Wartburg College in my hometown of Waverly, Iowa, where we won by a wide margin.

Next was a stop in Fargo, North Dakota, for a seven-team meet. It was snowing so hard when we arrived, the meet had to be moved indoors. Setting six new field house records, we won the meet handily.

Then we traveled to Mitchell, South Dakota, for the Corn Palace Relays. When we entered the hotel lobby, I went to the desk and announced that I wanted to check in the Western Kentucky track team. The woman behind the counter said, "I'm sorry, but your coach will have to check the team in." Apparently, I looked too young to be the coach, so I went up to pole

Western Kentucky's 1964 track and field team, with Roy Turner pictured in the center.

vaulter Paul Woodall, an Army veteran who looked much older than I did, and asked him to check in the team, which he did. There were fourteen colleges entered, and we won the meet easily, setting two meet records in the process.

When we returned home, we won a triangular meet over the University of Louisville and Bellarmine College, and then we defeated Middle Tennessee and the University of Kentucky. In the meet against Kentucky we set eight records—five school marks and three U of K track marks.

The next week, we went on the road to Murray and suffered our only dual meet loss of the season. They were much better than we were that night. Then we beat Eastern Kentucky before going to the Ohio Valley Conference meet. We finished second to Murray.

The next weekend we went to the Kentucky Federation Championships in Lexington, Kentucky, and the Memphis Relays in Memphis, Tennessee. We split the team for the two meets. Manager John Wallace accompanied half the team to Lexington, and I took the other half to Memphis. We won both meets.

The season was considered a very successful one. My fellow conference track coaches voted me Conference Coach of the Year, and I was awarded a Kentucky colonel's commission by the governor of Kentucky. The colonelcy is the same one awarded to Colonel Sanders of Kentucky Fried Chicken fame many years earlier.

My duties as an instructor at Western were changing. I taught a track and field course in the physical education department. But I also taught television production classes in the English department.

Judy taught the television journalism classes (everything in front of the cameras), and I taught the television production classes (everything behind the cameras). The classes never met together.

The TV journalism students wrote news copy and practiced reading the news on camera. The camera was a fake one, made of a wooden box mounted on a tripod, with a tin can on the front serving as the camera's lens.

Fortunately, the local television station, WLTV, didn't have a network affiliation, so they were happy to offer their station to us for any live programming we could provide. Four mornings a week, we aired a live, five-minute news program called "Topper Topics." The TV journalists took turns reporting on various campus activities, while the TV production students operated the cameras, microphones, and other equipment, both in the studio and in the control room.

Following the newscasts each morning, we aired a thirty-minute program, *Understanding Science,* hosted by Western science professor Dr. Earl Murphy. The program catered to rural schools that did not have the apparatus and equipment available to Dr. Murphy. On Mondays and Wednesdays, the program was seen by about 3,000 fifth-grade students. On Tuesdays and Thursdays, some 1,500 eighth-graders saw the program. I was the director for all of the news and science programs. With virtually no budget, but with talented, enthusiastic students, we laid the groundwork for what is now Western Kentucky's School of Journalism and Broadcasting, which has a staff of thirty.

My final two books published by Prentice-Hall were written with the help of two Cedar Rapids high school coaches. The first was *Athletic Journal's Encyclopedia of Football,* co-authored with football and track coach Bill Calloway. Published in 1978, the book was a collection of articles from past issues of *Athletic Journal* magazine, updated, edited, and sometimes rewritten. The follow-up book was *Athletic Journal's Encyclopedia of Basketball,* co-authored with basketball coach Don King. It was published in 1983.

In 1971, I started writing for Tafnews Press, the book publishing arm of *Track and Field News* magazine. My first book for Tafnews was a physics book for track coaches, *Track and Field Dynamics.* It explained how the laws of Newtonian physics could be used to improve performances in track and field technique. It was a simplified and Americanized version of a British book, *The Mechanics of Athletics* by Geoffrey Dyson.

After its release in the United States, the book was translated into Japanese and was republished in Japan. It was very popular with both American and Japanese track and field coaches, and the English version was revised and reprinted in 1974.

The next book for Tafnews Press was another, more specific physics book for coaches, *Track and Field: Technique through Dynamics.* It was published in 1976 in both the U.S. and Japanese markets. The English version was updated and republished in 1979.

I had some real fun writing the dedication for this book. I had been in Florence, Italy, the previous summer and had visited the Museum of the History of

Science. In the museum were many of the inventions of Galileo Galilei, the brilliant Italian scientist whose ideas were to become the basis for Newtonian physics. But he made one discovery that was not popular with the Catholic church. He announced that the Earth was not the center of the universe.

The pope had Galileo taken before the Inquisition, where he was threatened with torture, was forced to kneel and recant his beliefs before ten Dominican cardinals, and was then sentenced to live under house arrest for the remainder of his life.

While visiting the museum, I found one real curiosity. It was one of Galileo's fingers that had been amputated nearly a century after his death and was preserved inside a glass vessel. It was the middle finger of his right hand, and it is pointing straight up. (I have pictures to prove it.)

So, for the book's dedication, I wrote:

"This book is dedicated to a courageous scientist, Galileo Galilei (1564–1642), whose true feelings toward the Inquisition continue to be on display, unsubtly, in the Museum of the History of Science in Florence. May the remainder of his body rest in peace!"

In 2010, the Museum of the History of Science was re-opened to the public after two years of renovation and great expansion. The museum also underwent a name change. It is now the Galileo Museum, featuring all of Galileo's discoveries and inventions.

The museum also features more parts of Galileo's body, removed after his death. Besides the middle finger, mentioned above in my book's dedication, there is now a tooth, a thumb, and an index finger.

A short distance from the Galileo Museum is the Basilica di Santa Croce, where Galileo's tomb is located. At the tomb site, there is no mention that enclosed in the tomb is some, but not all, of Galileo's body.

The final physics book for coaches was *Basic Track and Field Biomechanics*. It was first published in 1985, revised in 1996, republished in 2015, and is still in print more than thirty years after the book was originally written. The Japanese version came out in 1999.

My books have been so popular in Japan that I have been invited to Hiroshima twice to give talks to track coaches, and even had a tree planted in my honor at the famed Wakanuga Gardens near Hiroshima.

I decided to begin writing my own Olympic history book in the summer of 1990. I went to the Greek Island of Naxos and began writing. I took an extra suitcase, just for some of the Olympic books, magazines, and notes that I had collected over the years. Because of that heavy suitcase, I developed a severe case of what my doctor called "suitcase elbow." When I returned home, a shot of cortisone ended the pain.

My original source for Olympic information was the book *An Illustrated History of the Olympics* by Richard Schaap. Of course, I had no idea I would eventually own more than 300 Olympic history books and biographies. As I began collecting more and more information, it became clear to me that most Olympic history books are filled with inaccuracies, embellishments, distortions, and fabrications.

Over the next five years, I continued to collect information on the Olympics and took detailed notes, placing the notes and other information in file

Photo provided by Galileo Museum, Florence, Italy

Galileo's finger, preserved inside a glass vessel, is on display at the Galileo Museum.

folders—one for each of the modern Olympic Games, beginning with the first Games in 1896.

In 1995, I received a telephone call from my publisher, Ed Fox. He wanted the book completed by early 1996 so he could have it printed and made available during the time of the 1996 Olympics in Atlanta. His plan was to include the book, which was to be called *Olympic Facts and Fables,* in the packets of the 1,400 people who were members of his Olympic tour.

I knew that assembling all of the disjointed pieces into a readable book would be a monumental task. I was already a retiree, so time was not a factor. I rented a small office with no windows in downtown Cedar Rapids and moved all of my reference books, notes, and files into the office. Then I began to write, from 4 a.m. to 4 p.m. every day until the project was finished.

Everything was written in longhand, so it was a long, difficult process. But the project was completed, and the book came out in time for the 1996 Olympics. The second edition was released in time to be given to the 580 people who were members of the 2008 Olympics tour to Beijing. It is still in print.

We opened the 1963 cross country season against the University of Florida in Gainesville. We wanted to take all of our top seven runners to Florida, so everyone agreed we would squeeze all eight of us into our four-door sedan. There were three in the front, three in the back with their feet resting on the front seat, and two on the floor in the back. The trip was 650 miles each way.

Even though we had cramped traveling conditions, and we decided to stop on the way down to sleep on concrete picnic benches in a state park, we won the meet easily.

When we returned home, we had dual meet victories over Middle Tennessee, the University of Cincinnati, and Eastern Kentucky. Then followed a big upset win over Murray, a team that hadn't lost a dual cross country meet in five years.

We won our next meet against Tennessee Tech to finish the dual meet season unbeaten. However, we were edged out of the OVC title by Murray. The next week we won the Kentucky Federation Championships to end a very good season.

The office in downtown Cedar Rapids, where I finished writing Olympic Facts and Fables.

30

The Opportunity of a Lifetime

In the fall of 1963, during my second year as cross country coach at Western Kentucky, I received a phone call from Raymond Kohn, deputy chief of the Division for Americans Abroad at the U.S. State Department in Washington, D.C. He asked me if I'd like to become an American Specialist and work with track and field coaches in other countries.

The American Specialist program had been developed when the Vietnam War was becoming controversial. The program was designed to improve America's image abroad. I don't know how Mr. Kohn knew about it, but he referred to the training program I had devised called Progressive Interval Training. Apparently that was my ticket.

He told me the assignments were usually short and could often be done during vacation times. He added that he had an opening for a trip through central Africa in two weeks, but I had to turn it down. It was the middle of Western's cross country season. However, I told him I'd be interested in an assignment during the summer, if he had one.

During that winter, Mr. Kohn called me back and said he had an assignment in Finland for three weeks in June. Would I be interested? Of course, I was. He said the salary would be good, and the State Department would pay all my expenses.

He explained that Finland was the only country that owed money to the United States at the end of World War II that continued to pay it back. The State Department was using that money to help fund American Specialists abroad, especially when Finland was included in the itinerary. He told me American Specialists were not just in sports. They could be from any profession.

Then he asked me if I would accept any additional assignments in Europe, as long as I would already be there. I told him I could be gone as long as ten weeks.

A few days later, he called back and said he had an additional four weeks in Sweden and three weeks in Iceland. At the age of twenty-nine, I was about to leave North America for the first time and work with coaches in Northern Europe for ten weeks. What I didn't realize was that the adventure would involve taking twenty-five different airplane rides and sleeping in forty-four different beds.

I thought back to the nights I attended school at Nazareth College in Louisville, when I was working toward earning a teaching certificate. A fellow student had just returned from a trip to England, and she was telling me how wonderful it was. I told her my dream was to someday cross the Atlantic and visit Europe. My dream was about to come true.

But first came my primary obligation: the 1964 track and field season. Our opener was a home meet against Middle Tennessee. A free track and field clinic for coaches and athletes, featuring Fred Wilt, was conducted in the afternoon. That evening we won the track meet easily.

Then we took a long road trip, with our first competition at the North Dakota State University Invitational in Fargo. We won the meet over eight other colleges, scoring more points than the next four teams combined. That lopsided victory prompted Del Johnson, a Fargo journalist, to write:

Tom Ecker, a young man in a hurry, gives the impression that he is capable of starting from any given point and walking off in all directions. At a track meet, it's as though he pulled the pin on a live hand grenade and then held on to it until the blast—because when it comes to Ecker, that's him all over

At yesterday's meet, he played will-o'-the-wisp as he flitted from place to place to greet his athletes as they crossed finish lines. Each time a Kentucky runner came home first in a running event or one of his boys wound up on top in a field event, there was young mister Ecker—hand extended, beaming brighter than the sun that shines bright on his old Kentucky home.

It kept him busy. The Kentuckians won nine of the thirteen events, breaking records in six.

Our final road meet was against the Big Ten champion, the University of Minnesota in Minneapolis. After we won that meet, 54-50, and had a nice dinner, the team presented me with a restaurant placemat dated April 11, 1964, with Western Kentucky vs. University of Minnesota printed across the top. It said, "To Coach from Us," with the signatures of the twenty-one athletes and one publicist, Dave West, who made the trip. At the bottom it said: "Murray, Eastern and OVC next." My enthusiastic athletes were predicting three more victories.

Within one week, we beat Murray in a home meet—their first dual meet loss in five years, and then we beat Eastern on the road. For the Murray meet, more than 3,000 partisan fans were in the stands.

The following week, we traveled to Murfreesboro, Tennessee, and won the Ohio Valley Conference meet held at Middle Tennessee, the first track and field conference title in Western's history.

Besides the amazing showing by the Western Kentucky track team that weekend, there was a little unexpected drama on the track. As Western's Tom Gard was beginning his approach run in the long jump, Eastern's coach, Conan Smith, decided to step onto the runway, obviously to interfere with the jump. Because Conan Smith was always unfriendly and was willing to do anything to try to beat us, we all referred to him as "Con Man Smith."

Long jumper Tom Gard, who had been reading George Orwell's *Animal Farm* in a literature class and who liked the Orwell character named Napoleon the Pig, yelled out, "Hey, Napoleon! Get your fat ass off the runway!"

Coach Smith, who was carrying a hammer that was used to pound nails into cinder tracks to anchor starting blocks, began chasing Gard with the hammer. Gard, who was not about to be caught by his over-weight pursuer, ran away. One of my graduate assistants, Joe Bugel, grabbed Coach Smith and calmed him down. (That's the same Joe Bugel who later coached in the National Football League for thirty-two years, five of them as an NFL head coach.)

Anticipating a good showing in the Ohio Valley Conference meet in Murfreesboro, I had called ahead to a nearby country supper club and ordered twenty-five steak dinners. When our bus arrived at the restaurant after we had won the meet, we entered and began sitting at the tables. Of course, Roy Turner, our only black runner, was with us. The manager called me aside and told me Roy would have to eat in the kitchen. I got up and, in an atypically loud voice, I announced, "We're not eating here. Everyone back on the bus." Farther down the road, we found a place where we could all eat together.

When the season was over, Tom Gard was named OVC Trackman-of-the-Year, and I was named OVC Track Coach-of-the-Year for the second time. Local journalist Al Stilley began calling the Western team "the Ecker Empire."

During the thirty-three years that Fred Wilt and I were friends, he often used me as a teacher/coach in his "international coaching clinics." Fred always surrounded himself with his favorite coaches, a group that became known as "Wilt's Rat Pack." Naturally, I was pleased to be included.

The summer of 1964 began for me in Slippery Rock, Pennsylvania, where I joined Fred Wilt as an instructor in a weeklong international track and field coaching clinic. Jack Mahurin, one of my top distance runners at Western Kentucky, helped me drive my car from Bowling Green to Slippery Rock. Jack signed up as a student at the clinic.

For the most part, it was a learn-by-doing clinic, with twelve instructors, including my friend Bill Huyck. My responsibility was teaching Progressive Interval Training.

Three of the other instructors were from Great Britain, headed up by a fun-loving triple jumper named Mike Turvey. One night, the entire learn-by-doing staff drove about fifteen miles to an out-of-the-way dance hall, where we listened to Beatles' music non-stop. At the end of the evening, after much beer had been consumed, the three Brits decided I should be knighted. They had me kneel in front of them, where they tapped me on both shoulders with a beer bottle and dubbed me Sir Thomas of Her Majesty's Forces in Pennsylvania. My official title was Minister of Mirth.

The lone lecturer at the Slippery Rock clinic was Geoffrey Dyson, the great British coach, who lectured on "The Mechanics of Athletics," which was also the name of a book he had written. (Mechanics, which later became known as biomechanics, refers to Newtonian laws of motion. Athletics is an international word meaning track and field.)

I attended all of Dyson's lectures and took several pages of notes. It was a new science for me and for all of America's coaches. I was determined to learn as much as I could about mechanics and to become an expert in the field. I bought a copy of Dyson's book and had him autograph it for me.

Because of Dyson's influence, I later began doing talks on mechanics, applying the laws of physics to track and field technique. The talks were supported by a remote-controlled 16mm projector, many props, lots of humor, and some audience participation. It became a very popular presentation.

Posing with Eero Uotila, one of Finland's national coaches.

Over the next twenty-five years, that talk, or variations of it, took me throughout North America and Europe. Billed as "humorous and informative," I gave the talk at several of Fred Wilt's coaching clinics, many state coaching associations, two NCAA national clinics, and meetings of sports delegations in England, Mexico, Sweden, Germany, Spain, New Zealand, Iceland, and Canada.

When the week in Slippery Rock was over, Jack Mahurin and I drove to the airport in Pittsburgh so I could catch a flight to Washington, D.C. Jack then drove my car back to Kentucky.

In Washington, I was to be briefed by different agencies the next day. On the short flight to Washington, the airline managed to destroy the footlocker I had packed for the trip. It was the footlocker I had bought in Alaska. Part of my briefing day in Washington had to be spent shopping for two suitcases to replace the badly damaged footlocker.

The briefings themselves were pretty funny. I would meet with a few people from one governmental agency, then hop in a taxi to the next agency, where I would meet with a few people, etc. There were four separate meetings, with everyone telling me how much I would enjoy the trip. No one gave me any advice. At one point, when I asked if they could provide me with maps, I was told to wait until I got there. Their maps are much better than ours, I was told.

That evening I caught an overnight flight to London and connected to a flight to Helsinki, Finland, later that morning. The plane to Helsinki lost an engine (one-half of the total), and we had to make an emergency landing in Gothenburg, Sweden. After a three-hour delay, the plane was back on its way to Helsinki, arriving at 10 p.m.

At the Helsinki airport, I was met by John Hughes of the American Embassy, who was upset that he didn't know I was coming until the day before. He said I'd be leaving immediately for Vierumäki with one of Finland's national track coaches, Eero Uotila. Vierumäki, which is located in the middle of thousands of acres of unspoiled wilderness, is the official training center for the Finnish Olympic teams.

Mr. Hughes introduced me to Eero and his wife, Ritva. Eero told me he had learned at 3 o'clock that afternoon that an American track coach was coming to Finland for a three-week visit. He would be in

The Soviet jet that had been converted from military service, that took me from Helsinki to Leningrad.

charge of my entire stay and would act as interpreter whenever I gave a talk. Eero's understanding of English was very good, despite his having had no formal training.

We put my two suitcases in the trunk of the Uotilas' Mercedes-Benz, and we made the one-hour drive north to Vierumäki. Even though it was midnight when we arrived, there was still enough daylight that Eero didn't have to turn on the car's headlights. I didn't see any American-made cars along the way, but there were many bicycles.

My duties during my stay in Finland were helping with coaching tasks, meeting with coaches and athletes, and delivering a few lectures. Eero was always there to translate for me. I always began my lectures by telling a joke. Usually, Eero and about half the audience would laugh when I finished the joke in English. The other half would laugh when Eero finished the translation in Finnish.

Throughout the three weeks, every time I met with coaches or athletes, there were journalists and photographers present. The newspaper coverage of my time in Finland was amazing.

I wasn't the first track and field coach to visit Finland as an American Specialist. Eero told me a story about a South Dakota coach named Jim Emrich, who had come to Finland two years earlier. The day Emrich arrived in Helsinki he was suffering from severe jet lag. So after checking into his hotel, he decided he would take a long walk until he was very tired—or lost—or both. When he left the hotel, he looked up at the sign

to be sure to get the name of the hotel. An hour or so later, when he was completely lost, he hailed a taxi, got in, and said, "Hotelli Ravintola." (Hotelli Ravintola means Hotel Restaurant.)

Several times during my stay in Finland, I was treated to the Finnish sauna experience. A sauna, usually built next to a lake, features a small room lined with wooden benches along its walls, with a stove heating several rocks in a corner of the room. Naked participants sit on the benches, with temperatures in the sauna often topping 212 degrees. Then the participants jump in the lake to cool off.

It is a very pleasant experience when the humidity in the sauna is low. But in Finland, there is always a bucket of cold water and a ladle near the stove. Daring participants splash water on the hot stones, which creates a cloud of steam and a burning sensation to the skin. That can be a very unpleasant experience.

One of the Finns told me that a common trick played on the occupying German troops during World War II was to tell the Germans that the way to cool off a sauna was to splash cold water on the hot rocks.

One day the first week I was in Finland, Eero and I drove to Pajulahti to pick up one of the British national coaches, Dennis Watts, who was traveling through Finland with two British pole vaulters, Trevor Burton and David Stevens.

We drove them to Turku for an international track meet with six different countries participating. Even though they were Britain's best, Burton and Stevenson finished fifth and sixth out of six pole vaulters.

While walking around Leningrad in the middle of the night, I photographed this woman who was working at a park. In the background is a statue of Peter the Great on horseback.

A friendly and fun guy, Trevor Burton blurted out the word "Shitteroo" every time he was happy about something. There was a huge, fancy banquet that evening for all the athletes and dignitaries. At 2 a.m., after much eating and drinking, and many more shitteroos, we all went to our hotel for a short sleep.

Early the next morning, Eero and I drove the three Brits to the Helsinki airport to catch their flight back to England. Then, while in Helsinki, I went to the embassy to collect my mail and salary money. I also asked if they could help me get a visa to the Soviet Union for a short visit.

The Uotilas were eager for me to see as much as possible on this trip, so they arranged a flight for me from Oulu, Finland, to Kirkenes, Norway, about 250 miles north of the Arctic Circle and very near the border of the Soviet Union. Actually, it was three flights up to Kirkenes and three flights back, all on twin engine DC-3s, with only twenty-one passenger seats.

The first stop was Rovaniemi, Finland, which is very close to the Arctic Circle. Next was Ivalo, Finland, which was well north of the Arctic Circle. Then to Kirkenes, where we were told that taking photographs was forbid-

den because of the proximity to the Soviet Union.

Then it was back to Ivalo to spend the night in a hotel. After a great Wiener schnitzel dinner, I stayed up until midnight to see the midnight sun. It was low in the sky but was well above the horizon.

The next day I flew back to Oulu and gave a lecture to the Oulu Track Club. There was a track meet that evening with several local track clubs participating. During my final days in Finland, we made several more trips, visiting various communities and speaking to track clubs throughout Finland.

We returned to Helsinki, where I went to In Tourist (the Soviet travel agency) to buy an airline ticket to Leningrad (or St. Petersburg after 1991) and to get a hotel reservation. There I learned that 1964 was only the second year that the Soviet Union had allowed tourists to visit the country.

I went to the Soviet embassy to pick up my visa. My last assignment in Finland was to attend a Fourth of July picnic at the U.S. Embassy. After the picnic, I took a taxi to downtown Helsinki, and a bus from there to the airport.

My flight to Leningrad was aboard a Soviet jet that had been converted from military service. The stewardess could have been a Soviet shot putter. I was told the jet had only two speeds—full speed and stop. The plane had to be towed to the runway before taking off and back to the terminal after landing.

I was met at the airport by an In Tourist taxi driver (called a Politruki by the Finns, from the Russian word Politruk, a person employed to keep an eye on you). He first took me to an exchange window where I was required to exchange $50 into Soviet rubles. Since the Soviet government had artificially established the ruble at $1.25, I received only 40 rubles.

Then he drove me to the Astoria Hotel, where he said he'd pick up the next morning to take me to the airport. When I was checking in, the woman at the front desk kept saying to anyone who would listen, that I was the American who had come to Leningrad to sleep. It was true I was checking in around 8 p.m. and would be checking out before 8 a.m., but I wasn't planning to sleep.

I went into the hotel's restaurant and ordered a big meal. When it was time to pay, they wouldn't take rubles, only dollars. There was a government store in the hotel, where I bought a Russian fur cap. I tried to

—119

pay in rubles, but they only took dollars. It turned out that dollars were accepted everywhere in the world; rubles were accepted nowhere in the world except in the Soviet Union.

I did find a small nearby souvenir shop that accepted rubles. I stood in a line to pick out a small carved wooden bear that I wanted to buy. Then I stood in a second line to pay for it. Then I stood in a third line to pick it up. The whole process took almost an hour.

Around midnight, I could hear laughing and singing coming from someplace a short distance from the hotel. I followed the sounds and found myself in a park next to the Neva River.

A street scene in Leningrad, with a mural featuring Vladimir Lenin.

There were hundreds of students congregating there, spending their Saturday night talking, drinking, and laughing. As soon as the students found there was an American among them, I was in great demand to join in conversations with the few of them who could understand and speak English.

After many interesting discussions, I took a break around 3 a.m. to write a Finnish aerogram to my parents, to be mailed from Helsinki later in the day. I wrote: "This is quite a place—beautiful in a way, but quite dirty. The people I've met all look like followers without a leader. They're satisfied because they don't know any other life exists. I know because I've been out talking with them and they're flabbergasted (and often unbelieving) when I tell them about American life. Language is a big problem during these discussions, but some know a little English and our sign language seems to be international. I'm going back out now for another hour's worth of chats."

I spent the next hour chatting with the English-speaking Soviet students again. Several of them wanted to know why their country had allowed me to come to Leningrad, but my country wouldn't allow them to come to America. I told them they are welcome to

come to America, but their country won't let them leave. None of them wanted to believe that.

When I checked out of the hotel at 5:30, my taxi driver (my Politruki) was looking for me frantically. He was most pleased to see me. He drove me to the airport where I learned I was not allowed to take rubles out of the country. I took some anyway.

I was searched three times before boarding the airplane. I don't think they knew what they were looking for. There certainly weren't any security concerns in those days. They even saw my collection of rubles, but they didn't take them from me. After boarding the plane, this time a very modern Finnair jet, I flew back to Helsinki.

There I was met by Eero, Ritva, and John Hughes from the American Embassy. They accompanied me to the gate for my flight to Stockholm, which was ready to leave.

When I got to Stockholm, I was the last person to pick up my luggage. My bags were the only two left on the carousel. A man—very excited—ran up to me and asked, "Is that Frank Sinatra's luggage?" Apparently, Sinatra also had just arrived, and his luggage was lost. I answered, "I hope not. My clothes are in them."

31

The Swedes and the Icelanders

When I arrived in Stockholm for my four-week stay, I was met at the airport by Håkan Bergenheim, who represented the Swedish track and field team. He explained that the entire team, along with coaches and other officials, were at a training camp in western Sweden.

He showed me some of the sights in Stockholm, including the Warship Vasa, which sank in the Stockholm harbor on its maiden voyage in 1628 and was only recently "exhumed" and put on display. Then he took me to Stockholm's central railway station so I could catch a train to Karlstad, more than 120 miles to the west.

In Karlstad, I was met by Sweden's chief national track and field coach, Gunnar Carlsson, and the team manager, Eric Ahldén. They drove me to Wermlandia, a resort hotel in the small town of Eksharad, one hour north of Karlstad. It was midnight when we arrived and time for bed.

In the morning at breakfast, I was introduced to other coaches and many of the track and field team members. On the breakfast table were two small flags—one Swedish and one American. When I went outside after breakfast, I saw two flagpoles, one with the Swedish flag and one with the American flag. I was very impressed.

The rest of the day was spent watching middle distance and distance runners in the morning and discus throwers and 400-meter hurdlers in the afternoon. Already I realized the Swedes were not as serious as the Finns and that their grasp of English was much better.

After the workouts were completed, I took a "bastu," the Swedish version of the Finnish sauna. A bastu is not nearly as hot as a sauna—only about 185 or 190 degrees—and the humidity is kept low. When I felt hot enough, I was told to jump into a nearby swimming pool, which was not nearly as cold as a lake.

Immediately, I decided I preferred the bastu.

The next morning, after breakfast, I rode back to Stockholm with Chief Coach Gunnar Carlsson in his new Ford Taunus. Gunnar, who spoke excellent English, had a keen sense of humor. We both spent a lot of time laughing during the long ride to Stockholm.

Gunnar told me of an old Swedish custom. He said when a Swede buys something, he always buys two, in case he loses one. He said when he bought his new Ford Taunus he thought he should buy a second one. But he decided not to when he realized how difficult it would be to lose a car.

Sweden's Chief Coach Gunnar Carlsson at Stockholm's Olympic Stadium

Meeting with two local track coaches, I'm joined by national coach, Gusti Larell, talking with the local coaches.

When we arrived in Stockholm, Gunnar checked me into a dormitory room at Skogshögskolan (College of Forestry). Then I went to the American Embassy, where I met my contact, Phillip Benson, who was originally from Iowa.

There was a big track meet—Sweden vs. Norway and Finland--scheduled at Stockholm's Olympic Stadium (built for the 1912 Olympics) the next two nights, so I attended the meet's scratch meeting that evening. Scratch meetings are held before big track meets to determine who would be running and what heats and lanes they would have.

At the scratch meeting, I met the other national coach, Gusti Laurell, who was as delightful a character as Gunnar. Gusti, short for Gustav, was originally from Finland, and while he was very funny, he was also very serious about his love for track and field. He talked about track training and technique whenever he had an opportunity. Gusti spoke Finnish, his native tongue, and was also fluent in Swedish, English, and German.

One of the few non-track and field things Gusti

and I discussed in those days was the Winter War of 1939—a time just before World War II when the Soviets were bombing Finland regularly before a planned invasion. Gusti was in the Finish army at the time, operating an anti-aircraft gun on the border between Finland and the Soviet Union.

When the Soviets invaded Finland, their men and equipment, including tanks, got stuck in heavy snow. The Finns, although heavily outnumbered, surrounded and attacked the Soviets on skis, wiping out several Soviet regiments. The Finnish battle cry was, "They are so many and our country is so small, where are we going to bury them all?"

During the Winter War, diplomats from Finland and the Soviet Union had regular meetings to try to settle their differences. The meetings were held in Stockholm, Sweden, a neutral site. The diplomat representing the Soviet Union was foreign minister Vyacheslav Molotov, which prompted the Finns to invent the Molotov cocktail. The Finns would fill empty whiskey bottles with gasoline and stuff rags in the bottles as fuses. When the Soviet tanks passed through the Finnish forests, Finnish soldiers, perched in the trees above the tanks, would light and drop the bottles on the Soviet tanks. One well-placed Molotov cocktail could knock out a tank and kill everyone inside it.

After attending the two-day meet at Stockholm Stadium, I was invited to Gusti's home in Lerum, a small town near Gothenburg in western Sweden. Gusti's wife, Rosemarie, was in Finland for the summer, so Gusti and I had the residence to ourselves. Lerum was our headquarters for the next several days, with side trips scheduled from there to meet people, to conduct workouts for area athletes, and to attend track meets.

One of the side trips was to visit the great Swedish distance runner, Dan Waern, at his home in the nearby countryside. Among his many accomplishments, Waern was best known as the first Swede to run a sub-four-minute mile, back in 1957.

Dan Waern had become a track coach but not a track coach like all the others we knew. Dan coached horses. He bought well-bred but unsuccessful race horses and trained them to become big money winners in thoroughbred races.

While all other horse trainers used over-distance as the primary training method, Dan's horse training secret was interval training. In theory, the horses would run several shorter distances to exhaustion, with an interval of rest in between. But early on Dan discovered that horses won't run repeated races to exhaustion. Unlike humans, when horses get tired they quit.

Dan solved the problem by constructing a large tank of water with a leather sling that would lower a horse into the water. The horse had a choice—swim to exhaustion or drown. Using this method of interval training, several of Dan's race horses became thoroughbred champions. As far as I know, Dan's system of training race horses has never been duplicated. To this day, horse trainers are relying on old-fashioned over-distance training.

One evening, Gusti and I went to a movie theater to see a James Bond movie, *From Russia with Love*. After the movie, we discussed how cool James Bond was. We decided the two coolest people in the world were James Bond and Bugs Bunny.

One of my proudest accomplishments while visiting Sweden (and later Iceland) was the introduction of cheeseburgers. I was often asked to fix them as word spread about how good they were.

Burgers were completely unknown to the Scandinavians in 1964. McDonald's and Burger King wouldn't appear until years later. I made cheeseburgers with the following rules: They had to be big and slow-cooked. They had to have a lot of cheese on them. No one was allowed to put any "junk" on them, except salt. (No catsup, no mustard, no pickles, no anything.)

My biggest challenge was finding burger meat, cheese, and buns. I would ask a butcher to grind up his best steaks (which the butcher was hesitant to do). Then I would find a block of the mildest cheese I could find, which had to be sliced by hand. Finally, since there were no buns available anywhere, I had to use slices of bread. My cheeseburgers were big, juicy, and very popular with everyone who tried them.

Our longest road trip took us to several international track meets. The first meet was in Norrköping, south of Stockholm, where two Swedish athletes I was helping to coach won their races against German opponents. At dinner that night, Norrköping's mayor presented me with a special bronze medal commemorating the 600th birthday of the city.

The next day we drove farther south to Ronneby, the home of boxer Floyd Patterson's training camp. At that time, Patterson considered Sweden to be his second home.

From Ronneby, we drove to the southern port town of Karlshamn for another international track meet. Karlshamn was the port where more than one million Swedes had immigrated to the United States during the early part of the twentieth century. There is a statue near the water's edge there that shows a Swedish man looking off to the New World while his wife is looking back at Sweden. It is very touching.

The next day, Gusti and I were invited to have lunch with a well-known Swedish sports journalist, Torsten Tegner. Tegner, who was then 76, wrote a column in the Idrottsbladet newspaper and was known for his regular use of capital letters and exclamation marks for dramatic emphasis.

It happened that Torsten's late mother, Alice, who had been the foremost composer of Swedish children's songs, was being honored that day. She was born in Karlshamn in 1864, and the entire community was celebrating her 100th birthday. There was a parade through town, and then the unveiling of a statue of Alice Tegner in the city's rose garden.

The only thing I remember now about the lunch is that was the only time I ever drank several shots of Swedish schnapps before noon. Torsten enjoyed toasting anything that was on his mind at the moment.

From Karlshamn, we drove to the town of Växjö, where we visited several nearby glass factories. I really liked Växjö, partly because it was the only five-letter word I'd ever seen that has five dots over the letters.

Then we drove back to Lerum to complete our swing through southern Sweden. I caught a plane in Gothenburg and flew back to Stockholm, where I was met by Gunnar Carlsson. We spent the next several afternoons working with athletes who were training at the Olympic Stadium.

One of the athletes was pole vaulter Hans Lagerqvist. Hans was twenty-four at the time, and since most American track and field athletes were retired by age twenty-two, I thought Hans was too old to be pole vaulting. But he was such a nice guy, I decided to work with him anyway.

Hans had trouble keeping his legs up before reaching the crossbar, so we put the bar up to seventeen feet and had him repeatedly vault and kick the crossbar off with his feet. (Little did I know that Hans would be clearing the crossbar at seventeen feet a few years later. He vaulted seventeen feet, eight-and-a-half inches in 1972, at the age of thirty-two.)

Another of my favorite athletes was discus-thrower Lars Haglund. Lars was already established as a world-class thrower, so I spent most of my time with him as an observer.

One afternoon, Hans invited Lars and me to the Lagerqvist home for dinner. That was the night I offered the two athletes a travel deal. If they could get to Bowling Green, Kentucky, the next spring to train with my Western Kentucky athletes, I would provide them room and board for as long as they wanted to stay. Their acceptance of that offer changed all of our lives.

After a Saturday afternoon press conference at the stadium, I was ready to pack my bags and fly to Reykjavik, Iceland, for my final three weeks on the road. I was met at the Reykjavik airport by a member of the Icelandic National Track and Field Association, Svavar Markusson, and an "immigrant" track coach,

Gabor Simonyi. Gabor had escaped from Hungary and had gotten as far as Iceland on his way to Canada, and, hopefully, to the United States.

Gabor stayed very close to me, hoping I might be able to provide him with a shortcut on his planned journey to the West. He offered me lunch in his home, he accompanied me to the American Embassy to pick up my mail, and then he offered me dinner in his home.

After two days in Reykjavik, I flew to the Westman Islands (within sight of Iceland's mainland), where I was met by Iceland's top discus thrower, Hallgrimmur Jonsson. He was also the island's chief of police. He told me there is no crime on the island because there is no place to hide. He said the only offense is drunkenness.

I conducted workout sessions on the local track every evening at 5 and 8:30 before flying back to Reykjavik to attend the Scandinavian decathlon championships. Before leaving Sweden, the Swedish Track and Field Association had named me the coach for the Swedish decathletes so they wouldn't have to pay for one of their coaches to be there.

When the competition was about to begin, everyone stood for the playing of the national anthems of

Pole vaulter Hans Lagerquist, only 24-years-old when we met, became a world-ranked vaulter eight years later.

In the Westman Islands, I climbed a small mountain and had a local boy shoot my picture.

anyone, he managed to get passage on a ship bound for Canada. The next time I heard about Gabor, he was making a name for himself as a Canadian coach.

My final days in Iceland were spent with a young javelin thrower, Páll Eiriksson, who was a medical student at the University of Iceland. Páll, who had a great sense of humor, led me on a great sightseeing trip. We flew to Akureri, on the north coast of Iceland and had two good coaching sessions with local coaches and athletes.

We spent the night in a fancy hotel in Akureri with a fancier restaurant, and then took a bus over winding, second-class unpaved roads back to Reykjavik. As I had heard, the countryside of Iceland looked like the surface of the moon, without any trees in sight. I spent one last night in Reykjavik.

Then it was time to go home. My official State Department itinerary had me flying to Washington, D.C., arriving there the morning of August 24. I showed up at my debriefing promptly at 9 a.m. The officer in charge saw me walk in and said, "Oh, my God. Is this your day back?"

Needless to say, they weren't ready for me. A short debriefing session was quickly arranged for me, and I was soon on my way home.

It had been an amazing ten weeks.

Norway, Denmark, Sweden, and Iceland. Gabor Simonyi stood next to me during the playing of the anthems and remarked, "Isn't it funny that the smallest nations always have the longest anthems?"

When the two-day decathlon championships were over, there was a large banquet for everyone involved. But Gabor Simonyi was not there. Without telling

32

The World's a Stage

When I returned from my European adventure, I was asked about the differences between life in the northern European countries and life in the United States. Although there were many differences, I pointed out that the main one for me was the various kinds of toilet paper that I had experienced while traveling abroad. The quality, I said, ranged from wax paper to sandpaper.

As noted earlier, the 1964 cross country season was a really good one for the Western team, culminating in the Ohio Valley Conference title, the first in Western's history.

I'm not sure why, but I took up wood carving as a hobby during Western's 1964 cross country season. Perhaps it was a way to relax after practice every day. I had read that Michelangelo, when he was sculpting his famous David statue, explained that sculpting requires

At Left: A carved piece of wormy birch, entitled, A Long Screw and a Short Screw, *was carved after returning to Iowa in 1967. At Right: A walnut carving called,* Swirly, *was completed at Western in 1964.*

removing anything on a block of marble that doesn't look like David.

So I became a wood carver, removing anything on a block of wood that didn't look like whatever I wanted to create. I bought a small sheath knife (which I still have), a variety of cutting and shaping tools, several types of wood files, and various grades of sandpaper. My first carvings were of walnut, an extremely hard wood that is difficult to carve, but later I carved some softer woods.

My first walnut carving required a great deal of effort. The final result was an abstract walnut figure, simply known as *Swirly.* There were nine more carvings over the next three years, including one I called *Statue of Limitations.*

One afternoon, after cross country practice, I hadn't bothered to change clothes when I began carving at the dining room table. I was trying to carve a small piece off the sculpture when I slipped and plunged the knife deep into my left thigh. With blood gushing out of the wound, my wife Judy came running in and screamed, "Your new slacks!"

(Four years later, after I had returned to Iowa, I continued wood carving as a relaxing hobby. One of my carvings called *Sticks and Stones* won a blue ribbon at the All-Iowa Fair in Cedar Rapids.)

In the middle of the Western campus, there was a large log building called the Faculty House. Dating back to 1918, it was a place for faculty members to drink coffee, grade papers, and socialize. In the 1965–66 school year, it was also the site of daily Scrabble matches, every weekday at noon. At the time, I was really taken with the game of Scrabble and had even written a booklet on Scrabble strategy.

There were two other Scrabble enthusiasts at Western. One was Dr. Allan Anderson, head of the mathematics department. Al and I were so evenly matched, we would play each other for ten cents a point, with neither of us gaining much advantage over the other. But when either of us was challenged by another faculty member, we had to spot the opponent 100 points ($10), but, still, we seldom lost.

The other Scrabble enthusiast on campus was Dr. Stephen Levensohn, the head of the philosophy department. In 1965, Steve and I began a marathon Scrabble game that lasted almost twenty-three weeks. We played one hundred fourteen matches, with Levensohn winning fifty-eight to my fifty-six. However, when you compare total scores, Levensohn had only 39,008 points to my 39,315. Obviously, we were pretty closely matched.

Steve once told me the difference between a track coach and a philosopher. If a track coach lies on a beach by the ocean for a long period of time, he is considered by many observers to be a beach bum. If a philosopher does the same thing, most observers say he must be thinking.

During the early 1960s, I kept in touch with my writer friend Don Hough. I learned that his wife, Berry, had died, and he had moved back to Jackson Hole, Wyoming, probably to try to relive the memories of his past. In the fall of 1964, after the Western Kentucky cross country season was over, I decided to spend the long Thanksgiving weekend trying to locate him. In those days, it was not easy flying out of Bowling Green, Kentucky, or into Jackson Hole, Wyoming. It took all day to get there.

Without telling Don I was coming, I flew to Idaho Falls, spent the night in a hotel, rented a car, and drove the ninety miles over the pass to Jackson Hole. I found Don living in a small one-room cabin near the center of town. He was very surprised and happy to see me. He showed me drawings and other mementos from his past. Then I drove him around the town so he could point out the places that were prominent in his book, *The Cocktail Hour in Jackson Hole*. He was loving the experience.

He had downgraded from expensive gin to cheap wine. He asked me if I would buy him a bottle of wine, which I did. It was obvious the drinking had taken its toll. He wasn't able to write anything anymore. And the things he would talk about constantly were exciting for him to tell, and interesting for a first-time listener, but boring for those who had heard the stories over and over. He was living in the past.

Late in the afternoon, we parted company so I could drive back to Idaho Falls to catch my flight. It was a sad farewell.

I would never see Don Hough again. In his book, *The Cocktail Hour in Jackson Hole*, he had written a chapter entitled "My cabin is on fire." As if he were predicting his own demise, his cabin caught fire while he slept one night in 1965, and he died as a result of the fire.

I wrote to Floy Tonkin, the mayor of Jackson Hole, to try to learn about Don's death. I explained to her that I had been one of Don's students at the University of Iowa and that I had become a reasonably successful writer because of him. She sent me a quick reply:

About Don Hough's death: I could not find a copy of the Jackson Hole Guide containing the account of his death, but since he was not burned, it was assumed he died of smoke inhalation. He had been drinking heavily for a long time. Anyway, the fire started apparently from a cigarette dropped in an overstuffed chair.

Don had a hard time finding a permanent place to live. He was so untidy that no one would let him remain very long. But the cabin, which he rented from the Shirvins, had been comfortable, and the Shirvins looked after him well, cleaning the cabin and running errands for him. In return, he kept his rent paid up; he was very particular about that.

When his wife, Berry, died, he was very depressed. She had nursed him and supported him for many years, then she had a nervous breakdown and could not live with him any longer, so he came to Jackson, which he remembered fondly from the old days. He was disappointed because the people he had chummed around with were either gone or too sedate to spend much time in the bars. They tried to be cordial and took him with them to banquets and clubs, but he always managed to embarrass them by either drinking too much or starting an unnecessary argument.

I may sound unduly hard on Don, but I have known him for a long time, and it made me very sad to see a brilliant mind wasted. He could have done so much with his life.

Don taught a lot of people how to write, and I, for one, think his books are priceless. He certainly enjoyed your visit and was looking forward to your return.

Donald Hough's grave is high on a hillside overlooking Jackson. I plan to stop there and pay my respects the next time I'm in Wyoming.

To cap the year, Western's mass media division of the English department produced a two-hour documentary called *Western 1964.* Since the local television station, WLTV, still didn't have a network affiliation, the station was happy to have us produce the live show.

Airing on the second Sunday in January at 2 p.m., *Western 1964* gave viewers a concise but comprehensive picture of the events that combined to make the year one of Western's most outstanding. The program featured nineteen student newscasters and eleven student production crewmembers. I served as the program's director.

In March 1965, Western Kentucky's drama department produced a popular musical of that time, *Bye-Bye Birdie.* One of the scenes in the musical was the set of the then-popular TV program, *The Ed Sullivan Show.* Since we had a fake TV camera that we were using in our television classes, I was asked to appear in the scene as the TV floor manager, along with the camera. It was my first appearance in a play since high school, thirteen years earlier. I had no lines.

Bye-Bye Birdie was a big hit on Broadway in the early 1960s. It was the story of a rock singer, Conrad Birdie, who was about to go in the Army and makes a final appearance on *The Ed Sullivan Show.* The character Conrad Birdie was a rough representation of Elvis Presley, who had been drafted into the Army in 1957.

In the cast of almost 100 Western students (and one track coach) were two actors who would later become stars of stage, television, and motion pictures.

One was Leo Burmester, who played Conrad Birdie in the musical. He later appeared in thirty-seven movies, made thirty-two TV appearances, and was in nine Broadway shows. When *Les Miserables* came to Broadway from the London stage in 1987, Leo was cast as Thenardier, one of the leading roles.

The other actor was David Schramm, who played the mayor in *Bye-Bye Birdie.* Although he later appeared in movies and on Broadway, his best-known role was Roy Biggins, the portly curmudgeon who owned the rival airline in the TV sitcom *Wings.* The show ran for eight seasons in the 1990s and David appeared in all 172 episodes.

I became friends with both Leo and David, and followed their successes throughout the years.

One of the funniest scenes in *Bye-Bye Birdie* was not written in the script. At one point, Conrad Birdie opened a can of warm beer after it had been well-shaken. Of course, the beer exploded all over the orchestra members who were sitting directly in front of the stage. The orchestra conductor, Virgil Hale, had a pop-up umbrella that he opened at exactly the right moment. Everyone was splashed with beer, except for the orchestra conductor.

When *Bye-Bye Birdie* closed in March after a three-day run, the production director, Dr. Russell Miller, asked me if I would consider appearing in another play. He thought that having someone prominent in sports participating in a theater production could help bridge the gap between athletics and the arts. The play's dates would be July 21 through July 23, 1965, well after the 1965 track season was finished.

The play was *Three Men on a Horse,* starring Leo Burmester in the leading role. Leo played a mild-mannered greeting card writer, Erwin Trowbridge. Erwin had the uncanny ability to take a daily racing form and predict all of the winning horses. Bored with his job, he decides to visit a local saloon, where he meets some unsavory horse players, who decide to use Erwin's skills to make money at the track.

I played Charlie, one of the unsavory horse players. In one of the scenes, the setting was the saloon, but we all pretended we were in a pharmacy. When the telephone rang, I answered it and told the caller I was the "pharmastist."

One of the nights, Judy brought all three children to see the play. Wendy was eight, Kerry was seven, and Kevin was five. When I first appeared on stage, Kevin yelled out, "That's my daddy!" Years later, when Kevin was appearing in many different stage productions, I always threatened to yell out, "That's my son!" As tempting as that was, I never did it.

33

The Long Spring Break

The 1965 indoor track season began with an unofficial indoor meet in Knoxville, Tennessee. We entered our mile relay team, the four runners and me making the trip in my car. The relay team was involved in a tight race, but anchorman Roy Turner came from behind to bring home the victory.

As it turned out, the relay race was not as exciting as our trip back to Bowling Green. Roy Turner was our only black runner. Because of strict segregation practices in much of the South at that time, we knew we would not be able to stay in a motel or hotel anywhere along the way. So we decided to drive straight back to Bowling Green after the meet. In the middle of the night, somewhere in rural Tennessee, we stopped to fill the car with gas.

Above the gas station was a large billboard that read: "We will not rest until the four Ks are dead." On the billboard were pictures of the late President John F. Kennedy, former Attorney General Robert F. Kennedy, civil rights leader Martin Luther King Jr., and the Soviet Union's Nikita Khrushchev. Not knowing how Roy would be received, I told everyone to stay in the car while the attendant filled it with gas. We left as soon as we could.

At that time, John Kennedy had already been assassinated. Martin Luther King would be assassinated in April 1968. Robert Kennedy would be assassinated in June 1968. The only one of the four Ks who died of natural causes was the Soviet Union's Nikita Khrushchev, who died of a heart attack in 1971.

In March, I flew to Cleveland, Ohio, with Henry Wadsworth, where he was to pole vault in the Knights of Columbus Relays. Transporting sixteen-foot poles was not easy in those days. They were carried in long cardboard tubes and had to fit in cargo holds with limited space.

When we boarded the plane in Louisville to fly to Cleveland, the pole in its cardboard case was on the tarmac, ready to be loaded in the cargo hold. One of the plane's cabin attendants asked Henry what was in the long tube. Without hesitating, he told her it was a snake being transported to the Cleveland zoo. He explained that snakes have to travel in straight tubes so they can't curl up.

The upcoming April issue of *Athletic Journal* was to feature a color picture of Wadsworth clearing a crossbar, which would appear on the magazine's cover. I took the cover photo. Inside were to be sequence photos of Wadsworth pole vaulting from three different angles, along with an article, "The Fiberglass Vault," which I had written.

Western Kentucy Pole Vaulter Henry Wadsworth

Getting the sequence photos for the magazine was not an easy task. *Athletic Journal's* publisher, Jack Griffith, had been planning to photograph Wadsworth sometime in March. As soon as we had a clear day, he would fly in from Chicago to take the pictures.

Early one March morning, I got a phone call from Griffith, asking how the weather was in Bowling Green. I looked out the window and saw nothing but blue skies, so I told him the weather was fine. He gave me his arrival time and said he'd see me in a couple of hours.

Shortly after that, I checked the outside temperature and realized we had had a sudden "cold snap" overnight. It was below freezing. And we all knew that fiberglass poles do not bend when they are cold. So, on my way to the airport, I stopped at a hardware store and bought an electric "pipe warmer," a long piece of electric wire used to wrap around outside pipes to keep them from freezing during the winter months

I met Griffith at the airport, and we drove to the track to meet Henry Wadsworth, who was wearing heavy clothing over his track suit. We took the cork plug out of Henry's pole, which was a hollow fiberglass tube, and plugged the wire into an electric outlet. Then we inserted the long wire into the tube. Immediately, the pole warmed up.

Henry stripped off his heavy clothing, removed the wire from the pole, and completed his first vault. He warmed the pole this way before several succeeding vaults. The system worked, and the sequence photos were perfect.

In April, it was time to start the outdoor track season. It was also time for two Swedish athletes to visit the Western campus. While I was traveling in Sweden the previous summer, I had invited two of the Swedish athletes, pole vaulter Hans Lagerqvist and discus thrower Lars Haglund, to come to Western Kentucky to train with my Western athletes. I told them that if they could get to Bowling Green, Kentucky, I would provide them with room and board for as long as they wanted to stay. They decided to stay for six weeks.

I provided a dorm room for the Swedes at Northeast Hall, and asked the Western Hills Restaurant if they would provide them with their meals. In exchange for the free meals, the Swedes appeared in a newspaper ad under the headline "International Athletes at Western Hills."

Since Western's spring break fell within the time the Swedes were visiting, I decided to take that week off and treat them to a "sightseeing" trip. I borrowed the athletic department's 1965 Dodge, which had "Western Kentucky Hilltoppers, Bowling Green, Kentucky" lettered on each front door. Then I asked two of my students, runner Tom Graham and radio announcer and writer Dave West, if they would trade off driving during the trip.

But first we had a Saturday afternoon track meet in Lexington, Kentucky, some 160 miles from Bowling Green. The entire Western track and field team, plus the two Swedes, participated in the Kentucky Federation Relays that afternoon. When the meet was over, we all climbed on the bus and returned to Bowling Green. By the time we had showered and packed a few things for the trip, it was after midnight.

We left early in the morning Sunday and returned on the following Sunday afternoon. The trip took us through sixteen states and covered 6,704 miles, averaging about 894 miles per day.

There were no speed limits in many of the states covered, which accounts for the great distances traveled in so little time. We averaged over thirty-seven miles per hour, even though we made many stops along the way. The price of gasoline was less than forty cents per gallon. The only sleep we got was in the car, while it was moving. While in Los Angeles, we did stop at a YMCA so everyone could take the only shower of the trip.

We had only two rules regarding sleep:

1) If the driver saw something that he thought everyone else should see, he was obliged to awaken any sleeping passengers.

2) If a sleeping passenger didn't think he should have been awakened, he was not allowed to complain.

We stopped forty-two times to fill the car with gasoline. At a stop in Rock Springs, Wyoming, the filling station attendant, noting that we had Bowling Green, Kentucky, printed on the car's doors, asked if we knew Pauline. We told him that we didn't know her personally, but she was well-known in our area. Apparently, Pauline was well-known outside our area, too.

Pauline was the madam at Bowling Green's only brothel. She "merchandised sex," as she called it, from 1931 until she retired in 1971. During the four years I was in Bowling Green, I heard stories about some of my athletes being "initiated" in some way at Pauline's, but I never heard any details.

There was a story about Pauline's that was making the rounds at that time. It seems that Pauline was planning to raise her rates for all new customers, but old customers were going to be charged the previous year's rates. One evening, a freshman at Western knocked on Pauline's door. When she came to the door, he said, "Well, back again!"

We made many sightseeing stops along the way, including a visit to the Capitol in Jackson, Mississippi, a stop on Bourbon Street and at an above-ground cemetery in New Orleans, and fancy homes along the Gulf Coast. We stopped to inspect a cotton field and to eat a watermelon from a roadside stand. We crossed the border into Ciudad Acuna, Mexico, and wandered the streets, where we bought cowboy hats and some Mexican liquor (to be consumed after the trip was over).

There were also times when we bypassed sightseeing opportunities in order to keep moving. When we went through San Antonio, Texas, in the middle of the night, we drove past the Alamo without stopping. As we passed it, I pointed and said, "Remember the Alamo."

We spent some time at the south rim of the Grand Canyon, taking many photos, including one of Lars hurling a discus into the Canyon. He claimed an unofficial world record of about one mile—down. The picture later appeared in the Bowling Green newspaper and on the front page of a Swedish newspaper.

We stopped on top of Hoover Dam and marveled at its size. After we had inspected Las Vegas on a very hot day, we drove up Mount Charleston, where my brother Don and his family lived. We had to leave the car and walk because of the heavy snow that had accumulated. After a quick meal there, we got back on the road.

In the Los Angeles area, we drove through Hollywood and Beverly Hills and spent the afternoon at Disneyland. We waded in the Great Salt Lake, where Lars stepped on broken glass, and we had to take him to a doctor. We then headed north toward Yellowstone National Park, but we had to change our route and turn east into Wyoming because of heavy snow.

We stopped at a saloon in Pinedale, Wyoming, to shoot a game of pool. We arrived at Mount Rushmore just as the sun was rising. Then we explored the Badlands and visited the Corn Palace in Mitchell, South Dakota. We got caught in floodwaters and had to take detours in Minnesota, stopped to visit my parents in Waverly, Iowa, and headed back toward Kentucky.

It had begun raining that Sunday morning, and the windshield wipers didn't work. I remember driving with my head out the window for a few miles that morning. All in all, it was a most memorable trip. Hans filmed the entire trip with his 8mm camera, and now all five travelers have DVD copies of the adventure.

Two days after we returned from the spring break trip, we had a home meet against Tennessee Tech. Western won the meet handily, but the highlight performance was in the pole vault, where Henry Wadsworth cleared a record sixteen feet, one-half inch, the best in the nation that season. It is still a school record more than fifty years later.

The next dual meet was at Southeast Missouri State College, which we won with ease. That was the last meet for the Swedes, who would be returning home the next week. During that week, we participated in the Indiana Relays, where we set two new records and won a dual meet at Middle Tennessee, 104-40. One of the local sportswriters referred to the Western Kentucky team as "Ecker's Eccentrics." I'm not sure why.

Then it was time to welcome a new foreign visitor--Coach Eero Uotila from Finland. Eero had been my guide and translator during the three weeks I was in Finland the previous summer. At my request, the State Department arranged for him to travel to the States and to visit the Western campus for three weeks.

Our final home track meet was against Eastern Kentucky. We printed a special program for that meet because it was the fiftieth anniversary of track and field on "The Hill." In the program we reprinted an article from *The Elevator* of May 1915, telling the story of that first track meet.

Also in the program were twelve photos of current Western Kentucky stars and photos of the previous Western coach, Turner Elrod, as a miler in 1923 and as he appeared in 1966. The program also included the schedules for the morning track clinic in the Snell Hall auditorium and the track meet against Eastern that afternoon.

The clinic, which was conducted for high school coaches and athletes, featured "Fiberglass pole demonstrations" by Tom Olsen, the inventor and manufacturer of the Thermo-Flex vaulting pole, and "Track and Field in Finland" by Eero Uotila. I served as the emcee. In the track meet, Western put on quite a show, beating rival Eastern Kentucky, 103-42.

The next week, we traveled to Morehead College for the Ohio Valley Conference championships. In the two-day meet, we beat Murray again to take the title. The league's coaches selected me as conference Coach of the Year for a third time. It had been a very good season for us.

In June, Fred Wilt again arranged for me to be a part of an international track and field coaching school, this one at Baldwin-Wallace College in Ohio. As usual, I taught progressive interval training.

One evening, when I mentioned to one of the other instructors, Englishman Mike Wade, that I was looking for a graduate assistant coach at Western, he suggested John Cooper, his former roommate at Loughborough College in England. Cooper, who had won two silver medals in track events at the 1964 Olympics, was a graduate of Loughborough.

Wade located the nearest pay telephone and put in a call to Cooper at his home in the village of Bitteswell in England. It was the middle of the night in England, and Cooper was sound asleep. Wade talked to him for a few minutes to make sure he was awake. Then, over the phone, I introduced myself and, on Mike Wade's recommendation, offered Cooper the graduate assistantship. Cooper accepted and said he would meet me in the fall when classes were to begin at Western. That was certainly a quick, long-distance decision

We began the 1965 cross country season by driving to Florida for a dual meet against the University of Florida, home of the Florida Gators. We took two cars so we wouldn't be as cramped as we had been in the past. Even though three of our runners got lost on the course, we managed to win the meet 25-30. In the team photograph taken after the meet, student assistant John Cooper was holding a two-foot baby alligator in his hands.

During the rest of the season, we had victories over Middle Tennessee, Southeast Missouri (their first loss in four years), and Murray. Our only loss was to Tennessee Tech. Again we won the Ohio Valley Conference championship, this time held at Morehead College.

During that cross country season, the team members formed an organization called the Thousand-mile Club. Club members had to run at least 1,000

miles in workouts and competitions to belong to the club. Four of the tracksters had run more than 5,000 miles since enrolling at Western.

Because the Thousand-mile Club was becoming well-known on campus, a headline in the school newspaper read: "Tracksters Feted for Feet Feat." When runner Tom Graham was told he'd have to sit out the season because of an injury, he commented, "I guess I'm in for my 5,000-mile checkup."

At Christmastime 1965, I scheduled a trip to Iceland, Sweden, and England. I told the press it was a good-will tour. Actually, the trip was planned so I could visit friends in Iceland and England. In Sweden, I not only visited friends but also secretly interviewed for the job of national track and field coach.

My final track season at Western was our best. We began by beating Indiana University, 75-61. We won thirteen of seventeen events to beat Southeast Missouri, 95-50. In a six-team meet in Fargo, North Dakota, we won six events, setting records in all six. At the Moorhead, Minnesota, Invitational, we won four events. On the same road trip, we participated in the Corn Palace Relays, setting five records.

At the Kentucky Federation championships in Lexington, we won twelve of the fifteen events and brought home sixteen trophies. In the final meet of the year, the Ohio Valley Conference championships, we won eight events and won the meet by fifteen points. The local newspaper's headline read: "Western Wins Third OVC Track Title."

The sub-headline read: "Toppers Stun Field; Ecker Bows Out." According to the article, "The victory marked the end of the Ecker Era."

To top off the season, the conference coaches again voted me conference Coach of the Year, for the fourth consecutive year.

In 1997, I was inducted into Western Kentucky's sports hall of fame. Attending the induction luncheon was one of my former hurdlers at E-town High School, long time friend Gary West. During my speech, I introduced Gary as the worst, I mean the <u>first</u> hurdler I ever coached.

34

Sweden, the Land of the Midnight Sin

In early June 1966, I packed my bags and left for Sweden. When I arrived in Stockholm, Matts Carlgren, the head of Svenska Fri-iddrotsförbundet (the Swedish Track and Field Association), had an older, two-room apartment ready for me. There was a critical shortage of available housing in Stockholm at that time, and apartments were almost impossible to get. Matts was a wealthy industrialist and apparently the apartment was part of his property holdings.

The partially furnished apartment was on the building's second floor, and there was no elevator. It was a short walk from the apartment to several museums, to some fine restaurants, to a large amusement park, and to the American Embassy. It was a great location.

My first day in Sweden, I was interviewed on Swedish radio, on a sports program that was broadcast throughout the entire country. I was asked about the great successes of American sprinters. "What is the secret?" I was asked.

"Breeding," I replied. As Stan Wright, a great American coach and dear friend once said, "The great sprinter owes his parents a great debt of gratitude." But the translator thought I said "breathing." For the next few months I had to explain to coaches and athletes that proper breathing has no effect on sprinting success.

The first thing I purchased when I got to Sweden was a new Volvo. The Swedes whom I knew were not taken with the famous Swedish car. They called it "the world's fastest tractor" and "an old man's racing car."

During the summer of 1966, Sweden had a very successful track and field season, winning every dual meet for the first time in recent history. We were so successful, the newspapers began referring to me as "Sveriges Turgubbe," (Sweden's good luck charm).

We participated in four two-day dual track and field meets against other nations. These were always hard-fought and completely sold out, making a lot of money for the participating countries. The first of them was against Norway, in Oslo, with the Swedish team winning, 121-91.

There were also many "open" track meets throughout Scandinavia, featuring the best local talent competing against top athletes from other countries. The success of these meets was based on ticket sales, so the meet promoters paid the best competitors well, even though it was illegal under the strict rules of amateurism of that time.

Several U.S. athletes came to Scandinavia to participate in track meets that summer. One of them was Bill Toomey, who was not so well known internationally but later won the 1968 Olympic decathlon championship. Because he could compete in so many different events, and since he wore his USA uniform, Bill received $100 every time he participated in an event.

Toomey, who trained in Santa Barbara, California, prided himself on being the picture of health. He ate only healthy foods and condemned the use of junk foods. With every meal, he would consume dozens of pills—vitamins, minerals, and other various food supplements. One of his doctors in California once told him, "You must have the strongest toilet in Santa Barbara."

One of Sweden's home dual meets was against Great Britain. The British, who arrived in Stockholm for the first day of the meet, were confident they would win with ease. However, they found themselves several points behind after the first day. Worried that they might lose the meet, their officials called back to London to have some additional athletes flown in for the second day. The replacement athletes arrived, but they couldn't close the gap. Sweden won in a big upset, 112-110.

Another home meet was against the Soviet Union. It wasn't the entire Soviet Union, as most people believed, but was the nearby Soviet-annexed nations of Estonia, Latvia, and Lithuania. It was still stiff competition, but Sweden won the meet, 122-90.

The next week the Swedish team flew to Budapest, Hungary, for the European Championships. At the same time, my brother Dick was a participant in the International Congress of Biophysics in Vienna, Austria. Since Budapest and Vienna are only 140 miles apart, we planned in advance to get together while we were there. That shows how naive we were. The "Iron Curtain" separated the two countries at that time, and there was no way either one of us would be able to cross it without a very good reason. And Brotherly Love wasn't one of the reasons.

Spending a week in Hungary was a special adventure for me. My communist "Politruk," a local person employed to keep an eye on me, had to be able to speak both Swedish and English. On my first day in Budapest, it was obvious to me that my Politruk was following me wherever I went. When I took a taxi somewhere, he was in a taxi behind me.

So I called him over and said to him, "Why don't we just ride in the same taxi from now on. It'll save a lot of money." He agreed. I learned that his regular job was as a professor at the Lenin School of Social Economics. For the next week, whenever I wasn't with Swedish coaches or team members, my Politruk friend was with me.

It had been just ten years since the Hungarian revolution of 1956. When I mentioned this to my Politruk friend, he said, "It was not a revolution. It was just a mild counter-revolution."

The week after the European Championships came to a close, Sweden competed in the biggest track and field competition of the year, and of every year. It was called Finnkampen, also known by the Swedes as the Finn Battle. It was an annual dual meet between Sweden and Finland that began in 1925. It was a two-day meet that always sold out.

In 1966, the Finn Battle was held in Finland's Olympic Stadium in Helsinki. In my brother Dick's memoirs, he wrote:

I was returning home from a scientific conference in Vienna, and I scheduled a side trip to visit my brother, who was in Helsinki attending a dual track meet. It was not surprising that Tom would be attending a track meet on the weekend in question. He had moved to Sweden

that year, 1966, to become one of three national track and field coaches, assisting the Swedish national team in its preparations for the 1968 Olympic Games in Mexico City.

On the airliner over northern Europe, the man in the next seat introduced himself.

"You are an American?" he queried.

"Yes," I replied, offering my hand.

He explained that he was a Finnish businessman returning from a meeting in Frankfurt to his home in Helsinki.

"And what takes you to my homeland?" he asked.

"I'm going to a track meet," I replied.

"Indeed," he responded with increased animation, obviously interested in my answer. "And do you have tickets to the meet?"

"No," I answered, puzzled by his familiarity with an event that I assumed would attract little attention except from a track nut like me. "Will there be limited seating?"

"Oh, yes. All tickets have been sold out for months."

"For months? You're kidding. How many people does the place hold?"

"Fifty thousand."

I sat stunned while the man unfolded the newspaper he was holding and showed me the front page. I didn't have to be able to read Finnish to understand that the big news in Helsinki that weekend was track and field.

He went on to explain that the "dual meet" I was planning to attend was the biggest athletic event of the year in both Finland and Sweden—equivalent in the United States to the World Series and the NFL and NBA championships all rolled into one. It was a fiercely contested rivalry that alternated between the two capitals each year. This year Finland was the host country, and as my traveling companion advised me proudly, the Finns had never lost at home.

When Dick's plane landed in Helsinki, he caught a cab to the stadium. I had told him to go to the pass gate at the north end of the stadium, where I would meet him. When he approached the gate, it suddenly swung open, wide enough for a car to go through. Dick was impressed with my planning, but he soon realized the gate wasn't opening for him. The president of Finland, Urho Kekkonen, was arriving in his limousine to attend the meet.

Dick explained to an official that his brother was one of the Swedish coaches and asked him to let me know he was at the pass gate. The official ran toward the stadium. Soon, Dick could see me racing to the gate to meet him. I said, "Hurry, we only have a few minutes before the national anthems. I want to record them."

Dick thanked the official for his help, and then raced after me toward the stadium. I handed him a metal pin with a blue and white ribbon attached to it, to show the guard at the stadium entrance. Then we ran past the guard, down some stairs and into a dark tunnel, which led us to bright sunshine and to the middle of the backstretch of the track.

A band marched onto the infield and played the two anthems. I still have the recording I made that day. The stadium went quiet and the Swedish anthem began. The small group of Swedes in the stadium sang their hearts out, but they were greatly outnumbered by the Finns.

When the Finnish anthem began, 45,000 Finns sang with great national passion. It was amazing how loud the Finnish voices were that day. As brother Dick wrote later, "Their voices must surely have echoed far into the surrounding countryside."

The Finnmatch itself turned out to be one of the most exciting track meets I've ever attended. And the result was equally exciting for me. Sweden won the meet, 208-199.

When the 1966 track season was over, I received a phone call from my friend Ron Pickering in England. Ron had resigned his position as national track coach of Wales to join the BBC as a sports broadcaster. Ron not only had an amazing command of the English language, he could talk for long periods of time without a script.

He told me the BBC wanted to produce a special national telecast on the use of anabolic steroids in sports. It was a topic of great interest at that time. Nationally recognized sports authority Norris McWhirter would be the program's moderator, and Ron and I would be the interviewed "experts."

Ron asked me if I'd be willing to fly from Sweden to London, at the expense of the BBC, to appear on the program. It was a slow time for track coaching in Sweden, so I agreed to do it.

When we all met at the BBC studios to record the program, I was very impressed with the program's moderator, Norris McWhirter. He and his twin brother, Ross, were co-editors of *The Guinness Book of Records,* the second best-selling book in the history of publishing. First was the Bible. The McWhirter twins, both with photographic memories, had come up with the idea of the Guinness book as a reference text to settle bar bets.

Ron and I were interviewed by McWhirter, live, for the hour-long show. Probably because of the topic, anabolic steroids in sports, the show was a big hit and received very high ratings across Great Britain.

To complete this story, I have to jump ahead nine years. On November 29, 1975, I was a guest in the home of Ron and Jean Pickering in the London suburb of Broxbourne. It was late afternoon when Ron received a telephone call from the BBC, informing him that Ross McWhirter had been murdered. McWhirter had offered a 50,000 pound ($102,000) reward for the arrest and conviction of any IRA (Irish Republican Army) terrorists.

To get their revenge, two IRA members hid in the bushes outside McWhirter's home and ambushed and killed both McWhirter and his wife when they arrived home. The BBC scheduled a special hour-long program on the life of Ross McWhirter. They wanted Ron Pickering to moderate the program, but he didn't have time to get from his home to the BBC studios.

The BBC engineers arranged for Ron to moderate the program over the telephone while still photos and film of Ross McWhirter's life appeared on the television screen. Ron would have no knowledge of what was going to appear on the screen next, so he had to do an hour-long, ad-libbing session. There were no commercial breaks on the BBC, so Ron had to talk non-stop.

When the program aired, Jean and I were sitting in front of the television set in the Pickering living room. Ron was on the telephone from his office in the next room. As we watched pictures and films of Ross McWhirter, we could hear Ron's voice, both from the office and over the TV set. He talked for a straight hour, always matching his narration with the pictures. Ron's wife, Jean, looked at me during the program and said, "I don't know how he does it."

35

The Nissen News

In the fall of 1967, I decided to leave Sweden and return to the States. After arriving back in Bowling Green, Kentucky, I wrote everyone I knew, telling them I was looking for a job. Within a few days, I received a phone call from my dear friend, George Nissen in Cedar Rapids, asking if I would like to work for the Nissen Corporation again. George told me the company, already the largest manufacturer of gymnastics equipment in the world, was expanding. They wanted me to design a line of track and field equipment for them.

I drove to Cedar Rapids and contacted an old friend from high school and college, L.W. Ward, who offered his couch as a place for me to sleep while I was becoming oriented to the ways of the Nissen Corporation. L.W. worked for KCRG-TV as a cameraman and lived in an apartment on Oakland Road NE.

One of the first things I had to do was to try to buy a house for the family. Nissen's executive vice president, Bob Bevenour, helped me find a house at 1908 Grande Avenue SE. Bob and I went there to see the house, but it was after dark and all we could do was look in the first floor windows. A woman came up to us as we were peering in the windows and said she was interested in buying the house. She asked how many rooms there were. Bob answered, "Only two rooms, one up and one down." The next day, I contacted the real estate agent and ended up purchasing the home for $20,000.

I first met George Nissen on Friday, July 16, 1954, in Monticello, Iowa, following my freshman year at Iowa. It was a meeting that would really change my life. We were both performing in a water show at the Monticello swimming pool. George, who was forty years old at the time, was doing a trampoline act with fellow gymnast, Claire Jennett. I was doing the lawnmower balancing act with my friend, Al Baker. Ours

George Nissen

were the only acts that were performed on the edge of the pool, not in the water. The star of the show was Beulah Gundling, billed as an "Internationally Famous Solo Swimming Star."

George was promoting his invention, the folding trampoline, by doing trampoline shows around the country and throughout the world. During that time, he performed on the trampoline with many partners besides Jennett, including his wife, Annie, and later with their two daughters, Dagmar and Dian.

From the first time I met George Nissen, I really liked him. He was a small, clean-cut, soft-spoken man, who appeared, in person, to be too shy to perform in front of audiences. But once the spotlight was on him, George became a top-flight entertainer. He was on a mission.

I stayed in touch with George for the next two years. In 1956, following my junior year at Iowa, I asked him for a summer job at his trampoline factory in Cedar Rapids. That summer I worked as a handyman at the Nissen factory, along with a daredevil gymnast named Obe (pronounced Obie) Ross. Obe and I did odd jobs for the Nissen Company throughout the summer. I drove back to Iowa City every day after work. Obe spent every night at the factory, sleeping on a trampoline.

George Nissen always had ideas for expanding his product lines. One of them was called the Hi-Guy, which was a two-coned top that rode on a string on two sticks or handles. (The Hi-Guy is difficult to describe and even more difficult to master.) It came in a small cardboard box and could be assembled easily. The generic name for the Hi-Guy was the Diablo (sometimes spelled Diabolo).

I began practicing with a Hi-Guy, and although the learning threshold was quite high, I was finally able to do several basic tricks. George was impressed enough that he transferred me from factory handyman to Hi-Guy demonstrator. I appeared on a popular local TV show with a cowboy named Marshall Jay, filmed a commercial for other TV stations, and even spent a day at Marshall Fields department store in Chicago, demonstrating the Hi-Guy to potential buyers.

At the end of the summer, I returned to the University of Iowa for my senior year. It would be more than ten years before I would rejoin the Nissen Corporation to design a line of track and field equipment.

One of the strengths of the Nissen Corporation over the years was the publication of a weekly newsletter, *Nissen News*. It was written by Bob Bevenour, who praised employees, and kidded those who could take it. I was a regular target for Bob's comments.

In the September 14, 1967, issue of *Nissen News,* there was a photo of Norm Barnes and me, with the following caption: "Two former Iowa U stars got together last week. Tom Ecker, who has just joined our staff to help us get into the track and field market is shown with Norm Barnes, Advertising Director, who might find Tom's journalistic skills also helpful to us." In that same issue, there was a photo of Buck Kelly, who had just been pro-

moted to management status in Research and Development. Over the next two years, Buck and I worked together on the development of many new and exciting products.

During that time, Bus Klinge, Nissen's sales manager, and I began looking into buying out other manufacturers' track and field lines. It was common in those days to purchase a line of a company's products, make improvements, and then sell the products under the Nissen name.

Nissen had purchased the Medart Company in St. Louis in 1960. Medart was a leading manufacturer of gymnastics apparatus. Nissen redesigned all of the Medart equipment, added chrome plating to anything that was metal, and became the largest manufacturer of gymnasium equipment in the world. During that transition, Nissen kept only one of the Medart employees—Bus Klinge, sales manager, who moved from St. Louis to Cedar Rapids.

Almost immediately, Bus Klinge and I became good friends. Bus was warm and friendly, but he had a gruff side as well. He once told me that whenever he and his wife had a houseguest, he would announce, "Dinner the first night is on me. Dinner the second night is on you. There is no third night."

Our first attempted acquisition was the Gill Company in Champaign, Illinois. Bus and I were given a tour through the plant and then met with the owner in his office. After analyzing everything, we were of the opinion that we could produce better products than Gill was offering without having to buy any-thing from them. So we passed. (Gill is still manufacturing track and field equipment.)

Practicing with the Hi-Guy, a spinning top that is maneuvered on a nylon cord.

Gunnar Carlsson, Sweden's chief track and field coach, visited the Nissen factory and inspected one of the company's hurdles.

But there was one area where we needed help from the outside—fiberglass products, including pole vaulting poles and crossbars. We could make things out of steel and wood and molded plastic, but we couldn't manufacture anything in fiberglass. So in December 1967, Bus and I approached the Shakespeare Company in Columbia, South Carolina. It was famous for manufacturing fiberglass fishing rods and archery equipment and was just beginning to make fiberglass pole vaulting poles. They were interested in selling that line, so we asked them to ship a half dozen poles to us in Cedar Rapids.

At that same time, two of my Swedish pole vaulters were visiting me on their way to California, and they said they'd be happy to test the poles for us. A Cedar Rapids *Gazette* article titled "Swedish Vaulters in C.R." ran on January 3, 1968, and included a photo of George Nissen and the two Swedish pole vaulters, Hans Lagerqvist and Ulf Bjuhr.

We tied the poles to the top of my car and drove to the University of Iowa Field House, where we tested the poles. The poles made terrible creaking noises when they were bent, and we knew that would frighten young vaulters. So we gave up on buying the pole vault line from Shakespeare.

In the October 26 issue of *Nissen News,* there was a photo of me clearing the new chrome-plated Nissen hurdle in the gymnasium, in a white shirt and tie, and wearing street shoes. The caption said: "It looks like we're finally making progress with our Track & Field equipment now that Tom Ecker is our take-charge guy. And naturally Buck Kelly is a big cog in the team. Tom says Buck is coming up with the best hurdle in the world. Here, Tom tests the new Nissen hurdle. Too bad he has such poor form."

In December, It was announced that the Nissen Corporation would merge with Wilson Sporting Goods. Part of the Wilson merger deal was that George would continue being president of Nissen, and he would also serve on the Board of Directors of Wilson Sporting Goods. When I asked George about the merger, he said, "If you own the ocean and someone comes along and offers you a lot of money for your ocean, but says you can continue to swim in it, you sell."

In May 1968, the Nissen employees were concerned about the proposed merger with Wilson Sporting Goods. It was reaffirmed the new corporation was to be divided into three corporate divisions—Wilson Sporting Goods, Wilson meatpacking, and Wilson Pharmaceuticals. Bob Bevenour called the three divisions "Baseball, Meatball, and Goofball."

36

By George, He's a Genius

George Nissen was a creative genius. His best-known invention, of course, was the folding trampoline, but he was credited with more than one hundred other inventions, including improvements on various pieces of gymnastics apparatus. Besides being an accomplished inventor, George had a number of fascinating sidelines during his career. Fortunately, he included me in many of them.

In October 1968, George asked me if I'd like to go with him to Mexico City to attend the Olympic Games. He said he would get me a credential as an equipment exhibitor. I already had credentials as a Swedish track and field coach, as a "stringer" for the BBC, and as a photographer for *Athletic Journal* magazine. With four credentials, I would be able to go just about anywhere I wanted on the Olympic grounds, including the Olympic Village.

I didn't spend much time with George during the Olympics. His interests were the gymnastics events and reuniting with his longtime Mexican friend, Joaquin Capilla. Capilla had been Mexico's greatest platform and springboard diver, winning medals in the 1948, 1952, and 1956 Olympic Games.

In Mexico City, my mornings were spent at the practice track with the Swedish coaches and athletes. During the two-day decathlon event, I sat in the BBC booth with broadcasters David Coleman and Ron Pickering as they highlighted the performance of American gold medal-winner, Bill Toomey. During the Olympic track and field events, I shot sequence photos of several events, and shot a color photo of the Olympic flag and flame, which appeared on the cover of a later issue of *Athletic Journal.*

When George and I returned from the Olympics, we faced a new challenge. One of George's traveling trampoline performers, Otto Schmidt, had fallen ill and wasn't able to complete his schedule of school assembly programs. The other trampolinists who were doing assembly programs for the Nissen Corporation, Eddie Cole and Ronnie Munn, suggested to George that I replace Otto Schmidt until he could get back on his feet. George thought it was a great idea, even though I could barely bounce on a trampoline.

We decided I would do a comedy physiology show, not using a trampoline at all. I would bring the school's top athletes out of the audience and, using a spirometer, check their lung capacities. (It was always easy to identify the smokers.) And, using a twelve-pound shot put, I would test each athlete's arm strength and muscular endurance. All of this was done with friendly comedy banter that often embarrassed the athletes. The kids in the audience loved it.

The scheduling of school assembly programs was done by a firm in Chicago. They scheduled two shows per day, one in the morning and one in the afternoon. They made sure there wasn't a great distance between the schools scheduled for the same day. Eddie Cole, Ronnie Munn, and I were all on salary at Nissen's, so the pay for the assembly shows, $700 a week, was sent to the Nissen Corporation.

My assembly programs were all in Wisconsin. I got to perform in such places as Neenah, Pulaski, Shiocton, Beaver Dam, Oostburg, and Walworth. My reviews ran from a low of "He did an adequate job for a substitute" to a high of "One of the finest programs I've attended in quite some time." I was on the road for two-and-a-half weeks and did a total of nineteen shows.

Early in 1969, George decided to sponsor an appearance of the famous Harlem Globetrotters basketball team, featuring the amazingly talented Meadowlark Lemon. The Globetrotters played the Washington Generals in the new Five Seasons Center in downtown Cedar Rapids. The halftime show was a thrilling and humorous trampoline performance,

One of the Soviet acts I photographed was this spectacular four-high sports acrobatics performance.

Olympics would be pretty routine.

George's plan was to have trampolining become an event in sports acrobatics, thus paving the way for the trampoline to be part of the 1980 Olympic program. George then asked me if I'd like to be the second American member of IFSA.

In 1974, I got my first taste of IFSA membership. George and I were invited to attend IFSA meetings in Moscow in June. On my Soviet visa application, I was listed as a photographer so I could take photographs freely during our time there. We stayed at the huge Russia Hotel, then billed as the largest hotel in the world.

During our four-day stay in Moscow, I got to meet the IFSA Executive Committee—Stoil Sotirov of Bulgaria, Emil Glessner of East Germany, Marian Golema of Poland, Anatoly Ropov of the Soviet Union, John Atkinson of Great Britain, Todor Koukouvanov of Bulgaria, Matias Heglyi of Hungary, and, of course, George Nissen of the USA. I also learned that I was a member of the IFSA Technical Committee, along with IFSA members from the Soviet Union, Poland, East Germany, and Bulgaria.

which was George's purpose in booking the Globetrotters. He was always promoting the trampoline. It was a very entertaining evening for everyone who attended, especially for my three children, who were twelve, eleven, and nine. George arranged for them to sit on the bench with the Globetrotters.

In the early 1970s, George mounted a major effort to get trampolining into the Olympics. His plan was to join and become involved in a new sports organization, the International Federation of Sports Acrobatics (IFSA). IFSA's main goal was to get sports acrobatics into the 1980 Olympics in Moscow. Since many of IFSA's leaders were from the Soviet Union, including Russia and other Eastern Bloc nations, it was thought that getting sports acrobatics into the Moscow

We had meetings, with plenty of time for translations, acrobatics demonstrations, and a banquet with an abundance of food and drink—especially drink. At each place setting, there was a bottle of wine. Between each two places was a bottle of vodka to be shared by the two people.

After the banquet, one of the Russians wanted to show off his new car to the British representative, John Atkinson, and me. There were very few cars in Moscow in those days. Even though we had all been drinking at the banquet, or maybe because we had all been drinking at the banquet, John and I accepted the invitation.

Our host drove us all over Moscow, playing his radio so we could hear the Soviet Union's jamming of

Posing with George Nissen and Antoly Ropov of the Soviet Union.

non-Soviet radio stations. The jamming was done by broadcasting a loud buzzing sound on the same frequency as the station they wanted to jam. Our host would turn the dial on his radio until there was a loud buzzing sound. "That's 'Voice of America,' " he said. He turned the dial to the next buzzing sound and said, "That's the BBC." This went on until he had covered all of the radio stations broadcasting into the Soviet Union from free countries.

On our final night in Moscow, after the meetings and demonstrations were over, the Soviets put on a show that was so truly amazing that it was difficult to describe to people when we returned home.

The opening act was the famous Soviet gymnast, Olga Corbett, performing on the balance beam. Corbett had become the darling of the 1972 Olympics just two years earlier. That was followed by two hours of circus-like acrobatic performances, all on a raised stage in the middle of the arena. When the performances were over, a curtain at the end of the arena was raised, and there was a rock band, as professional as I had ever seen or heard, performing until well into the night.

During the stay, I took many photographs, some of which later appeared in two American magazines, *Acrobat* and *AcroSports,* and one Soviet magazine, *Sports in the USSR.*

In October, George called me on my home phone in Cedar Rapids. My phone number was 366-6933. When I answered, he asked, "Is this 3, triple 6, 9, double 3?" I knew right away who was calling.

George told me we were invited to IFSA meetings in Warsaw, Poland. But he had a conflict and couldn't go, so he sent me as the sole representative of the United States. I flew to Sweden and stayed with my friend Hans for five days before continuing on to Poland.

During the next week in Warsaw, I hung out with John Atkinson again. It was easier communicating with him than having to wait for translations, although many of our Polish hosts were quite proficient in English. One night, John and I were walking in downtown Warsaw, where there were very few electric lights and no electric signs. I commented, "A dearth of neon." John laughed. Several years later, I returned to Warsaw and was surprised to see there were so many bright lights and neon signs it looked like a large American city.

The following May, the Nissen Corporation hosted an International Sports Acrobatics meeting in Cedar Rapids. A delegation of IFSA executives from Russia, Bulgaria, Poland, and Great Britain, including a Russian translator, arrived at the Holiday Inn, which was then on Williams Boulevard SW in Cedar Rapids. None of the Russians understood any English.

One of the Russians brought a small suitcase of bottles of Russian vodka with him. Nissen employee Ron Munn and I were sitting in a motel room with the Russians, when one of them poured vodka into several glasses and handed them to everyone in the room. In those days, I always had a Pepsi-Cola in my hand, so I began pouring some Pepsi into my glass of vodka. The Russian jumped up and yelled, "NYET, NYET!" I then realized I was polluting his gift.

That night was a time for rest. The next morning I arrived at the Holiday Inn and found that all of the

Eastern Bloc IFSA members were gone. Of course, I went into a state of panic, thinking we were experiencing a mass defection. Then we learned they were all across the street at the Kmart, marveling at all the things we had that they had never seen before.

During that day, there were several IFSA meetings, which went very well. That night, a Saturday, we took the Russians to a lively bar in the Czech part of town, which we simply called 16th Avenue. There was live music, and the Russians began dancing with some of the local women.

We never let on that we were hosting Russians, and I'm sure the people of Czech decent would not have been pleased had they known they were partying with Russians. Alexander Dubcek, the former leader of Czechoslovakia, who was very popular with the Czech people, had been deposed only a few years earlier.

On Sunday, all of our IFSA visitors packed up and left Cedar Rapids to go back to their home countries.

In November 1975, George Nissen and I were invited to attend the Volkov Cup in Moscow. Again, there would be meetings and acrobatic demonstrations. As usual, I flew first to Sweden for a few days before going on to Moscow. When I arrived in Moscow, they had no

George Nissen's dream was to have trampolining included as part of the Olympic program. He saw his dream come true at the 2000 Sydney Olympics.

record at immigration control that I was coming. When I showed them my letter of invitation, they let me in, but I didn't know where to go after that.

I took a taxi to the Hotel Russia, where I had stayed previously, but they had no record of George or any other IFSA member staying there. There was an English-speaking man standing in the hotel lobby, who advised me to go to the American Embassy. He wrote the address on a piece of paper and handed it to me. As I left the lobby, another man ran up to me, snatched the piece of paper out of my hand, read it, and then gave it back to me. Obviously, it was the KGB at work.

I took a taxi to the American Embassy, where a woman at the front desk explained to me that the Soviets had "lost me." She said it happened quite often. As far as the Soviets were concerned, I didn't exist. She said I was free to go anywhere I wanted in Moscow.

She also said I could sleep on a lobby couch. The embassy would provide me with an army blanket and a pillow. And I could eat American food, using dollars, not rubles, and watch American movies at the embassy's commissary.

On my last day in Moscow, I received a telephone call from one of the few English-speaking Russians who attended the IFSA meetings. It seems they moved the meetings to a small town outside Moscow and hadn't told me. He said he had some gifts for me, but he didn't want to meet in the American Embassy. So, at his suggestion, we met under a large clock a few blocks from the embassy, where he gave me several beautiful gifts.

The next day, I flew home and regained my existence.

One of George Nissen's biggest, and probably one of his most expensive endeavors, was the filming of the motion picture, *Dribble*, in 1979. George had formed a women's professional basketball team called the Iowa Cornets, and George paid $50,000 for the team to join the newly formed Women's Professional Basketball League. George said, "I wanted a name the entire state could be proud of. And since corn is always associated with Iowa, I decided on the name Cornets." George named me to the board of directors of the Cornets.

One of the things George wanted to do to help make the Iowa team successful was to schedule games in eight cities around Iowa. "We want the entire state to identify with the Cornets, not just one metropolitan area," Nissen said. "Why locate the team in an area of just 300,000 people like Des Moines, when you have an entire state of three million people to choose from?"

The Iowa Cornets played their "home" games in Des Moines, Cedar Rapids, Cedar Falls, Spencer, Bettendorf, Council Bluffs, Ottumwa, and Sioux City. There were only three home games played in the Cedar Rapids Five Seasons Center in 1979, which had opened earlier that month. I went to see the Cornets play the New Jersey Gems in Cedar Rapids and found the game enjoyable, but not well-attended.

The Cornets traveled in a customized recreational vehicle called the Corn Dog. Described as a home-away-from-home with all the modern conveniences, the Corn Dog had a capacity of thirty.

I'm not certain how the making of a movie featuring the Cornets evolved, but it did. A director and actors came to Iowa from Hollywood to make the movie. The "stars" were people who were completely unknown to us. And still are. The leads were Freya Crane, Myra Taylor, and Charles Fatone. The only "star" in the film that I had heard of was the great basketball player, "Pistol Pete" Maravich, and he was billed only seventh in the list of actors. Maravich, who was an amazing ball handler and shooter, died ten years later at the age of forty from a previously undetected congenital heart defect. Of course, the Iowa Cornets were featured in the film. Movie extras were cast from the hundreds of locals who wanted to be in a movie.

George decided that Gus Schrader, the sports editor of the Cedar Rapids *Gazette,* Bob Brooks, sportscaster for KCRG-TV, and I would be cast in the movie as bench officials during one of the movie's basketball games. We each received a check for $75, signed by George, which was our pay for serving as extras in the film.

The first night of filming the game, which was at McKinley Junior High School in Cedar Rapids, was the same evening as my daughter Wendy's wedding rehearsal dinner. Choosing between the two events was a difficult decision for me, but I chose being in the movie. I missed the second day of shooting, which was at Regis High School, because of the wedding itself. There were two more days of shooting at Regis, but I missed those because of my job in the school district.

The following January, I attended the world premiere of *Dribble,* which was held at the Iowa Theatre in Cedar Rapids. Before the movie began, all of the Iowa Cornets were introduced, dressed in very fancy tuxedos.

Then followed the movie, which was terrible. When I returned to my apartment in the Cedar River Tower, I called a friend in California who knew about the movie. I said I had bad news and good news about *Dribble.* "The bad news: It was perhaps the worst movie I'd ever seen. The good news: My scenes were cut out of the movie."

Even though he had paid $1.3 million to make the movie, George Nissen was not pleased with *Dribble.* The producer-director-writer, Michael de Gaetano, had taken great liberties with the storyline and had included scenes that did not jibe with George's wholesome outlook on life. There were scenes, for example, that included growing marijuana for profit. And there was the use of rather raw language, which George did not appreciate. But, worst of all, the movie was called a comedy, and George didn't think it was funny.

As far as I know, the movie didn't play in any other theaters after its world premiere in 1979. But in 1982, and again in 1992, the movie was released on videotape with the new title *Scoring.* In the 1982 version, Pete Maravich was fourth billed. In 1992, Maravich was listed as the star. The opening line on the VHS box was: " 'Pistol Pete' Maravich stars in this hilarious hotbody sex romp."

I have a copy of the movie's original script, and it is obvious that the movie has been altered from the original, with many of the scenes cut and many new ones added. My guess is that George paid for the alterations. Although *Scoring* is a sanitized version of *Dribble,* it is still a bad movie.

George's dream to have the trampoline included on the Olympic program was finally realized in 2000 Games in Sydney, Australia. The 86-year-old Nissen and his daughter, Dian, made the trip to Sydney to see his longtime dream come true. One evening during the Sydney Olympics, I met George at his hotel and interviewed him for an article that appeared in the Cedar Rapids *Gazette* the following Sunday.

The article, "Triumph for the Trampoline," ends with George saying, " 'Of course, it's a big thrill to have trampolining in the Games, but success is a gradual process. People had told me in the 1950s and '60s that I'd never live to see trampolining in the Olympics. They said it'll be the year 2000 before that ever happens.'

"They were right. And George was there to see it, too."

37

Most Parents Have Daughters

It was obvious to me in the spring of 1969 that the Nissen track and field line was not going to be a part of the Wilson merger. Bill Alley, the former Olympic javelin thrower, offered to buy the Nissen track and field line, and the Wilson people were happy to sell it.

Later that spring, I was interviewed for the job of athletic director in the Cedar Rapids school district. (Actually, the job title was coordinator of athletics, but the superintendent, Craig Currie, jokingly told me that if I was introduced at a meeting as the athletic director, it was OK for me to stand up.)

Until I was eighty-two years old, I believed that I was one of many people interviewed for the job. In 2017, I learned from Craig Currie, at his ninetieth birthday party, that he had already selected me for the job and I was the only person interviewed. He told me he was impressed when he heard me deliver a speech about the 1968 Olympics at a local Rotary meeting. And he said he had heard good things about me from one of his golfing partners, my friend Gus Schrader, sports editor at the Cedar Rapids *Gazette*. Also, he said he had heard positive comments from sportscaster Bob Brooks and from George Nissen.

The job of coordinator of athletics included overseeing all of the sports programs in the three high schools and six junior highs. The interview team was made up of the top five administrators in the district, led by the superintendent. Throughout the interview, it was obvious to me that they didn't want to hire a typical jock for the job.

After answering many questions, I said I'd like to ask them a few questions, if that would be all right. My initial question was: "Did they think it was possible for the school district to offer a comprehensive sports program for girls?" They all thought it was a great idea.

At the time, small schools in Iowa offered only girls' basketball and girls' softball, which were very popular with the public. The girls' state basketball tournaments always drew bigger crowds than the boys' state tournaments, which were played a week later. Large schools didn't offer any girls' sports, except for golf and tennis in a few cases.

As soon as I was hired, I announced that my plan was to offer a totally equitable—not necessarily equal—sports program for girls within five years. Equality is providing everyone the same thing. Equity is providing everyone fairness. I called it our five-year plan, and I had the complete support of the superintendent and the other central office administrators, but not any support from the high school principals or the high school athletic directors. I always joked it was helpful that the superintendent had three daughters.

Naturally, with such drastic changes being proposed, I was asked by several PTAs to talk about these changes at their meetings. To my surprise, I found there was as much support from the fathers attending the meetings as from the mothers. It was then I realized that most parents have daughters.

At the same time, with the total support of the superintendent, I initiated a strict no-cut policy in every sport at every level. If sports are good for kids, as sports people often argue, then they should be good for all kids, not just the athletically gifted. Any student who went out for a team was a member of that team until the season was over. Any coach who "cut the squad," or even suggested that a student should quit a team, was fired. That was made very clear to the coaches, who knew I had the backing of the administration.

When teams became so large that it was difficult for the coaches to handle everyone, we simply added coaches. At one time in the early 1980s, we had 345 coaches in our nine secondary schools, and we were scheduling more than 1,500 sports events a year.

Our largest turnouts were in junior high sports. In football, we played a fifth quarter, to accommodate those who hadn't yet played. In basketball, where we always had the biggest turnouts, we had an A team, a B team, a C team, etc., so that everyone could play. In swimming, there were additional heats of the twenty-five-meter swim. In track, there were additional heats of the hundred-meter dash. Using these and other ideas, we made sure that everyone who wanted to participate in sports could do so.

But as difficult as it was to get coaches to accept the no-cut rule, it was even more difficult to get the high schools to accept the inclusion of girls' sports. The principals and athletic directors simply weren't going to cooperate. As I was told so often: There isn't room or time for girls' sports.

In the fall of 1969, I called a meeting of the six junior high principals, and they agreed that we should offer two sports for girls at the ninth-grade level, which was part of our junior highs in those days. They said they had the money to pay salaries comparable to the salaries for the boys' coaches.

My idea was simple. If a large number of girls enjoyed participating in competitive sports while they were in the ninth grade, there would be a demand to continue participating when they reached high school the next year. The pressure would be on the high schools to finally offer girls' sports.

The junior high principals said I should meet with the twelve female junior high physical education teachers to decide which two sports we could offer first.

We would have one season in the fall and one in the spring, in case either or both of the selected sports would require use of the school's gymnasium. The gym was already used for seventh-, eighth-, and ninth-grade boys' basketball in the wintertime.

The female physical education teachers were very pleased we were going to be starting a sports program for girls. One of them even wrote me a note the next day that said, "Thank you so much for realizing that girls want to be a part of the competitive sports program."

The teachers were unanimous in selecting volleyball as the fall sport and basketball for the spring. Then I asked them which of them would be willing to coach. Not one hand was raised. It was then I knew that we would have to rely on men to coach girls' teams, which, as it turned out was a good thing. At that time,

it was much easier for a man to get changes made in sports than it was for a woman. (I made that observation when I gave the keynote speech at a national physical education convention in Atlantic City that year, and it prompted loud booing from the women in the audience.)

But it was true. Our girls' sports program grew quickly because of the strong influence of so many male coaches. We did have some women coaches later on, but the majority of them were always men.

As it turned out, we were way ahead of our time. The Cedar Rapids program was well on its way toward sports equity when the U.S. Congress passed the Education Amendments of 1972. The part of the law requiring schools to offer equitable sports programs for females was called Title IX. It took the government until 1975 to develop guidelines for implementing the new law, and schools were given an additional three years to comply.

Because the addition of girls' sports program was now required by law, our high school principals and athletic directors quickly joined the cause. They didn't have any choice.

It was the year that schools were required to be in total compliance with the law, 1978, that Time magazine devoted six pages to a cover story on women in sports. Although most of the Time article was devoted to the difficult struggle women have had gaining equity in athletic programs, the final half-page was about the future of women's sports. In part, the article stated:

One city in which the future is now is Cedar Rapids, Iowa. In 1969, well before law, much less custom, required the city to make any reforms, Cedar Rapids opened its public school athletic programs to girls and, equally important, to the less-gifted boys traditionally squeezed out by win-oriented athletic systems. Says Tom Ecker, head of school athletics, "Our program exists to develop good kids, not to serve as a training ground for the universities and pros. ..."

Some 7,000 students, nearly 3,000 of them girls, compete on teams with a firm no-cut policy. Everyone gets a chance to play. Teams are fielded according to skill level, and a struggle between junior varsity or C-squad basketball teams is as enthusiastically contested as a varsity clash. Cedar Rapids schoolgirl athletes compete in nine sports, guided by 144 coaches. Access to training equipment is equal, too. The result has been unparalleled athletic success. In the past eight years, Cedar Rapids boys and girls teams have finished among the state's top three sixty-eight times, winning team championships in ten different sports.

Throughout the 1970s, Cedar Rapids staff members were being asked to participate in seminars in the parts of the United States in which schools were slow in complying with the law. Presentations outlining the Cedar Rapids sports philosophy and program, most of them sponsored by women's groups, were made from California to New Jersey. During one of the seminars, a representative of the Office of Civil Rights in Kansas City described the Cedar Rapids program as a model for others to emulate.

From the beginning, the girls' sports program in Cedar Rapids has been growing steadily. In 1969, only golf and tennis were offered for girls. There were six coaches and 74 participants. By 1973, there were eight sports and 84 coaches. Today, there are ten sports and 144 coaches for girls' sports. There are now more girls than boys participating in basketball, swimming and tennis.

The Time article summarized it best: *"Girls athletics have become an accustomed part of the way of life in Cedar Rapids."*

We had a few sex discrimination complaints during my years with the school district. My favorite was filed during the third year of our five-year-plan. We weren't offering a totally equitable program yet, but we were close. The Cedar Rapids Women's Caucus filed the complaint against us, even though we were the only school district in the state that was working toward complete equity.

As a courtesy, I agreed to meet with members of the caucus. They sent two women to meet with me to discuss the situation. One had children in the nearby Marion school district, which was way behind us in providing sex equity in sports, and the other, Bev Mitchell, didn't have children. Among other things, they were complaining that we didn't allow girls on the boys' teams. I explained about the differences between male and female athletes because of male androgenic and female estrogenic hormones. It simply isn't fair to have girls competing in the same program as boys. Bev Mitchell responded, "We don't appreciate you talking about our glands." Since we were in complete

compliance with the law, the complaint was dropped. Over the following years, I gave many talks throughout the country, usually to women's groups, about our successful sports programs for girls. I always started the talks with humor, first mentioning the conflict with the Women's Caucus and the "we don't appreciate you talking about our glands" line.

Continuing the humor routine, I said that one of the caucus members asked me, "How many coaches do you have in the school district, broken down by sex?" I answered, "Most of our coaches are broken down by alcohol."

Then, I continued, another woman asked me to name any job a man can do that a woman can't do just as well. I answered, "Sperm donor." (Pause) "But that's all I could think of."

The talks themselves covered the physical differences between boys and girls, and how they affect performance and coaching. Emphasized were strength levels, cardiovascular capacity, aggressiveness, emotions, and injuries. The biggest myth at the time was that sports participation could damage a girl's reproductive system. I explained that boys are much more vulnerable in that area than girls are.

Besides giving sex equity speeches around the country, I was also delivering many sports banquet and commencement speeches throughout the Midwest. In a ten-year period, there were twenty-nine banquet speeches and forty-four commencement speeches. The biggest year for commencement talks was 1976, the year of the nation's Bicentennial. That year, with patriotism as the theme, I delivered thirteen commencement talks during the month of May.

In December 1980, I was asked to be the emcee at the banquet of the National Conference of Directors of Athletics in Atlanta, Georgia. The conference was held at the Peachtree Hotel. The hotel's ballroom, where the banquet was held, was filled to capacity—more than 2,000 athletic directors.

I was on the main stage at one side of the ballroom, where I was to begin by warming up the crowd with a comedy routine. Next was a dance group called The Possum Trot Cloggers, who were setting up on a different stage at the end of the ballroom. The final act, back on the main stage, was a series of performances by outstanding local high school performing arts students.

When I finished my comedy routine and was getting ready to introduce the Possum Trot Cloggers, I received word that the Cloggers weren't ready, and I would have to fill the time until they could get their sound system set up. I didn't think that would be a long time, so I told one of my borderline (semi-naughty) jokes, which got a big laugh.

The Cloggers still weren't ready, so I continued telling jokes. It was almost a surreal experience. Whenever I told a joke, I could visualize the next joke's punch line on a list that I had created years before. My joke-telling, which, fortunately, had everyone in stitches, lasted for more than forty-five minutes. Finally, the Cloggers were ready, and I introduced them. I was exhausted.

After the show that night, one of my high school athletic directors from Cedar Rapids, Dudley "Dude" Draxton, came up to me and said, "You were hot tonight, Eck." To me that was the ultimate compliment.

One of my duties as athletic director in Cedar Rapids was managing Kingston Stadium, a 16,000-seat stadium on the west side of town. Kingston was the home field for the three Cedar Rapids high schools, Jefferson, Kennedy, and Washington, the two Catholic high schools, Regis and LaSalle, and Coe College. There were high school football games scheduled almost every Thursday, Friday, and Saturday night during the fall. Coe played on Saturday afternoons.

The Cedar Rapids school district received rent from Regis, LaSalle, and Coe for their games played at Kingston. Receipts from the three Cedar Rapids high schools' games were distributed to the home teams' booster clubs.

After the first game was played at Kingston that fall, I realized that the distribution of money to the schools' booster clubs wasn't fair. Jefferson High School was having a series of winning seasons, drawing big crowds, and the other two high schools were not. Plus, it was convenient for Jefferson fans to get to the stadium, which was near their high school. Jefferson's gate receipts were projected to be more than twice the receipts of the two east-side high schools combined.

Also, the Jefferson boosters received all the money from the stadium's four concession stands because they had owned all of the equipment (popcorn poppers, grills, coolers, etc.) since the stadium first opened in 1952. Jefferson had always provided many boosters to operate the concession stands at every game.

So I went to the superintendent, Craig Currie, and told him I wanted to socialize the stadium's financial operation. All gate receipts would be put into a central fund and distributed evenly among the three high schools, with a lesser amount given to the six junior highs. The superintendent thought it was a great idea, but the Jefferson Booster Club did not.

The president of the Jefferson Boosters contacted me and demanded I appear the next night at their booster club's monthly meeting to explain the new procedures. I went to the all-male meeting and sat in the back until it was time for me to speak. When my time came, the booster president gave me the shortest introduction I've received in my more than sixty years as a public speaker. He said, "Well, he's here."

I'm sure I didn't convince the group that night, but I tried to tell them that no kids should be deprived of an opportunity just because he or she lives in a different part of the city. I also told them they would thank me someday. And a few years later, when Jefferson's football glory had faded, they did.

One of the first things I noticed when I first visited Kingston was there was no telephone in the entire stadium. I found out later that one of my predecessors would often leave his office mid-afternoon, telling his secretary he was going to Kingston for the rest of the day. With no telephone at the stadium, no one could locate him. Since I felt Kingston Stadium was an important school district facility, I had a telephone installed in the Kingston press box, in the booth where Irv Nelson, the public address announcer sat.

The telephone in the stadium caused me a small problem during a football game that first year. Irv Nelson told me that I had a telephone call. When I answered the phone, the voice on the other end said, "Tom, this is Craig Currie. It's started to rain, and I want the game called off."

I responded, "Craig, you know we don't call off games because of rain." He said, "I don't care, I want the game called off." Then I said, "Craig, let me have your phone number, and I'll call you right back." The caller hung up immediately.

At that time, Kingston Stadium was by far the best, most secure, local arena in which to play football games. A newly formed local professional football team, the Rapid Raiders, wanted to play their home games at Kingston. When I mentioned this to the superintendent, he told me to keep them out. We had heard of beer drinking and fighting in other communities' stadiums, so he said he didn't want to take the risk.

I decided the way to keep the professional team out of the stadium was to set the rent so high they couldn't afford it. When I met with one of the owners of the Rapids Raiders, I told him the rental price would be $1,000 a game. He said, "We'll take six games."

38

Never Give Up

In the fall of 1970, my secretary, Vicki McAllister, handed me a mimeographed sheet of word puzzles that she urged me to try to solve. Among the puzzles were such brainteasers as LINE READ LINE (Read between the lines) and NIGHT CHRISTMAS (Night before Christmas). I found them fascinating.

Later, I learned this type of puzzle is a form of rebus—a word and symbol puzzle that dates back more than 2,000 years to the Persian Empire. The secret to solving a rebus is to determine the missing "concept," such as in, on, over, under, before, after, between, etc.

I began creating my own rebuses, calling them Wurdles (word hurdles). When a sufficient number of Wurdles had been created, I began sending samples to book publishers and newspaper syndicates. But no one was interested.

When my collection grew to 200, I sent some of the Wurdles to my old high school buddy, Bill Wiederanders, who was living near New York City at the time. I asked him to seek out book publishers in the city to see if anyone might be interested. I thought the personal touch might be better than mailing them in. But, again, there was no interest.

Then, when I was looking through an old puzzle book (copyright 1959), I found a section with puzzles called Wordles. I knew that was close enough to the name Wurdles that I would never survive a legal challenge, should my puzzles ever become popular. So I changed the name of my puzzles to Wuzzles (word puzzles).

For the next twelve years I tried to sell Wuzzles, with no success. I tried many different formats. Every time I changed the layout for the puzzles, I would have to pay a printer to typeset the new format so it would look professional. There were many different formats during those years, some with a single Wuzzle in a box, some with two Wuzzles, and once I did a format with six Wuzzles.

By 1982, there were more than 3,500 Wuzzles in the collection, using about 200 different concepts. I was getting ideas by poring through standard, slang, and idiom dictionaries. But it didn't matter. Nobody was buying.

In February 1982, I decided to try to market the Wuzzles one last time. I went to a local printer and had a new format typeset, this time featuring three Wuzzles, side by side, labeled Easy, Medium, and Difficult. I took the new format to John Robertson, the managing editor of the Cedar Rapids *Gazette,* who looked them over, shaking his head. I suddenly realized that he wasn't able to solve any of the three Wuzzles. I then knew I shouldn't have sprung the puzzles on him without a bit of explanation. I thought that was the end of the project forever.

But after I gave him the answers and explained how to "read" them, he said he'd like to field-test Wuzzles in the *Gazette* for a two-week period. That meant I had to go back to the printer to have additional Wuzzles typeset.

At that time, the school district had a superintendent who did not want his employees "moonlighting." So, in order to keep my identity secret, I created the pen name of Tom Underwood, which itself is a puzzle if the word Tom is written below the word Wood. *Gazette* staffers agreed to keep Tom Underwood's identity secret. (Ten months later, when that superintendent resigned, the *Gazette* ran a page-wide headline, "Who's Tom Underwood? The answer will surprise you.")

On February 28, the Wuzzles began the two-week run in the *Gazette.* At the bottom of the feature was a box with the words: "The Wuzzles word game is being field-tested in the Cedar Rapids *Gazette.* Your reactions to this new feature will be greatly appreciated."

On the first day after the two-week run was completed, I called the *Gazette* to see what the reaction had been. I couldn't get through to the switchboard. People had tied up the lines complaining that the

Wearing a sweat shirt that says "Working under pressure," I'm sitting in a stack of fan mail received by the Gazette *in 1984.*

Wuzzles weren't in that day's paper. When I finally reached the editor, he said the paper would pay me to provide Wuzzles to them on a daily basis, beginning the next day, and they would set the type. We were in business.

The Wuzzles ran without missing a day for the next two years. On January 23, 1984, I received a phone call from Dale Larson, the *Gazette's* new managing editor. Dale wanted me to come to his office to meet John Killian, the Midwest sales representative for News America Syndicate in Irvine, California. When we met, John told me he thought Wuzzles would make an ideal national feature, so he took the idea back to California with him.

When that happened, I had my attorney search the files of the U.S. Patent and Trademark Office for

the trademark Wuzzles. When it turned out that there weren't any "paper products" trademarked with that name, we had the name registered.

News America Syndicate contacted me a week later and offered me a contract, but it took more than a year to get the syndicate's contracts into a form that was acceptable to both parties. I made two trips to California during that time—one to meet the syndicate's editor and one to give a talk to the News America sales staff.

When I met with the editor, we decided the daily feature would have two Wuzzles and the Sunday version would have three. That would be fifteen puzzles per week, or 780 per year. He also showed me the stack of mail he received every day from people who want to have their features syndicated. (I later realized that the editor had rejected my Wuzzles on two previous occasions.)

We also created three Wuzzles booklets available by mail-order, *The Best of Wuzzles, More of the Best of Wuzzles,* and *Wuzzles for Kids.* An additional book, *Wuzzles for Presenters,* was published by Creative Training Techniques in Minneapolis.

The *Gazette* was interested in two of my other puzzles, "Crypto-Quote" and "Diamond Crisscross." It was decided they would start running those two puzzles in the *Gazette* on the same day that the syndicated Wuzzles would begin running.

The agreement with the syndicate was finally signed on May 2, 1985, three days after the syndicate's sales staff had begun marketing Wuzzles. The target day to start the feature nationally would be August 29, 1985.

But a month before that starting date, my trademark attorney received a challenge from Hasbro-Bradley, the toy producer, and Walt Disney Productions. They were using the name Wuzzles for Hasbro's line of stuffed animals and a Disney TV cartoon program about the animals. They had not yet registered the name.

A Disney attorney argued that the type of use for a trademark and the geographical area are important factors in such cases. He said, "Just because you sell Wuzzles candy in Oregon doesn't mean you can stop somebody from selling Wuzzles T-shirts in Chicago." But he forgot to mention that the Wuzzles trademark, which I held, was for paper products, and Hasbro had already produced several different Wuzzles books.

When Hasbro and Disney admitted they were in the wrong, they offered me a deal. They would pay me

Wearing an apron that reads "A little behind in my work," I am posing as Tom under wood.

$200 for the trademark and own it forever, but I could continue to use it. I turned the case over to the syndicate's attorneys, who wanted a slightly better deal.

In the final settlement, I retained ownership of the trademark, the syndicate received a settlement of $100,000, and Hasbro-Disney could use the name for their animals.

In the meantime, News America Syndicate was purchased by King Features in New York, the largest newspaper syndicate in the world. It took fifteen years of persistence to get Wuzzles before the public, and they're still going strong more than thirty-five years later in newspapers throughout the world. About 6.5 million people see them every day, which is a pretty low number when compared with most syndicated features.

When I look at the size and scope of the King Features family, with such popular comics, puzzles, and columns, I know I'm a small fish in a very big pond. But I'm happy just to be in the pond.

The highlight of every year for the King Features' employees and contributors was the annual Christmas party, held at the Waldorf-Astoria Hotel in New York. Besides limitless food and drink, and music from a full orchestra, there was the chance to meet and chat with some of King's well-known contributors.

One year I spent much of the evening chatting with three of King's female contributors, Dr. Ruth Westheimer, Dr. Joyce Brothers, and Heloise Evans. Ruth Westheimer, a sex therapist, created the column "Ask Dr. Ruth" and had a radio program called "Sexually Speaking." (I later told friends that Dr. Ruth wanted to get some sex tips from me.)

Dr. Joyce Brothers, who was known as "the face of American psychology," wrote a daily advice column for King Features.

Heloise rarely used her last name. She was just Heloise. Her column, "Hints from Heloise," contained many useful household hints. The column was begun in 1959 by her mother, the original Heloise. The present Heloise took over the column in 1977 when her mother died.

Another year I went to the King party armed with a sketch pad. I went to all of the cartoonists there, asking if they would draw a cartoon for my young grandson. I came away with personalized drawings of many cartoon characters, including Beetle Bailey, Hagar the Horrible, Hi and Lois, Curtis, Popeye, Wizard of Id, and Dennis the Menace.

While chatting with Chance Browne, who drew Hi and Lois, he invited me to his holiday party the next day. Chance is the brother of Chris Browne, known for drawing the popular Hagar the Horrible, which at that time appeared in 1,800 newspapers.

In typical cartoonist style, Chance took out his sketch pad and wrote across the top: "The Brownes' Holiday Party 2-6 PM." Below that is a bearded cartoon character, saying, "Take Merritt Pkwy North to Exit 40." Then I told him I wasn't driving. He wrote, "Forget it. By Train: Metro North to Westport. Cab to Indian Hill, Wilton."

I followed the instructions and arrived in time for one of the best parties I have ever attended. Chance was a gracious host, but he couldn't spend much time with the many guests. Besides being the host, he played guitar with his musical group, The Twinkles, who entertained throughout the afternoon. At 6 p.m., I left the party and took the train back to reality.

39

Lawsuits and Stalkers and Nerves, Oh, My!

In the 1970s, after I had left the Nissen Company to become the athletic director for the Cedar Rapids school system, George Nissen was faced with his biggest manufacturing challenge. The Nissen Corporation, along with other sports equipment manufacturers and sports programs across America, were being threatened with extinction by multimillion dollar lawsuits filed by lawyers on behalf of injured athletes.

Since I was the Cedar Rapids athletic director, I realized that all of our sports programs were ultimately going to be in jeopardy if something wasn't done. I began to write newspaper and magazine articles, and I gave speeches on the evils of general and product liability litigation.

It was easy for me to get information about product liability at that time. The Nissen Corporation, which was the largest manufacturer of gymnastics equipment in the world, was facing an average of one multimillion dollar lawsuit every week. And it was losing all of them, even when the evidence showed the company's equipment had not been at fault.

Lawyers were using the "deep pocket" theory of litigation. Whoever had money, usually the equipment manufacturer and the school district, were the ones who were sued, whether they were at fault or not.

Sympathetic juries (usually made up of people who weren't smart enough to get out of jury duty) always took the side of the injured athlete because "someone has to pay." Why not just collect from the company or the school district with the deepest pockets?

The Nissen Corporation was sued so often that it could no longer get liability insurance. So it became "self-insured," putting aside some funds to cover lawsuits. One day, George Nissen received a telephone call from a lawyer who said he was filing a lawsuit against the company. The lawyer asked, "How much insurance do you have?" When he was told the company

didn't have any insurance, the lawyer responded, "Good, I've always wanted to own a gymnastics equipment company."

To help fight some of the lawsuits, the Nissen Corporation brought in my friend Jim Hay as an expert witness. Jim, who was the biomechanics professor at the University of Iowa, had a knowledge of sports movement that was invaluable in providing evidence that helped the Nissen lawyers win some of the later cases.

Jim and I spent a lot of time with George Nissen, going over many of the details of the lawsuits. It was during that time that Jim told me that George treated me like the son he never had. He was probably right. For forty years, George had always treated me as someone special. I always appreciated his kindness.

When I gave speeches about frivolous lawsuits during those days, I used actual cases as examples. One was about a woman who was hit by a cable car in San Francisco. She wasn't seriously injured, but she filed a lawsuit claiming that the accident had turned her into a nymphomaniac. She said she had little interest in sex before the accident, but she had a need to be with as many men as possible afterwards. The jury awarded her $50,000. The local newspapers dubbed the case "A Cable Car Named Desire."

Another case was about a woman who took off her clothes and climbed up on top of a dresser so she could check out her hemorrhoids in the mirror. She fell off the dresser and injured herself. She sued the furniture manufacturer and won.

By 1983, the problem of general and product liability was becoming a serious problem for school districts. In Cedar Rapids, our insurance premiums had been growing excessively every year. The use of trampolines, which had been an important part of our high school physical education and sports programs, had to be discontinued because of a lack of available insurance. Eventually, we

152—

had to drop our entire gymnastics programs.

Pole vaulting was another casualty. Our district had purchased expensive pole vault landing pits for our nine secondary schools. The next year the manufacturer began making an "even safer pit." Our lawyers advised us to drop pole vaulting from the school program. They explained that any opposing lawyer could prove easily that our landing pits were not the safest available. The state of Iowa followed our example. There hasn't been any secondary school pole vaulting in our state in more than thirty years.

I wrote one magazine article at that time that really made the rounds. It was called "Will We Allow the Courts to Kill Sports?" It was written originally for *Athletic Journal* magazine, but was reprinted in other magazines and journals. It was even read into the *Congressional Record.*

Most of the lawsuits against the Nissen Corporation were based on "failure to warn." If the opposing lawyers could convince a jury that their client was not adequately warned of the dangers of using the Nissen equipment, the jury ruled in favor of the plaintiff.

In 1982, two of Nissen's executives, trying to find a way to thwart lawsuits against equipment manufacturers and school districts, came to me with an idea. If they could raise the money, would I be willing to produce a short warning film, designed to educate student-athletes and their parents about the possible dangers of participating in sports?

The color film would be short, only twelve minutes in length. It would be titled *Warning: It Could Happen to You.* The film would be reasonably priced, without the intention of making a profit. The two executives only wanted protection from lawsuits against equipment manufacturers and school districts.

I was put in touch with an Arizona trial lawyer, Rick Ball, who specialized in athletic injury litigation. He agreed to narrate the film. I contacted some friends at the University of Iowa Motion Picture Unit, who wrote the script and shot and edited the movie. In the film credits, I was listed as "Producer."

The film came out in May 1983. There were brisk sales nationwide, and enough money was made that the executives got their investment back. It was great for me to be able to fall back on my cinematography experiences from the University of Iowa.

In 1990, I received a letter from one of the secretaries at King Features syndicate in New York, warning me that they had received a letter from a "deranged person" who wanted to "locate" Tom Underwood. The secretary said she wouldn't have bothered me, but there had been an incident in New York that she thought I should know about. It seems a man had gunned down a stagehand outside the NBC studios in downtown Manhattan because the TV networks were spying on him—bugging him, taping his phone calls, and sending rays through his TV set. He said he couldn't take it anymore. So he shot and killed the stagehand.

The syndicate wanted me to know that my life might be in danger, so they forwarded the letter to me. It was handwritten by a woman in Denver, Colorado. She wrote:

"This letter is regarding your syndication in the *Rocky Mountain News,* The Wuzzles. My understanding is that this work is sub-contracted by others submitting packets of work.

"I'm in a very life-threatening dilemma. In 1989, I was involved in a very severe vehicular accident. At the time of my surgery, as insane as the deed sounds, the plastic surgeon inserted implants for the hearing impaired (which was without consent or knowledge) and he had arranged this sick act with others that work in media-type capacity as a link. In other words, my actual thinking is being held back because the person(s) I'm linked with who have a far lower sense of self-confidence, esteem, and work capacity than myself. Highly abnormal, undereducated while being physically, mentally and verbally abused by the beholders of the receptor to include professional studio equipment with the way the press and television are producing such low-quality work.

"My situation is that the parties sending in these packets are fully aware of said situation and I need their names and addresses in order for my attorney and private investigator to contact these people for statements. They have been using my life, my education, my body and mind to produce what an average child could produce. This matter needs your immediate attention as a life sustaining means. I'm not the only person that 'King Trash' is liable for doing this to. There is far too much to be a mere coincidence and direct reference to this started in the Wuzzles the week of March 11, 1990—i.e.: Everything's intact, Pain up, Tendons."

(The letter writer was referring to some of that

week's Wuzzles answers. In those days, the *Rocky Mountain News* ran the Wuzzles seven days a week, with the answers appearing the following day. The letter writer said one of the answers was "Pain up," when it was actually "Doubled up with pain.")

The letter continued: "The situation is still being directly referred to and my health is rapidly deteriorating due to the misuse of equipment, not by any means to medical factors which has been and will be very well substantiated.

"I realize this will undoubtedly be handled by your legal department. Immediate response is of the utmost urgency. Thank you for your cooperation in this matter."

Then she signed the letter, gave her address and phone number, and listed the names of her private investigator and her attorney.

The Denver area was my biggest market for Wuzzles. I had upcoming book signings in two Denver bookstores, so I had to try to find out if this woman was dangerous. I could envision her stalking me at one of the book signings, asking for an autograph, and pulling out a gun. Stranger things have happened.

So I called both the private investigator and the attorney, to find out more about the woman. Was she dangerous? Neither would tell me anything.

As a last resort, I flew to Denver—as Tom Ecker, not Tom Underwood—to try to learn more about the stalker. When in Denver, I learned the home addresses of both the private investigator and the attorney. I called both and asked if I could come over for a chat. Neither would see me. Then, at the advice of my attorney in Cedar Rapids, David Good, I went to the Denver public library to check the files there to see if there were any court records concerning the woman. I found some references to her, but nothing incriminating. So I canceled the Denver book signings and returned home.

During my final ten years with the Cedar Rapids schools, I was the director of information. In other words, I was in charge of the school district's public relations. My longtime secretary and PR partner was Robin Barnes. I called myself Mr. Information. Robin called herself Miss Information.

Although my new position required a strong background in journalism, my job was to be an advocate, not a journalist. A journalist is supposed to tell all sides of a story. An advocate tells whatever sides of the story favor the school district. There were times when we said our job was spray-painting the manure pile.

Besides being the public information wing of the school district, we also took over the responsibilities of operation the district's TV station and print shop.

The TV station, which had two employees, televised the district's board meetings, high school graduations, and other events of interest to the public. I was the director for many of the live telecasts, allowing me to fall back on the TV skills I had learned as an undergraduate student at Iowa.

The print shop, with seven employees, printed programs and newsletters for all of the district's forty schools. In the early 1990s, the print shop was threatened with extinction by—guess what?—lawsuits. Some employees filed lawsuits against the district and me because the employees were being "poisoned" by fumes from chemicals used in some of the machines. One of the printing equipment manufacturers was also sued for several million dollars, and the manufacturer, in turn, countersued me for several million dollars.

My nerves were so frayed by that time that I went to my doctor to see if he could prescribe something to settle my nerves. He wrote out a prescription and asked, "How long do you have until retirement?" I said, "One year." He asked, "How much sick leave do you have coming?" I answered, "One year." He smiled and said, "You're out of there."

After twenty-six years in the school district, I retired on December 2, 1993, at the age of fifty-eight.

*Serving as the TV director of a school district
board of education meeting*

Posing with "Miss Information," Robin Barnes

40

A Paramount Idea

The magnificent Capitol Theatre was opened in downtown Cedar Rapids on September 1, 1928. The large brick building, which was six stories high, housed the beautiful theater, some commercial offices, and a few street-level shops. The theater was designed to feature vaudeville acts, with dressing rooms on all six levels, plus a "Hall of Mirrors" between the box office and the theater, fashioned after those in Versailles, France. Another of the theater's features was the "Mighty Wurlitzer" organ, which provided musical accompaniment for the vaudeville acts. Throughout the theater, there were expensive oil paintings, sculptures, and antique furniture.

In 1929, with the advent of silent movies, vaudeville was dying, and the Capitol Theatre became one of the many Paramount movie theaters in the United States. Movies were shown at the Paramount continually from 1929 until 1948, when the Paramount fell into a serious state of disrepair and closed.

In December 1975, local businessman Peter Bezanson, who had purchased the

A plaque in the lobby of the Paramount Theatre lists the City officials and the members of the Performing Arts Commission.

Paramount building to utilize its retail stores and offices, sold the run-down Paramount Theatre to the city of Cedar Rapids for one dollar as a tax write-off. If the theater was going to be refurbished, it was going to be the city's responsibility.

The mayor of Cedar Rapids, Don Canney, named me to a new fifteen-member commission the City Council had established. It was called the Performing Arts Commission. The charge from the city was to restore the run-down Paramount Theatre to its original elegance and to have quality entertainment available to the community.

Members of the commission, along with me, were former Paramount Theatre owner Peter Bezanson, Barnes O'Donnell, and architect Leo Peiffer, who would deal with architectural problems, including having the theater's leaky roof repaired.

Other members were George Baldwin, Joy Bickel, Dawn Chapman, Sid Hayman, Ken Hastie, Dianne Koepsell, Stanislavs Reinis, Georgene Stapleton, William Shuttleworth, Sandra Skelton, Charles Swore, and Peggy Whitworth. Several commission members had interesting vocations, but my favorite was Sandra Skelton's. She was a belly dancer.

The commission held regular meetings, chaired by Barnes O'Donnell, determining individual commissioners' responsibilities and forging plans to raise $400,000 to restore the 1,900-seat theater, without using any tax revenues.

I had a new book coming out at that time, so to help the cause I donated all future royalties from that book to the Paramount restoration effort. While exploring the storage areas on the theater's upper floors, I discovered two ornate wooden candy machines that offered candy bars for five cents. I decided to use some of the royalty money to have the two candy machines restored and later placed in the theater's lobby.

The plan for the Paramount was to host live entertainment as a source of income to pay the costs of the theater's maintenance. Only three local organizations were going to be allowed to use the theater rent-free: the Cedar Rapids Symphony Orchestra, the Dieman-Bennett Dance Theatre of the Hemispheres, and the Cedar Rapids Community Theatre. It was agreed that movies would never be shown again at the Paramount.

The commission members set up a rental schedule and selected me to be the theater's booking agent. As soon as word got out that I would be handling the Paramount's bookings, two promoters—Jim Fox from Waterloo and Dean Lenz from Minneapolis—told me they wanted to provide the theater with entertainment. Often, acts that performed in Chicago, Minneapolis, the Quad Cities, Des Moines, or Omaha, and that had an open date on their calendars, would want to play Cedar Rapids.

Fox promoted rock bands, so his acts appealed to a younger crowd. Lenz promoted acts that appealed to more mature audiences.

Some of the commissioners thought the high decibel noise level of a rock band might be harmful to the theater's inner walls, but it was decided to give it one chance. To help win me over, Jim invited me to the Waterloo Hippodrome to see a live performance of Aerosmith, with lead singer Steven Tyler. He said I could bring my sons, Kevin and Kerry, ages sixteen and eighteen. We had backstage passes and were impressed that the small musical group needed seven semi-trucks to transport everything, including one entire truck to generate enough electricity to keep the sounds and lights going.

Another trip to Waterloo, at Jim's invitation, saw my sons and me backstage at a KISS concert, which was quite an experience. The KISS members wore gaudy makeup and strap-on spiked platform boots. Their appearance and shrewd marketing had made them one of the top heavy metal bands in the world.

We not only had backstage passes but were allowed to walk under the stage to the area between the front of the stage and the heavily guarded security fence. No one could have been closer to the performers. We looked up at them as them as they played, sang, and dropped guitar picks, which my sons were quick to retrieve.

On April 30, 1976, the Paramount Theatre had its first live performance since the days of vaudeville, almost fifty years earlier. Jim Fox booked in the rock band, REO Speedwagon, with singer-guitarist Bob Seger and the Silver Bullet Band as the opening act. It was a great (and loud) performance, but the audience was small. Jim lost money.

Dean Lenz, the promoter from Minneapolis, offered us two outstanding performances that season. One was the very entertaining pianist-comedian Victor Borge, who more than sold out the Paramount. The other was a live dramatic production, *John Brown's Body*, featuring film stars Rock Hudson, Claire Trevor, and Leif Erickson.

Victor Borge's show not only sold out the main theater, but Borge suggested that additional chairs be arranged in an arc around his piano, so he could talk with the main audience with his microphone, and to the onstage audience with asides that were not heard elsewhere in the theatre. My friend, Bob Foley, was in one of the onstage chairs, and he told me later that Borge's asides, often a little bawdy, were the funniest parts of the show.

I arranged for one of the classiest restaurants in downtown Cedar Rapids, the Flame Room, to close early the night of the Victor Borge concert. After the show, Borge, his accompanying opera singer, Marilyn Melvey, promoter Dean Lenz, my friend, Loren Olson, known to all as "Oly," and I could have a private dinner in the Flame Room. When the waitress came to our table for drink orders, Victor Borge asked for water. Oly said he'd like a beer. Immediately, Borge said, "Change that. I'll have a beer, too."

After a very pleasant dinner, Victor Borge and Ms. Melvey excused themselves and left, while the rest of the group went to Oly's apartment, drinking and laughing until the wee hours of the morning.

John Brown's Body, the Civil War-based play by Stephen Vincent Benét, was playing in theaters on the West Coast in May 1976, with Rock Hudson in the leading role. The plan was to take the production on the road, playing in theaters throughout the Midwest, including Minneapolis, where Dean Lenz was handling the booking. Lenz contacted the producers and suggested the road company also play Cedar Rapids for one night. They all agreed that the Paramount Theatre would be an ideal venue.

According to Lenz, Rock Hudson and the other lead actors, Leif Erickson and Claire Trevor, were really looking forward to playing a theater in Cedar Rapids, where they were sure they would be performing for an appreciative rural audience.

When I suggested to Lenz that the show's stars have dinner with me in my apartment near the top of the Cedar River Tower, he thought that was a great idea. He had visited me on the 22nd floor of the Tower, a short walk from the Roosevelt Hotel, where the actors would be staying. That would provide them with great views of the city and would help shield them from the throngs of admirers they faced whenever they were out in public.

But, alas, it never happened. I received a phone call from Lenz, canceling the performance. The show had played to small audiences in its early days on the road, so the remainder of the run had to be canceled.

I never got to meet three of my favorite movie stars.

When the Five Seasons Center (now the U.S. Cellular Center) was under construction in April 1977, an outsider, Mike Gebauer, was hired by the city to book acts into both the Paramount Theatre and the Five Seasons Center. So I was out of the entertainment business again.

However, Gebauer and I struck a deal. He would allow me to use the center, rent free, for the school district's three high school graduations each June. (Since 1970, I had been overseeing the graduations in the horseshoe end of the school district's Kingston Stadium, a facility that offered no protection from inclement weather.) In return, I provided him with an annual citywide pass for all Cedar Rapids High School athletic and performing arts events. It was a good trade.

Five years later, Mike Gebauer resigned from his position as manager of the Five Seasons Center to take a similar job in Tacoma, Washington. The Cedar Rapids Area Convention & Visitors Bureau decided to host a "roast" in his honor. I was selected to be the final "roaster." There was a large audience, including the four City Council members.

Here is part of the story that appeared in the Cedar Rapids *Gazette* the next day: "Then it was Tom Ecker's turn. Introduced as the Don Rickles of Cedar Rapids, Ecker first took jabs at the City Councilmen in the audience and, after unloading many unkind comments on Gebauer, decided it was time to introduce the guest of honor.

"I'd like to present a man of great leadership, a man impossible to replace. But Mayor Don Canney couldn't be here, so I'll introduce Mike Gebauer instead."

41

The Ex Club, the Rotary Club, and Detachments

In the 1970s, I learned of a small, unorthodox civic organization called the Ex Club of Cedar Rapids. I knew of the club because they occasionally asked me to be the speaker at their weekly meetings. Among my topics were the Olympic Games, drugs in sports, and sex equity in sports. They liked me because I would take on controversial topics, I sprinkled the talks with humor, and I could respond quickly to the club's occasional hecklers.

Originally, the club was part of the National Exchange Club, an organization that boasts itself as the "only service organization exclusively serving communities in the United States, with core values of family, community, and country."

The Cedar Rapids Exchange Club's affiliation with the National Exchange Club ended in 1974 after some of the National Club's officials complained that the Cedar Rapids club printed bawdy, off-color jokes in its newsletter.

When the Exchange Club of Cedar Rapids no longer existed, its name was shortened to a more appropriate Ex Club. But club members are not as rowdy as they once were, I'm told. After having been kicked out of several restaurant meeting places over the years, the club now meets at the prestigious Cedar Rapids Country Club.

When I moved to Cedar Rapids in 1967, I joined the 300-member Downtown Rotary Club. One of the first times I spoke to the Ex Club, I said, "At Rotary, we have more of our members in the hospital than you have in your whole club."

I decided to join the Ex Club in 1999, eventually even serving as its president. I call the club the city's counter-culture civic organization. But there is one thing the club members keep to themselves. They quietly give money annually to several youth charities.

During the course of their weekly meetings, the Ex Club's president calls the meeting to order and recognizes guests. Then, members give travel reports, try to answer trivia questions, tell off-color jokes, hope to win the weekly drawings for bottles of liquor, and listen to a speaker.

One of the best Ex Club tongue-in-cheek claims is: "We sponsor a half-way house for girls who won't go all the way."

Shortly after I moved to Cedar Rapids in 1967, I became close friends with the *Gazette's* sports editor, Gus Schrader. My job as an advocate for Cedar Rapids public school sports, and his as an editor, reporter, and columnist for the *Gazette,* first brought us together.

We had lunch together at the Dragon Restaurant every Thursday. It was a chance for us to swap our latest jokes, and for Gus to try out his column ideas on me. He was writing six columns a week at that time, so he needed lots of ideas.

At that time, Gus and I were fellow Rotarians. Rotary meetings were held at the Montrose Hotel, which was later torn down. There were no women Rotarians. There were Rotarians and their wives, who were called "Rotary Anns."

When Gus was elected president of the Rotary Club in 1973, he asked me to deliver special comical reports during the meetings. Often, I teamed up with Jack Laugen, fundraiser for Coe College, to deliver the reports. We became so popular, club members would begin laughing as soon as we were introduced. Because of that popularity, both Jack and I were elected to Rotary's Board of Directors.

It turned out Gus had a plan for me. I didn't know it at the time, but he wanted me to become president of the club. But that would take time because of the needed succession of officers. Three years later, I became president of the Rotary Club for the 1976-77 year.

In the nation's bicentennial year, 1976, the Shell Oil Company began running a series of informational ads on television, called the Shell Bicentennial Minute. Jack Laugen and I, along with a few other Rotarians, produced a weekly "Schmell Bicentennial Half-minute" for our club meetings. Jack wrote most of the material, which was really funny.

When I took office as president in July 1976, the Rotary meetings were being held at noon on Mondays at the Roosevelt Hotel. My goal was to have the club experience the wildest, craziest year ever.

The first thing I did was gather all of the funny Rotarians around me, so I could call on them to help keep the meetings lively. Our club's song leader, Torry Carlson, often turned the club's singing sessions into very funny scenes. Dr. Kasam Fathie, an Iranian-born neurosurgeon whose accent was very heavy, provided many humorous moments. Gus Schrader was always available to provide funny one-liners. After Gus was introduced at one of the Rotary meetings, he told the Rotarians that he had just gotten a sitting ovation.

Jeweler Joe Hoyt had an extremely dry sense of humor and delivery. Designer Mike Evans, who often wore his full-length raccoon coat to meetings, was the Rotary Flasher. With his back to the audience, he would flash members walking by him, so only the flashees could see what Mike had on under the coat. And, of course, there was the master humorist, Jack Laugen, one of the funniest people I have ever known.

Privately, we called our Monday meetings "crazy shit at twelve o'clock." We kidded some people. We joked about others. But mostly, we insulted people.

At one meeting, Duane Arnold was introduced as a guest. He was well-known in the community because he had constructed the only nuclear power plant in Iowa just northwest of Cedar Rapids. From the podium, I asked him if he had a fallout shelter at his house. The Rotarians loved it.

When Mrs. Virgil Hancher, widow of the longtime University of Iowa president, told us of her efforts to restore Old Capitol as a campus landmark, I asked her if it wouldn't have been cheaper just to tear it down.

Rotarians visiting from other clubs were usually very quiet when they stand to be recognized. On one occasion, a visiting Rotarian from Ohio stood up after being introduced and began raving about the culture and beauty of Ohio.

I didn't make any comments about the man from Ohio until the meeting was coming to a close. I stood at the microphone and asked, "Is anyone here from Ohio?" The man jumped to his feet and let out a large whoop. I said, "Welcome to America."

The biggest and most daring Rotary project I was involved with began in 1990 when I asked Linda Golden, a former teacher from the Quad Cities, to speak at a Rotary meeting in Cedar Rapids. I had met Linda the previous year, while traveling by train along the rim of the Copper Canyon in northwestern Mexico.

Linda had a unique story. Two years earlier, she sold all of her possessions and withdrew her fifteen years of teacher retirement money to become a volunteer teacher in a one-room schoolhouse near the Copper Canyon. The school, which is in the village of San Jose de Pinal, served the Tarahumara Indian children who lived in the canyon. Linda's new goal was to establish a health clinic in the corner of the school to serve the needs of all of the Tarahumarans who lived in the area.

During her speech, Linda told the Rotarians that the peaceful, cave-dwelling Tarahumarans are on their way to extinction. They were dying from usually curable diseases, such as respiratory infections, malnutrition, and dehydration caused by diarrhea. The life expectancy of the Indians was between forty and forty-five. Infant mortality, at 50 percent, was among the highest in the world.

Linda's speech sold me on trying to do something to help the Tarahumara Indians. I decided to raise money, buy medical supplies for the Indians, and take a group of Rotarians to deliver the money and supplies to the Copper Canyon school. The trip would require travel by airplane, train, taxi, bus, and pickup truck.

There were three Catholic nuns in the village who were prepared to staff the health clinic—a registered nurse, a nursing assistant, and a chemist/lab assistant. The three nuns made a list of medical supplies that were needed for the clinic and sent the list to me.

An initial donation of $2,500 was made by the Cedar Rapids Rotary Club, followed by individual donations from members of all three local Rotary Clubs. We had more than $5,000 to buy blood pressure cuffs, a stethoscope, bathroom and baby scales, syringes, aspirin, vitamins, and a variety of different medicines. All of the items were purchased in Cedar Rapids and packed in suitcases for the trek to the canyon.

I knew it would take a few people to carry the medical supplies in the extra suitcases, so I decided to set the number of travelers to ten Rotarians. However, only four Rotarians opted to go on the trip, so we opened it up to any of our friends who were willing to pay for the trip. When we had our ten travelers, KCRG-TV approached me and asked if they could send a reporter/cameraman along. That brought our total to eleven participants.

We flew from Cedar Rapids to El Paso, Texas, where we crossed the border into Mexico in taxis. We joked that it was probably the only time anyone had ever smuggled drugs *into* Mexico. From there, we traveled to Chihuahua by bus and on to the Copper Canyon by train. Then followed a two-hour ride in the back of a pickup truck over barely passable roads and a three-hour walk over rugged mountainous terrain.

The trip was very successful. And it was well-publicized. KCRG television ran daily reports on the trip's progress and ran a special program about the adventure when we returned. I wrote an article for the Cedar Rapids *Gazette*, "Iowans Race to Save a Society," which ran the next week, complete with five color photographs.

When we delivered the medical supplies to the school, five days after leaving Cedar Rapids, we all had feelings of pride in the new clinic and the work it would do and feelings of relief that our mission was finally accomplished.

When I was attending Rotary Club meetings in the 1970s and 80s, it was not unusual for fellow members to make reference to my many ex-wives. People always assumed there were more than there really were. At one of the Rotary meetings, member Jack Evans said I was a lot like Johnny Carson. He clarified that he didn't think I was as funny as Carson, but I had as many ex-wives.

There was one Rotarian, Tom Parks, who had more ex-wives than I did. I was presiding during a meeting one Monday noon, and I announced that my ex-wives were going to challenge Tom Parks' ex-wives to a basketball game. "But it wouldn't really be fair," I said. "His team has a stronger bench."

The truth is that I've been married three times and divorced three times. Basic math would tell you I'm not married at the moment, but that isn't true. One of the divorces was annulled after a year.

Judy Koch and I were married for ten years, were divorced and lived apart for a year, and then had the divorce annulled. (We even received an annulment present from our daughter, Wendy.) Although they are rare, divorce annulments are legal in most states.

We then spent the next ten years together before the second divorce. Years later, I told people that Judy and I had a ten-year contract with an option for another ten years.

My second marriage was to Karen Hatch. We decided to get married in Merida, Yucatan, Mexico, on January 1, 1983. Since January 1 was a holiday, we had to bribe a judge to perform the service. The time we were married was not much longer than the divorce proceedings, which lasted one-and-a-half years.

It didn't take me long to realize that ours wasn't a match made in heaven, so in 1985, I decided to end the marriage. I asked my attorney and good friend, Dave Good, who had set up the corporation for Tom Underwood Enterprises, how much I should pay him for his legal work. When he said I should pay him $2,000, I told him I'd pay him an additional $2,000 if he could also get me divorced. That turned out to be a great deal for me but not such a great deal for Dave.

Karen learned that I was planning to leave her during a ceremony celebrating the lighting of the Paramount Theatre's new marquee. The marquee was to be lighted for the first time on Friday evening, December 13, with Mayor Don Canney standing in front of the theater to throw the switch.

Most of the members of the Performing Arts Commission were there. Pete and Loraine Bezanson were standing in the crowd on the sidewalk in front of the theater. I was there with my then-wife, Karen, who did not know that I planned to split with her.

I had quietly rented two adjoining apartments for Tom Underwood (my nom de plume) on the twenty-fifth floor of the Cedar River Tower. The Bezansons lived in the Tower's penthouse, which was the entire twenty-sixth floor, the size of eight apartments on any other level. (I told people that Pete thought I lived in his basement. Actually, he lived in my attic.)

As Karen and I were chatting with the Bezansons, Pete commented that he and Loraine were looking forward to having us as neighbors. Karen, who realized for the first time that I was planning to leave, glared at me. She was not happy.

The divorce required thirteen different appearances in court and had a final trial lasting a day-and-a-half. During the time of the divorce, I suffered a great deal of anguish, primarily because the opposing lawyer was trying to make the ordeal last as long as

Peter Bezanson's apartment in the Cedar River Tower was the entire twenty-sixth floor.

possible. My lawyer, Dave Good, taught me a valuable lesson. One day, when he saw that I was particularly distraught, he asked me, "What's the worst thing that can happen to you?" I thought for a few moments and said, "I guess I could lose some money." "That's it?" he asked. "That's it." "Well," he answered, "money is a renewable resource."

Then he explained to me that most things in life don't really matter much. He taught me to face most of my potential problems with the line, "It just doesn't matter." And usually that's the correct response. It just doesn't matter.

On the evening of the completion of the trial, there was a party to celebrate the end of the long ordeal. The party was planned weeks in advance, so it

was a good thing the trial ended when it did.

The computer-generated invitation read: "You are cordially invited to DETACHMENTFEST (A Celebration of Freedom) Stouffer's Five Seasons Hotel, Cedar Rapids, IA. Friday, February 13, 1987." Inside it read: "Come help celebrate the detachment (Or come help celebrate Groundhog Day belatedly, if you're not into detachments). Room 1509. Drop in anytime between 5:00 and 8:00 p.m." On the back of the card was printed: "My computer is finally doing something I understand!"

We rented a large two-level room at Stouffer's Hotel in downtown Cedar Rapids. We also rented the adjoining rooms on both sides. We filled the bathtubs in the adjoining rooms with ice and ninety bottles of champagne. The food was catered in from the nearby Amana Colonies. Friends Ellen Ilten and Jane Welsh served the food and poured the champagne.

At the door was a used guestbook, with the front pages torn out, and a wedding cake, with just a groom on top. Some 149 people signed the guestbook, including a few uninvited guests—the roadies from the Alice Cooper rock concert, which was playing in the adjoining Five Seasons Center the next night.

Everyone who attended the party was served champagne or a soft drink in a souvenir champagne glass with printing on the side that read: "Detachmentfest/Stouffer's Five Seasons Hotel, February 13, 1987." We almost ran out of the 144 glasses that had been ordered for the party.

The Wuzzles that appeared in newspapers around the country that day were divorce Wuzzles—"It's over at last" and "Freedom from bondage." Enlargements of those Wuzzles adorned the room's walls. A friend living in Topeka, Kansas, saw the Wuzzles in her local newspaper that day and called to congratulate me.

There were lots of friends there, and it was great fun. (Karen heard about the party later and was not amused. Apparently, nobody told her, "It just doesn't matter.")

Ten years later, I met my most-recent wife, Carol. It all began in 1996, when I was in charge of hospitality for the *Track and Field News* tour to the Olympic Games in Atlanta. One of my assistants was a charming young woman named Helen Faw from Eugene, Oregon. Helen, an elementary school teacher, was the girlfriend of one of the other *Track and Field News* staff members, Tom Jordan. I had never met her before.

One of Helen's responsibilities was to greet the 1,400 tour members, distribute packets of information to them, and give each family a copy of my new book, *Olympic Facts and Fables.* Helen and I became good friends.

When the Olympics were over, I never thought I'd see Helen again. Yet a year later, when I was attending the World Veterans' track and field championships in Durban, South Africa, she was there, again with her boyfriend. I had been invited to Durban by my Swedish pole vaulting friend, Hans Lagerqvist, who was still pole vaulting at the age of fifty-seven. (As of this writing, Hans is still vaulting at the age of seventy-eight.)

Helen, Hans, and I spent a great deal of time together during our stay in Durban. When I told Helen about my word puzzles, Wuzzles, she began to call me Mr. Wuzzle.

At one point, I told Helen that I had been single for ten years and that I was "hunting again." She said, "I've got the perfect woman for you if we can get her to dump her boyfriend she's had for the past eleven years." The "perfect woman" was one of Helen's fellow teachers in Eugene, Carol Clarke. Helen gave me Carol's email address.

Emails were in their early stages in those days, and I was (and still am) very low-tech. When I returned to Iowa, I emailed Carol, but there was no response. So I tried again, still with no response. I emailed Helen to tell her Carol was not writing me back. Helen immediately went to Carol and said, "You'd better be answering Mr. Wuzzle."

Finally, on October 3, 1997, I received an email that began: "Hallo! (That's German, you know.) Well, how do, how do. I'll bet you could make a puzzle out

Photo by Helen Faw

My dear friend, Hans Lagergrist of Sweden, won the pole vault competition in Durban, South Africa. Here he is on the victory stand, after receiving the gold medal from the South African lady standing in front.

Here I am welcoming Sports Editor, Gus Schrader, (with eye patch) to the party.

Other party goers (I am holding the cup) are from left: Dave Good, Terry Osmanski, Terri Hoyland, Bruce Eichacher (partly hidden) Charlie Kolkmeyer, and Jack Laugen.

of that, couldn't you? Helen has told me a lot about you, and I must say you sound VERY interesting."

Over the next two months, we exchanged 277 emails. The record was twenty-three emails in a twenty-four-hour period. Many of the emails were about when and where we would eventually meet.

In November, Carol had a family get-together over the Thanksgiving weekend. Invited were her two children, a daughter-in-law, and two grandchildren. Her plan was to fix a big turkey dinner on Thursday and to relax the rest of the weekend. On Sunday evening, after everyone had left, she had "boyfriend" Bill over for leftovers. That's when she broke the news to him that she had a chance to meet someone new.

I was in Japan at the time, meeting with track and field coaches and athletes, but I knew Carol's plan was to end it with Bill that Sunday night. So I called her Monday morning before she left for school. With the seven-hour time difference between Japan and Oregon, I had to make the call at midnight. When she answered, I asked her how it went. She said it was over. Then I asked her when she'd like to have me come to Oregon so we could meet.

I was scheduled to go to Australia for a birthday party, but I canceled that and said I could come to Eugene on Tuesday, December 9. She said she'd meet me at the airport. And that's where we met. She was holding a stuffed koala to give me, in exchange for my canceled trip to Australia. To this day, the koala is resting comfortably on a shelf in our bedroom in Cedar Rapids.

42

My Own Escort Service

In 1968, while attending the Olympic Games in Mexico City, I decided I wanted to be a part-time tour escort during vacation times, getting my way paid to watch over people as they visited exotic places. I learned early on that there is a big difference between a tour escort and a tour guide. A tour guide has to know something.

During the Mexico Olympics, I spent a lot of time with Jack Griffith, the publisher of the *Athletic Journal* magazine. It was my thought that he and I could become partners in operating a tour to the 1972 Olympics in Munich. Advertising the tour in his magazine would attract a lot of attention from the thousands of coaches who were subscribers. I knew that *Track and Field News* had operated the largest tours to all of the Olympic Games since 1952. But I thought there would be room for us, too, since our people would be interested in all sports, not just track and field.

In 1970, we began running ads in *Athletic Journal* for our tour to the Munich Olympics, and people from all over the country began signing up. We limited the tour to 132, a number we thought we could accommodate. The travel arrangements were all handled by a Cedar Rapids travel agency, American Travel and Tour, so we didn't have to worry about any of those details. But we did have to go to the Munich area to make the housing and bus arrangements. I went back in 1970, twice in 1971, and twice in 1972, making certain there were no flaws in our arrangements. We had found excellent housing in the picturesque village of Reit im Winkl. It was a perfect Tyrolean setting, but it was an hour's bus ride daily to the Olympic grounds.

Our Olympics tour included the following: Round-trip jet flights from New York or Chicago to Munich and back; airport transfers; a selection of tickets for each day of the Olympic games, including opening and closing ceremonies, all final track and field final events, and assorted tickets for other sports; first-class hotel accommodations in Reit im Winkl with continental breakfast included; daily bus transportation to the Olympics grounds; Olympics trading pins; an Olympics travel bag; and the services of well-known U.S. coaches who acted as tour escorts. The cost for all this was $750 per person.

My trip to Munich in the summer of 1970 was part of an educational tour that my friend, Johnson Elementary School Principal Tom Moran and I planned and escorted. The tour included one week in London, one week in Zurich, and one week in Copenhagen. We took twenty people, mostly Cedar Rapids educators. The cost was $585 per person.

While we were in Zurich, Tom Moran and I rented a car to drive to Munich, where a German Olympics Organizing Committee member, Henrietta Dubbel, showed us around the Olympics grounds. She also introduced us to Timofey Pokorov, a Russian monk who claimed to be 2,000 years old. After World War II, Pokorov had taken up residence on what was to become the Olympics grounds and refused to move. Olympics organizers had to build the Olympics complex around Pokorov's humble home.

In the summer of 1971, Tom Moran and I escorted another educational tour to Europe, this time to London, Paris, Stockholm, Salzburg, and Barcelona. We took twenty-eight educators. The cost was $595 per person. We arranged the trip so there would be a full week in Salzburg, which was within easy driving distance of Reit im Winkl.

In December, I returned to Reit im Winkl to meet with the Klaus Lehrberger family, our travel agents in Germany. They took me on inspection tours of all of the hotels we would be using and said they would make all of our bus transportation arrangements during the Games.

In February 1972 we made our final pre-Olympics trip to Munich. Traveling together were Jack Griffith of the *Athletic Journal*, Chuck Rohe, my then-wife Judy, who took the pictures, and me. Our German contact, Henrietta Dubbel, showed us around the Olympics construction site for photo opportunities.

In the April issue of the *Athletic Journal*, there was a three-page article entitled *"Athletic Journal* Goes to the Olympics." Accompanying the article were seven color photographs Judy had taken. The article pointed out that our tour had been sold out for months, but we were able to get eight more tour packages. As soon as the magazine came out, those were sold, too.

We wanted to be sure we had experienced tour escorts helping us, so I enlisted some of my friends who were well-known in the sports world. The *Athletic Journal* article concluded with the following:

One of the main factors contributing to a successful tour is experience. And the Athletic Journal *tour escorts are certainly qualified in that department.*

Jack Griffith, publisher of the Athletic Journal, *has traveled throughout Europe and Asia, has led one sports tour to Germany (1969), and has visited the Olympic site on two occasions.*

Tom Ecker, author of six sports books, former Swedish national coach, will be leading his fourth tour to Europe. Tom has been in Germany every summer since 1964 and visited the Olympic site in 1969, 1970, twice in 1971, and once in 1972.

Chuck Rohe, a member of the U.S. Olympic Committee and one of the best known coaches in America, traveled throughout Germany in 1969 and 1972 and is experienced in leading tour groups.

Fred Wilt traveled to Europe in 1948 and 1952 to compete in the Olympics and has traveled to Europe seven other times, including once in early 1972. Fred has written a number of sports books and is known throughout the world for his scientific approach to sports coaching.

Jimmy Carnes, track coach at the University of Florida, served as one of the coaches of the United States national team, which toured Europe in 1970.

Geoffrey Dyson, head coach of the British team in the 1948, 1952, 1956, 1960, and 1964 Olympics, will join the group in Munich. Geoff has written sports books and has traveled throughout the world lecturing on various aspects of sports.

Three of our Olympic tour escorts in 1972. I am seated between Fred Wilt and Geoffrey Dyson.

Because of an unexpected windfall, we turned an even bigger profit from the Olympics venture than we had originally expected. By early 1972, we had received full payment from our tour members, so we had almost $100,000 deposited in a local savings and loan account. But we needed deutschmarks to pay for the rooms, buses, and other expenses in Germany. Our plan was to buy travelers checks in deutschmarks before making the trip.

My travel agency ordered $50,000 worth of American Express traveler's checks in deutschmarks and held them until we were ready to buy. The agency had an arrangement with American Express that allowed the purchase of traveler's checks at the previous day's exchange rate. Naturally, I checked the rate every day, looking for the best deal. I even made a graph showing the daily fluctuations.

On April 3, 1972, I was driving home from work at the Educational Service Center when I heard on the radio that the United States was devaluing the dollar by 10 percent. That was a surprise break for us. I turned the car around and drove to the savings and loan, where I withdrew $50,000 and took it to the travel agency to buy deutschmarks. It would have cost an additional $5,000 if I had waited until the next day.

The tour itself turned out to be very successful, despite the horrible terror attack on the Israeli team in the Olympic Village. All of our tour members were touring in the Alps that day and did not know there had been an attack until it was over.

After we returned home from Germany, I sent out surveys to all of our Olympics travelers, asking how we had done. The reports back were very positive. Planning ahead really paid off for us.

Jack Griffith and I were already planning our next Olympics venture—a tour to the 1976 Games in Montreal. We had already run ads in *Athletic Journal* and had signed up a number of people, many of them repeaters from Munich. As we learned more about the upcoming Olympics, however, we realized it was going to be much more difficult than Munich. Dealing directly with the French Canadians, we found, was going to be nearly impossible for us because we simply didn't have any connections.

So we went to the owners of *Track and Field News.* I met with the publisher, "Bert" Nelson, whom I knew quite well, and offered him our list of Olympics tour members. He was happy to take them, of course. Then we contacted everyone on the list to let them know it was their choice whether to go with *Track and Field News* or not.

Jack and I were suddenly out of the Olympics tour business, but I didn't give up on Montreal completely. Bert Nelson asked me if I'd like to be in charge of hospitality for the *Track and Field News* Olympics tour, which totaled 2,920 people. I liked a challenge, so I agreed to do it.

The hospitality center for the tour was a collection of several large ballrooms, called the Complexe Desjardins, in the Hotel Meridien, in downtown Montreal. There were television sets along all of the walls, telecasting in English or French. At one end of the largest room was a raised stage with two large spotlights, where I could schedule our seminar speakers every night.

On the day of the closing ceremonies, the tour's Gala Party was held at the Place des Arts, a large theater that could accommodate the 2,920 guests, the *Track and Field News* staff of twenty-three, and many of the athletes who had participated in the Games. The program consisted of on-stage interviews of some of the best-known athletes.

I was the opening act. In the book, *Olympic Images,* which was published a few months after the Games had closed, there was a picture of me in my leisure suit, with a microphone in my hand. The picture's caption reads: "The inimitable Tom Ecker 'warms up the crowd.' "

We made extra money in Montreal by offering three Olympics courses for credit from California State University at Hayward. One of my assistants in the hospitality room was Jim Santos, the track coach at Cal State Hayward, who arranged with their extension office to offer the Olympics courses. Many of the people on the tour wanted to pick up the three hours of college credit. All they had to do was attend the Olympics and our nightly seminars and write a paper on an Olympics experience.

The instructors for the courses were all of the coaches, athletes, doctors, and others we could enlist to speak at our seminars. Our most prominent speaker was Great Britain's Sir Roger Bannister, the first man in the world to run a sub-four-minute mile.

Track and Field News printed and distributed brochures and advertized the classes in several magazines, for which they received a share of the profits. We had 282 registrants. When it was all over, Santos and I each cleared $5,918.

We planned to offer courses at the 1980 Olympics in Moscow, but those Games were boycotted by the United States, and we had to put off our plans until the 1984 Olympics in Los Angeles. Besides working with Jim Santos at the Los Angeles Games, we added a new partner, Dr. Stanley Clark, the head of the Cal State Hayward's physical education department.

I approached my two partners with the greatest money-making idea of my entire career—offering college credits *for watching the Olympics on television.* After we received approval from Cal State to offer the courses, we again hired *Track and Field News* to print brochures and advertize the classes, for which they received a substantial payment up front. We also hired three Cal State professors to teach the classes. That year, we had 552 registrants. After expenses, Jim Santos made $5,087, Stan Clark made $2,208, and I made $5,315.

Between 1984 and 2006, we offered courses at five summer Olympics, five winter Olympics, the 1990 Goodwill Games and Freedom Festival, and the 1996 political party conventions. My total income from offering college credits during that period was more than $380,000.

When I was working for the Cedar Rapids schools in the 1970s, I was escorting tours for several different travel agencies during summer vacations. Sales representatives from two different airlines were always eager for me to select their airline for the tours. Lufthansa (the German airline) and SAS (Scandinavian Airlines) had sales representatives who visited the Cedar Rapids travel agencies.

The two representatives taught me about "inaugural flights." An airline was allowed to reward favorite travel agents or other travel industry employees with a free seat on a flight if it was an inaugural flight—the first time the airline had flown between two particular foreign cities. The airlines not only provided the inaugural flights, they also provided the flights from Chicago to the inaugural flight and from the inaugural flight back to Chicago.

Selected people were offered the trip, which they could either accept or reject. If, at the last minute, there were still seats available, I would get a call from the airline representative, either from SAS or Lufthansa, asking if I'd like to take the trip. It was not unusual for me to get a call on a Thursday, with an offer to take an inaugural flight on Friday.

In my case, I would have to pay for an airline ticket from Cedar Rapids to Chicago and back, but the airline paid for all of the other flights. But there was an additional benefit. As long as it didn't take more than a total of thirty days, I could fly anywhere else in the world I chose to go on that airline, as long as it was done before returning home. And all of that extra flying didn't cost me anything.

Getting time off from my job was not difficult. My contract with the Cedar Rapids schools included six weeks of vacation time, plus ten paid holidays. Although there were certain times when I had to be on the job, most days could be taken as vacation days, as long as the work got done. While teachers were

expected to be on the job 190 particular days a year, I had to be on the job 221 days a year of my choice. What that meant was that I could apply for and receive vacation time with very little notice.

One of the inaugural flights I took on SAS in 1977 was from Zurich, Switzerland, to Dar es Salaam, Tanzania. First I had to get to Zurich. SAS flew me from Chicago to Montreal, Copenhagen, and Zurich. The inaugural flight was Zurich to Entebbe, Nairobi, and Dar es Salaam.

We arrived in Dar es Salaam at 8:40 in the morning. At the airport, I had to wait in line for almost an hour to clear passport control. The delay was because our plane had landed in Nairobi earlier that morning, and the Kenyans and Tanzanians weren't on the best of terms. When I got to the head of the line, I convinced them I hadn't gotten off the plane in Kenya, so they let me in.

I had the entire day to kill in Dar es Salaam, since my flight out was scheduled for 10:35 that night. For most of the day, I explored the city and purchased a few wood carvings. Late in the afternoon, I decided to try out the bar in a fancy hotel. I approached the bar and was told I couldn't go in without a coat and tie. When I pointed out that other people were getting in without coats and ties, I was told they were in their native costumes. I said I was in my native costume, too, but they still wouldn't let me in.

That night I flew from Dar es Salaam back to Nairobi, Entebbe, Zurich, and Copenhagen. But them I took advantage of the "additional benefit" and flew to Stockholm to spend a few days with my friends there. Then it was time to head home, from Stockholm to Oslo, Copenhagen, Montreal, and Chicago.

My costs were $72 for the Cedar Rapids-Chicago-Cedar Rapids air tickets and cheap taxi fares and wood carvings in Dar es Salaam.

Frank Colonna of SAS and Maynard Solomonson of Lufthansa were both friends of mine. They were the ones who told me about the inaugural flights. Whenever Frank and Maynard were in town, usually not on the same day, my two travel agents, Jane Welsh and Ellen Ilten, and I would spend time with them. And it was always fun. It was not unusual for us to spend an evening having dinner together at the nearby Amana Colonies. On one occasion when we were going to have dinner with Frank at a "dungeon" restaurant in South Amana, we convinced Frank that he would have to wear leg irons during dinner.

Jane, Ellen, and I loved to poke fun at Frank, who was usually serious and was easy to kid. One of Frank's callings in life was as a poet. He published a book of ninety-two of his poems titled *Life's Happenings through Poetry*. Most of the poems are about love or Christianity. Here is a sample of Frank's work, "A Gift of Love."

If my love is strong to be,
Then humbly I will share it with thee,
For to give of love is like a gift received,
To give again a love perceived.

Frank made the mistake of giving me a copy of his book of poetry. I went to a local print shop and had a poem printed on a page that looked exactly like the pages in Frank's book, using the same size and style of type. The page was pasted into the book so it looked like it belonged there. The poem was entitled "Honor and Offer."

She offered her honor,
He honored her offer,
So all night long,
It was honor and offer.

43

Swedish Golf Balls

When I started my junior year at the University of Iowa, my roommate was John "Sky" Marschall. Sky was an outstanding golfer on the university team and was the only Iowa athlete, in any sport, to serve twice as the team captain. The previous year, as a sophomore, he was the medalist in the NCAA golf championships, shooting a blistering sixty-six.

I gave Sky his nickname. It was from Damon Runyon's short story, "The Idyll of Miss Sarah Brown," which was later a Broadway musical and motion picture, *Guys and Dolls*. The main character was Sky Masterson, who got his name because of his betting skills—"Sky's the limit!"

"Sky" Marschall attempting to drive a golf ball from the Hillcrest parking lot across the Iowa River.

Sky Marschall was also an avid bettor. He would bet on just about anything. He was watching raindrops on a window one day and gave odds that the raindrop he'd picked would be first to the bottom of the pane.

Sky was also one of the people in our dormitory the previous year who bet me I couldn't hitchhike to South Carolina and back on a weekend without missing any classes. That was the day we first met.

Some of Sky's adventures became part of campus lore, and no one was ever sure whether the stories about Sky's exploits were true of not. One of the stories was about Sky's weekend trips home to Hampton, Iowa. He would go to the bookstore to sell his classroom books so he'd have enough gas money to get home. When he got home, he'd get enough money from his dad to gas up the car for the trip back to Iowa City, and enough more to buy his books back.

Our junior year at Iowa, Sky and I became partners in a money-making scheme. I owned a small plastic roulette wheel and a chuck-a luck game. We would spread the word during lunchtime that there would be "games" in our room right after lunch.

We set up the roulette wheel or chuck-a-luck game in our room and encouraged everyone to join us. Many of our "customers" were freshman football players. I served as the "house." Sky acted as the "shill" and encouraged players to double or triple their bets. We made quite a bit of extra money that year.

One of our betting schemes that didn't work involved Sky's skill as a golfer. One night, well after dark, we went to the grassy area near the Hillcrest Dormitory's front door, where Sky teed up a golf ball. With a driver, he hit the ball to the east to see if it would go across the Iowa River and land on the other side. If the ball landed in the river, we would hear a splash. If it made it to the other side of the river, we would hear a thud.

He drove several balls, and we could hear they all

made it across the river. So the next day at noon, when Hillcrest residents were returning from their classes, Sky stood on the grass with driver in hand and a golf ball on the tee, while I took bets on whether he could hit a golf ball across the river. Quite a large crowd was assembled and many bets were made that he couldn't drive a ball over the river. We knew we had a sure thing.

But then, a dormitory proctor came out of the building and told us to get off the grass. He said Sky could hit the ball from the parking lot, but there would be no way he could tee up the ball. Sky gave it a try but hitting the ball from a blacktop surface was very difficult. The ball landed in the river, and we lost and had to pay off all the bets.

It has never been a secret that Sky and I weren't very scholarly during our days at Iowa. In fact, we often talked about writing a book called *How to Flunk Out of College in Ten Easy Lessons—and Five Hard Ones.*

Sky had been a pole vaulter when he was in high school, but he hadn't touched a vaulting pole since. During the indoor track season his senior year at Iowa, track coach Francis Cretzmeyer asked Sky if he would consider pole vaulting in an upcoming meet against Minnesota. If Sky could finish third, he would score a point. (There were only two other vaulters entered in the meet, so Sky only had to clear the opening height.)

The opening height was ten feet, which Sky cleared to score a point for the Iowa team. As it turned out, Iowa didn't need the point, winning the meet 59-55. In a write-up in the Iowa City newspaper, a columnist wrote: *"Golf Coach Glen Devine is vacationing in Texas. I expect a minor explosion in the Field House when Glen returns to find his links ace risking life and limb going over that crossbar."*

Sky spent all of his working days as a golf professional and, as his dad once said, "He never worked a day in his life." Sky was so good, he began shooting his age when he turned seventy-one, and he's done it every year since, now into his eighties. In 2018, he made his eighth hole-in-one at the age of eighty-two.

So you'd think, with a golf professional so close at hand, that I'd take up the game. But it didn't happen. Actually, I tried playing golf one year in the 1970s, but as I've so often told people since, "I tried it once, didn't get a hole-in-one, so I quit."

Fifteen years later, I was suddenly a golf promoter, entirely by accident. Some of the Swedish track and field athletes I'd been coaching during the 1960s were living and training in California, to take advantage of the warm weather in the wintertime. While there, they learned to play, and to love, the game of golf. But when they returned to Sweden, there was no place for them to play. There were a few golf courses, but they were exclusive and expensive.

My Swedish friend Hans Lagerqvist wrote me a letter on March 23, 1970, asking for help. He wrote: "I don't know if I told you that I bought golf equipment last summer. When I tried to play here, they wanted 5-600 kronor ($125-$150). You have to be a member of a club. Now I want to ask you if you happen to have a card that looks like a member card in a golf club. I want to fool those bastards (is that how you spell it?). They said it will be OK with a foreign country club."

If the Swedes belonged to a golf and country club—anywhere in the world—they could play at the Swedish golf courses. So I formed The Pembroke Golf and Country Club, 1908 Grand Avenue, Cedar Rapids, Iowa. It was my home address, and the golf course was my small front yard.

I had membership cards printed, signed them as the club president, and sent them to a few golfing friends in Sweden. There was a sudden demand for

My longtime friend, Hans Lagergrist, returned to Sweden from the U.S. with the desire to continue playing golf.

more cards, and at one time we had more than 300 Pembroke members in Sweden. Golf had become very popular among the Swedish track and field athletes.

On August 31, 1974, three of the athletes decided they would compete in the first annual Pembroke Open, an eighteen-hole contest played at the Sollentuna Golf Course. Ulf Bjuhr, who organized the event, announced to the others that I was the "founder" of the Pembroke Open, even though I wasn't there. Ulf, Hans Lagerqvist, and Christer Lignell were the first participants. Ulf won, shooting 104. Christer shot 109, and Hans followed with 111.

The next year, 1975, former decathlete Kenneth Andrean joined the competition at the Djursholm Golf Course, bringing the number of competitors to four. Also, a handicap system was added, but it didn't change the finish. Ulf still won, and Hans finished fourth instead of third.

In 1976, only Ulf and Hans competed in the Pembroke Open. The sun was setting by the time they got to the back nine. By the fourteenth hole, it was so dark out that they would each hit three balls, hoping to find one. They gave up the game after hole fourteen. Again, Ulf won, and Hans finished second—his fourth consecutive last-place finish.

But Hans turned his game around the next year, winning over Christer and Ulf. That was the final year for the Pembroke Open to be held at the Djursholm Golf Course. From 1979 on, the competition has moved from course to course around the Stockholm area.

Over the following years, membership in the Pembroke Open has grown continually, with the numbers reaching as many as thirty-two golfers. Most of the members are former track and field athletes, including many national champions, some world record holders, and one Olympic champion.

Over the 1997-98 winter break, an extra Pembroke Open was held in Pembroke Pines, a golf resort in southern Florida. Fourteen Swedish golfers and their wives made the trip to Florida to participate in the special event. My old college roommate, Sky Marschall, played a round of golf with some of the Swedes, and then impressed everyone when he conducted a very entertaining golf clinic/demonstration.

I made the mistake of showing up at the Florida Pembroke Open in shorts. Sky saw my white legs, which hadn't seen sunshine since my first bout with skin cancer, and asked, "Are those legs or out-of-bounds markers?" I haven't worn shorts since that day.

My white legs are even mentioned in an online publication called the Urban Dictionary, which anyone can see. Under "Ecker White," it says: "A shade of white which is almost absolute white, named after Tom Ecker, former Olympic track coach who spent his entire life shielding his body from the sun. *That guy's legs are Ecker white.*"

As this is being written, the 46th annual Pembroke Open is in the planning stages. A record number of golfers are planning to participate in this year's event, which is scheduled for September 2019. Usually, I attend the two-day competition, and I'm going to try to attend again this year. If so, it will be my 56th consecutive year to travel to Sweden.

44

The Somersault Long Jump

At some time during my many years of studying track and field technique, I was intrigued to discover that new techniques always originate with athletes, not with coaches or theorists. When an athlete, through trial and error, improves his performance with some new style, or a new variation, coaches begin to teach their athletes the new or improved style.

There have been many examples of athletes creating new techniques, but the most obvious one is the high jump style originated by Dick Fosbury in the 1960s. The Fosbury "flop" was considered just another unorthodox technique until he won the 1968 Olympic high jump title. When Fosbury enrolled at Oregon State, his coach even tried to get him to switch to a "better" jumping style, but Fosbury couldn't make the change. Today, all good high jumpers use the flop.

In 1972, biomechanics professor Dr. Jim Hay and I decided we would be the first theorists to come up with new track and field techniques that would improve performance. For our experiment, Jim selected the high jump. I chose the long jump.

Jim Hay's idea was to have the high jumper emulate the technique of a horse jumping over a barrier, except the human jumper would have to take off from only one leg. His plan was to have a jumper approach the crossbar straight on, dive headfirst over the bar, and then raise his upper body to clear the legs with an equal and opposite reaction. That's the way horses do it.

We brought in John Roach, a high jumper from Western Illinois University who was willing to try the new technique. We conducted our practice session at the indoor track at the University of Iowa, where Jim worked. Jim coached the jumper for most of a day, and although we got some great pictures of him over the crossbar, the jumper could never clear his trailing legs. Jim's idea was great in theory, but it didn't work.

My idea was to have a long jumper use a somersault

(or flip) in the jump. When looking through some old notes recently, I realized that I first had the idea for a somersault long jump on June 19, 1969, at a track and field coaching clinic at the University of Tennessee in Knoxville.

I was sitting in a classroom, listening to a lecture on sprinting by Stan Wright, who coached at Western Illinois University at that time. Among the notes I took that day there were sketches of a long jumper somersaulting.

When my first of three biomechanics books was published in 1971, I decided to include information on the somersault long jump, even though, as far as I knew, no one had yet tried it.

There was so much positive response from coaches and jumpers from all over the world that I decided to begin promoting the somersault technique. First, I had to find someone willing to try it. In March 1973, I called John Ask, the track coach at Cedar Rapids Jefferson High School, to see if he might have a long jumper who would give the new technique a try. He came up with a jumper named Scott Fleming, who could do the somersault, but he couldn't get up enough speed to flip completely before landing in the sand. We did get some pictures of Fleming that ran in the Cedar Rapids *Gazette* and later in some newspapers in Europe.

Then I had a stroke of luck. F.X. Cretzmeyer, my track coach when I was at the University of Iowa, was attending a district track meet at Kingston Stadium in Cedar Rapids. While we were chatting, he mentioned that he had a pole vaulter on the Iowa team, Dave Nielsen, who was using the somersault in the long jump. Dave hadn't tried it for distance; he was just experimenting with the technique. Of course, I was ecstatic. I wanted to meet this somersaulter as soon as possible.

Dave and I met the next week, and we arranged to do a photo shoot in June. I had to wait until I could get a 35mm, slow-motion sequence camera from my friend, Jack Griffith, at the *Athletic Journal* magazine in Evanston, Illinois. I also borrowed a 16mm motion picture camera from Jim Hay.

The photo shoot was held at the University of Iowa track, where Nielsen jumped for distance for the first time ever. He jumped, and was filmed fourteen times. He was landing about a foot farther than he could manage with the standard technique.

From the 35mm film, I selected a sequence of nine photos and had them printed on eight-and-a-half-by-eleven inches information sheets, with a frame-by-frame explanation of the advantages of the somersault written below. I had several hundred copies made at a local print shop.

From the 16mm film, I had 1,000 feet of film of the best jump produced repeatedly on a single reel. At home, I had a complete film editing table. I took the 1,000-foot reel and spliced together hundreds of separate film loops. Each loop could be threaded into a 16mm projector so a coach or athlete could see the somersault technique over and over. I bought clear plastic boxes for shipping the film loops and sold the loops for $3 each.

I placed a small ad in *Track and Field News,* advertising the somersault loop films. In the ad there were three pictures of Nielsen, one at take-off, one upside down in the air, and one at landing. Requests for information began pouring in, from both the United States and from many foreign countries. Those who paid $3 for a loop film received the loop, plus the information sheet. Those who just wanted information received only the information sheet.

Then I contacted sports magazines with information sheets and original photographs of the technique so those magazines could write illustrated articles about the somersault. Articles appeared that year in magazines in the United States, England, Australia, New Zealand,

The somersault long jump, as performed by Iowa student, Dave Nielsen.

West Germany, East Germany, Poland, Czechoslovakia, India, France, Ireland, Canada, the Soviet Union, Argentina, Italy, Greece, South Africa, Mozambique, Belgium, Sweden, Iceland, and Denmark.

Since we had excellent footage of Dave Nielsen's somersault style, it was easy to analyze the advantages of this new technique. I wrote an article for *Athletic Journal* magazine, explaining the advantages of the somersault long jump. On the magazine's cover was a fifteen-picture color sequence of Nielsen using the new technique.

I was sent a copy of a picture magazine from Denmark, showing photos of three Danish college students, all using the somersault long jumping technique. A track coach in Jamestown, New York, sent me clippings with pictures of six somersault long jumpers on his team. I was being deluged with either letters asking for further information or news and pictures of successful flippers.

The BBC in London contacted me to ask if they could send a film crew to Iowa City to get color sequence photos of Dave Nielsen in action. They said I could have any leftover pictures for my own use. There were many leftover pictures, giving me a stock of color sequence photos to be used in my lectures and for use in any publications that wanted color sequences.

I was leaving on a vacation trip to Europe the next month, so I contacted athlete friends in Iceland and Sweden, asking if I could meet with groups in those two countries to discuss the somersault long jump. Both responded that they had made the arrangements. My first stop was Reykjavik, Iceland. The track and field leaders there were so excited about the new technique, they asked me if I could arrange to send Nielsen to Iceland to do a demonstration during a six-nation track meet in early August. They would provide his air tickets and his lodging in Reykjavik.

I contacted Nielsen, and he agreed to go to Reykjavik to demonstrate the somersault long jump, but I asked him if he would extend his trip to include Stockholm, Sweden. He could stay in the home of my good friend Hans Lagerqvist. In Stockholm, he could get more extensive publicity than in isolated Iceland.

Nielsen's experiences in Reykjavik and Stockholm were very positive. He demonstrated the somersault several times in the competition between Iceland, Denmark, Holland, Belgium, England, and France, to the delight of the spectators in the packed stadium. In Stockholm, he demonstrated the new technique at the Olympic stadium for a reporter and a photographer from the newspaper, *Dagens Nyheter (The Day's News)*. The article covered two pages and included five photographs of Nielsen.

A few days later, a writer for the Swedish magazine *Aktuellt (Of Current Interest)* called Hans Lagerqvist, asking if Dave Nielsen could take a few jumps for their photographers. When Hans told them Dave had already returned to the States, the writer asked if Hans could do it. He didn't want to try it at first but soon changed his mind and said he would give it a try. Keep in mind that Hans was an accomplished pole vaulter and only long jumped for fun.

Hans met with the writer and a photographer at Stockholm's Olympic Stadium, and for the first time attempted to do a somersault long jump. He had trouble getting all the way over at first but soon realized that a tighter tuck after take-off would put him into a better landing position. The article and photos appeared in the September 1973 issue of *Aktuellt*.

The next month, Hans received a telephone call from a German television station in Frankfurt. They said they had read the article in *Aktuellt* and had also read in a Soviet sports magazine that the Russians had analyzed the somersault long jump and found it to be a superior technique. The representatives from the German TV station asked Hans if he would be willing to come to Frankfurt to demonstrate the somersault technique on live television the following Saturday night.

On Friday, Hans flew to Frankfurt for the demonstration. In order to get enough run-up distance for a decent jump, the raised runway ran through two TV studios, with a doorway in between. There was more than enough sand (300 cubic feet) in the landing area. Fans sat in some ten rows of seats around the sand. After the demonstration, there were many telephone calls to the station. Other people wanted to try this new technique.

The somersault long jump was so successful, Hans was later invited to somersault in another indoor meet, this one in Bremen, Germany. There, he had the best jump of his life, almost twenty-four feet. Remember that his all-time best was a wind-aided twenty-three feet, three inches. His normal results were around twenty-two feet.

Little did I know how big (and how controversial) the somersault long jump would become. In my personal collection, I have newspaper and magazine articles from all over the world, in many different languages. Some of the articles include photos of local jumpers, but most of them featured sequence pictures of Dave Nielsen, which I had provided.

Sports Illustrated wrote three articles on the somersault long jump, including a major piece titled "The flip that led to a flap." The article states: "The somersault long jump had been written about and discussed before the last Olympics Games by Tom Ecker, a coach and authority on biomechanics, who is the flip's No. 1 advocate, if not it's modern day originator."

The article goes on to tell of a thirty-two-year-old West German long jumper, Bernhard Stierle, who used the somersault technique to win the West German indoor long jump championship. Somehow, Stierle was later credited with inventing the new technique.

In January 1974, Jim Hay and I flew to his native New Zealand to attend the British Commonwealth Games in Christchurch. Actually, Jim attended the Games, and I had been asked to give a presentation on the somersault long jump at the International Conference of Health, Physical Education, and Recreation at Lincoln College, which preceded the Games.

The local newspaper, the *Christchurch Star,* published a nine-photo sequence of Dave Nielsen performing the flip long jump, along with a long article, telling of the advantages of the new technique. The article was titled "No Flippant Boast."

On the way home from New Zealand, I stopped off in Fiji for two days. During that stop, I decided to try to do a forward somersault into the motel swim-

ming pool where I was staying. I had one of the pool attendants take my photo so it looked like I was somersault long jumping. When I returned home, I had two photographs printed on the front page of a card. One was a picture of me long jumping the traditional way when I was in high school. The other was the picture taken at the pool in Fiji. The caption read: "You CAN teach an old dog new tricks." I sent that card to a lot of people around the world, including every member of the International Amateur Athletic Federation's technical committee, which would later ban the somersault long jump in international competition.

The last time I saw the somersault performed was in Louisville at the 1974 Mason-Dixon Games. Hans Lagerqvist entered the competition as both a pole vaulter and a somersault long jumper. On February 9, the day of the Games, the *Louisville Courier-Journal* ran a picture of Hans' somersault long jumping in mid-air, along with the caption: "Hans Lagerqvist will perform the somersault long jump at the 14th annual Mason-Dixon Games."

I was in the audience that night to witness the 1974 version of the Games. It was disappointing to see that the meet had evolved from an entertaining circus-like affair to a very dull track meet. The appealing voice of the animated announcer of the 1960s, Tom Conner, who was largely responsible for keeping the audience informed and entertained, had been replaced by a voice that could put people to sleep.

I enjoyed watching Hans do the somersault long jump and hearing the cheers from the appreciative crowd. That was my last time to experience the Mason-Dixon Games. And, it was my last time to see the somersault long jump in competition.

The picture of me in Fiji doing the somersault long jump—into a swimming pool.

45

Breakfast of Champions

In the early 1970s, many long jumpers began using the somersault long jumping style. The most prominent of those was Bruce Jenner, who used the somersault in the long jump portion of the decathlon. Before Jenner became the patriarch of the Kardashian reality show family, and before he announced in 2015 that he was transitioning into a woman, he was best known as the world's greatest athlete, the 1976 Olympic decathlon champion and world record holder.

Jenner got the idea for flipping in the long jump when he read about it in my first biomechanics book, but he didn't try it until 1974. He then used it in competition several times, including in the 1974 USA-USSR-West German triangular decathlon competition in Tallin, Estonia. At that competition, the Soviet Union's Igor Ter-Ovanesyan, a former world record holder in the long jump, said to Jenner, "I think it is a style with a lot of potential. A guy with a lot of speed could go crazy with the flip."

Another outstanding flipper was John Delamere of New Zealand, who used the somersault style to jump twenty-five feet, six-and-three-fourths inches. Delamere wrote me, asking how he could get into a better landing position at the end of the flip. I wrote him back, advising him to tighten his tuck in the air, which would cause him to turn over faster.

My youngest daughter, Kjerstin, loves to tell her friends that her father was on the Wheaties box once. She makes it sound like I'm some sort of sports legend, like Tiger Woods or Michael Phelps. Actually, my picture wasn't on a Wheaties box, but my name was.

My Wheaties' adventure began in July 1972. I had decided to spend part of my summer vacation attending the U.S. Olympic Trials in Eugene, Oregon. The trials are staged every four years, a month or two before the Olympics, to select athletes for our team. In the individual sports, the first three in each event make the team.

July 4 was a warm, cloudless day in Eugene. It was the second day of the decathlon, a two-day, ten-event test of human speed, strength, stamina, and skill. Twenty-two athletes were vying for the three spots on the Olympic team.

Bill Toomey, the 1968 Olympic decathlon champion, who was working for ABC-TV at that time, had invited me to watch the events with him from the top of the camera tower ABC had constructed in the infield. The decathlon events were not being telecast those two days, so the ABC cameras weren't there. We had the best seats in the stadium.

Toomey, an avid decathlon fan, was keeping a running point total for some of the top athletes in the competition, using a special decathlon reference book that lists the points awarded for every possible time or distance in each event. Decathlon scoring is complicated. Often, when the competition is close, the athletes themselves aren't sure how they stand.

Toomey continued to calculate the leaders' point totals until mid-afternoon, when the ninth event, the javelin throw, was completed. The final event, the grueling 1,500-meter run, would begin in a few minutes.

"Do you have any idea who will make the Olympic team?" I asked.

"Bannister and Bennett will finish one-two," Toomey said, "but it looks like a three-way fight for third."

Steve Gough looked like the best bet for third with 7,291 points, Fred Samara had 7,257 points, and Andrew Pettes had 7,156.

"What about Bruce Jenner?" I asked.

Toomey looked up from his notes. "Why do you want to know about Jenner?"

"Just curious. He goes to school in Iowa."

Quickly, Toomey added up Bruce Jenner's points, something he had not bothered to do previously.

"Hey, he's got a chance," Toomey said as he

continued figuring. "In the 1,500, Jenner has to finish ahead of Pettes, beat Samara by fourteen seconds, and beat Gough by twenty seconds."

The athletes were gathering for the start of the 1500-meter run as I quickly climbed down the ladder and ran over to the starting line. Jenner was sitting at the edge of the track, tying his shoes.

"Hi, Bruce," I said. "I don't know if anyone's told you, but you have a chance to finish third and make the Olympic team."

"You're kidding," was his quick response.

"No, you really have a chance. But you'll have to run the 1500 of your life. Bill Toomey figures you have to beat Samara by fourteen seconds and Gough by twenty seconds."

It might have sounded like an easy challenge, but Jenner knew that beating Gough by twenty seconds would be no easy task. The margin of victory would have to be more than 120 yards.

Sixteen of the twenty-two athletes who had begun the competition the day before lined up for the start of the final event, the 1500-meter run.

When the gun was fired, Bannister and Bennett, the two best decathlon 1500 runners in U.S. history, were surprised to see Jenner take the lead. Throughout the race Jenner continued to build up that lead, even though everyone in the crowd was certain he would finally falter and would be overtaken by the favorites.

But Jenner didn't falter. He continued to widen the gap, hitting the finish line ahead of the entire field, in 4:16.9, the best 1500 of his life and almost ten seconds ahead of favorites Bannister and Bennett. Pettes and Samara were out of contention, but Steve Gough, who merely had to stay within twenty seconds of Jenner, appeared to be about 120 yards behind when Jenner finished.

Finally, the announcement came over the loudspeaker. Gough had run 4:38.9—twenty-two seconds slower than Jenner. Gough's point total for the decathlon was 7,822; Jenner's was a career-best 7,847.

Bruce Jenner, the unknown from Graceland College in Lamoni, Iowa, was on the Olympic team.

Two months later, Bannister, Bennett, and Jenner took on the world at the 1972 Munich Olympic Games. But it was Jenner, our third-place qualifier, who showed the most promise. In twenty-third place after the first day's events, Jenner came through with an incredible second-day performance, finishing tenth in the 1972 Olympics—much higher than anyone thought was possible.

It was because of that surprise finish, and his belief in himself, that Bruce Jenner made the decision to devote the next four years of his life to training to become an Olympic champion in 1976. But he couldn't do it alone. In order for him to be able to train on a full-time basis, his wife Chrystie worked as a cabin attendant for United Airlines.

During that four-year period, Jenner began using the somersault in the long jump portion of the decathlon. He was quoted in the *Des Moines Register:* "I first thought of flipping in 1971, after reading Tom Ecker's book, but never tried it until last winter. My first jump was a personal best."

Jenner continued to use the somersault technique until September 1974. That's when we all learned that the somersault long jump had been banned by the International Amateur Athletic Federation at its meeting in Rome. It was banned because it was "so different that it is not the event traditionally known as the long jump." (If that is the case, how do you explain the flop high jump, fiberglass pole vaulting, and spin shot putting?) Anyway, that was the end of the somersault long jump.

At the end of the long jump section of the IAAF rule book, there is a terse addition: "The employment of any form of somersaulting is not permitted."

So, I decided to write a letter to the editor of the magazine *Track & Field News.* I wrote: "We've all heard of the flop high jump and the flip long jump. I have just invented a new pole vaulting technique called the floop, which will guarantee vaults of more than twenty feet. However, because somebody might try to ban it, I'm not going to tell anyone how to do it."

Jenner's four years of training full-time paid off. He won the Olympic decathlon title handily at the 1976 Olympics in Montreal, setting a world record in the process.

Almost immediately, Jenner became the spokesman for the breakfast cereal, Wheaties, and pictures of him were on the front of the Wheaties boxes. He also was named chairman of a new organization to "encourage sports participation and physical fitness," The Wheaties Sports Federation.

Jenner selected eight people to serve with him as

directors of the Wheaties Sports Federation. Probably because I was the one who gave him the information in Eugene, or because of the somersault long jump, I was one of the eight directors. And we all had our names printed on the back of the Wheaties box.

The following January, the Wheaties Sports Federation Board held a press conference in downtown New York. I was very excited to be able to attend, since I knew and admired most of the people who would be there.

The schedule called for everyone to arrive in New York on January 9 and to check in at the United Nations Plaza Hotel. At 7 p.m., the Wheaties Sports Federation Board members would meet in the "Wheaties suite" for cocktails. Then the group would be transported in limousines to Paul's Landmark Restaurant for dinner. After dinner, the limos would take us back to the hotel.

The next day, we were to go to Norman Thomas High School, again by limo. We were then to be escorted to the school auditorium for the press conference. First, Bruce Jenner would introduce all of the board members to the press. Then Bruce was to make general announcements about the Wheaties Sports Federation.

The meeting was then to be open for questions and answers. The meeting had to be wrapped up by 3:15, when Bruce would have to leave for CBS-TV to appear on the *Captain Kangaroo* children's program.

I so wanted to be in New York for the meetings, but the weather wouldn't cooperate. I was snowed in at the Cleveland airport and never got to New York. Bruce sent me a very nice note, voicing his disappointment.

Later that year, when my daughter Kjerstin was in the fifth grade at Erskine Elementary School, Bruce Jenner came to Cedar Rapids to give a speech. I drove him to Kjerstin's school so she could meet him. She still has the photo I took of them that day.

He also signed a copy of his autobiography, *Bruce Jenner's Decathlon Challenge,* for me. He autographed it: "I don't know of anyone I'd rather be on the Wheaties box with." I've often commented that I prize that inscription, even though he ended it with a preposition.

46

Testing the Waters

In 1973, when I was in my fourth year with the Cedar Rapids schools, I was asked by the city's Civil Service Commission if I would be interested in developing physical qualification tests that could be given to prospective police officers. The "agility tests" they were using at that time were being challenged by some of the people who had failed them. The commission wanted tests designed to measure actual physical abilities required for police work. I agreed to do it on a consulting basis.

The first thing that needed to be done was to get a team of respected people to contribute their ideas. The following became the test-constructing team: Dr. N. Peggy Burke, professor of physiology at the University of Iowa; Dr. James Hay, professor of biomechanics at the University of Iowa; Dr. Judith Grencik, professor of criminology at California State University at Long Beach; and Dr. Frank Verducci, professor of tests and measurement at San Francisco State University. My job was to coordinate the project.

In order to determine what was required of police officers on the job, we received permission from the Cedar Rapids chief of police to ride in the back seat of patrol cars, so we could observe police officers at work. Jim Hay and I rode several times, with our notebooks in hand, sometimes riding all night. Peggy Burke rode in the back seat with us on a few occasions.

After observing police activity for several weeks, we put together a battery of five PQ (physical qualification) tests: Backyard Pursuit Test, Stretcher Carry Test, Check-out Climb Test, Emergency Lift and Drag Test, and Pursuit Run Test.

The title of our final report to the Civil Service Commission was "The PQ Tests for Police Candidates— A battery of job-related physical qualification tests designed to determine the physical performance levels of prospective police officers."

When I presented the final testing booklet to the commission, the chairman asked for my bill. "You probably can't afford it," I said, "but I'll make a deal with you." I told the commission I would like to own the tests myself, but I would provide them to Cedar Rapids free for three years. Then they would have to pay for the tests, the same as any other police department that used the PQ tests.

Bob Moorman and I served as models for the PQ clothing line.

The commission agreed to the terms since it would less expensive for them in the long run.

I'm not a businessman. There's no way in the world I could market the tests to other police departments, so I contacted a businessman friend, Bob Moorman, and took him in as a 50-50 partner. Besides being a good businessman, Bob had a great sense of humor. He would introduce himself as "Bob Moorman, the same as the religion, but with two o's and one wife."

My job was to provide the testing research. Bob's was to provide the startup funds. He already had an office, a secretary, and an open line on his telephone system, so we were in business. We formed American Physical Qualification Testing Corporation (APQTC), which would be selling the tests, and Physical Standards Research Foundation, made up of the people who had developed the tests.

We had advertising brochures printed and mailed to every police department in the country. We also had stationery, contracts, instruction manuals, and score sheets printed. We even had a brochure marketing PQ professional wear, silk-screened t-shirts, jackets, and caps. Bob and I served as models for the photographs advertising the clothing line.

We knew we had a gold mine on our hands. Police departments around the country were being sued regularly by police candidates who had failed "agility tests," which didn't have any bearing on a person's ability to be a police officer. Our brochure told the story. Under the heading "Are the PQ Tests Non-Discriminatory on the Basis of Sex?," it said: The PQ Tests discriminate against the weak, the overweight, the uncoordinated, the physical inept, the out-of-condition. They do **not** discriminate on the basis of sex (or, of course, on the basis of race, religion, or national origin).

The cost to police departments for administering the tests was $50 a year, plus a charge per candidate, ranging from $8.50 down to $4, depending upon the number of candidates tested.

The individual departments administered the tests, following the instruction manual, and they recorded the results on score sheets, but the test results had to be computer-scored by APQTC. There was no way the local departments could know if someone passed the tests or not without our computer scoring.

At that time, some human rights agencies required

that police candidates be provided with a training program to assure that all candidates had an equal opportunity to train for the PQ Tests. Jim Hay and I sat down at my favorite bar, the Fox and Hounds, to tackle the problem. As part of the Physical Standards Research Foundation, we created a training booklet. Because most of our writing was done in a bar, the illustrations in the booklet were drawn by Jim on cocktail napkins. The booklet was made available to police departments to be distributed to police applicants. We charged the police departments fifty cents per booklet.

In the summer of 1974, APQTC purchased a booth at the International Association of Police Chiefs' convention in Los Angeles, where Bob and I distributed brochures. We also had a computer in the booth to demonstrate our method of computer scoring, which was unique at that time. We would ask for a potential customer's name, which we would enter on the computer's keyboard. Then the computer printed out a list of famous lawmen (such as Wyatt Earp and Dirty Harry) with the customer's name on the list. It drew a lot of people into the booth.

We were challenged only once by people who had failed the test. Bob and I flew to Sioux City, Iowa, in his single-engine airplane, to testify in the case. When we arrived in the courtroom, we saw the challengers— two short, very overweight women. We won the case.

In 1977, we decided to add a PQ Test for Fire Fighters to our testing lineup. The seven-part test was originally created in 1972 by Dr. Frank Verducci of San Francisco State, but we updated it and began advertising the test on a national basis. As with the police tests, the potential firefighters had to complete tasks that were similar to those required of firefighters.

I wanted to learn more about firefighting, so I went to the Cedar Rapids fire chief, Edsel McMickle, to ask him if I could participate in some of their firefighting exercises. He told me they would be burning down an old farm house the next Saturday, and they would let me participate, if I could be there.

When I showed up at the central fire station on Saturday, they outfitted me in a full firefighter's outfit, complete with a fireproof suit, helmet, gloves, boots, goggles, and an oxygen mask. The mask was equipped with a loud bell that would ring if my oxygen supply ran low. They explained to me that it is difficult to see, and impossible to breathe, in a smoke-filled room.

We rode in a fire truck to the site of the empty farmhouse, near the Cedar Rapids airport. There, some of the firefighters set fire inside the house, and our test group entered the house, with hoses in hand, to fight the fire. What we didn't know was that every time we had a fire under control, someone would set a new one. We ended up fighting fires inside that house for several very exhausting hours.

At one point, I was on the second floor, and I realized the floor was burning beneath me. My alarm bell sounded, and I knew it was time to go down the stairs and exit the house. It's a good thing I did. When I got outside, I realized my boots were on fire. It was a wonderful experience, but I decided that day to leave firefighting to others.

In 1979, when I was facing financial challenges because of my divorce from Judy, I began giving my shares of APQTC to her, in exchange for some income tax bills she said I owed her. (She was still doing my taxes.) Eventually, all of my shares were gone, and I was out of the testing business. The company kept going for thirty years before finally giving it up. It was a great venture, and I know Judy really profited from it.

47

The Cedar Rapids *Gazette*

For more than fifty years, I've been working closely with staff members in many different departments of the Cedar Rapids *Gazette*. I've written columns and articles, taken photos, created puzzles, and fed the staff many news tips and ideas. I've even designed display advertising.

From 1978 through 1984, at the request of the chief editorial writer, I wrote an "Outlooks" column once every eight weeks, where they appeared on the *Gazette's* op-ed page. The columns were up to 1,000 words long and included my photo and an explanation box which read: *"Outlooks ... periodic observations from some thoughtful Eastern Iowans invited to express themselves here. The topics are unlimited. The views are theirs."*

My Outlooks' columns included a variety of topics, including the 1979 controversy over the appearance of the rock group KISS. The group was to appear at the Five Seasons Center, and the howls of protest were heard in schools, in churches, and in the *Gazette's* letters to the editor. Dozens of letters, most of them condemning KISS, appeared in the *Gazette*.

Among the many letters were the following comments:

"If you listen carefully to their music, you hear references to the drug culture, references to witchcraft, slogans that are anti-Christian and anti-American. This is easy to understand when you know that KISS stands for "Kings in Satanic Service."

"Rock music is being used by Communists to bring Communism into America."

"Hell is at the end of a Christ-rejecting life. This, KISS fans, is the real issue."

"At a time when Pope John Paul is exhorting people to follow good, not evil, it is a shame we have the KISS appearance."

"The members of KISS are deeply into witchcraft and belong to the Satanist Church of America. This informa-

tion comes from a man who was a 13th level witch before being saved into Christianity."

"They use makeup to make themselves resemble satanic clowns or witch devils out of the ancient jungles."

There also were letters to the editor supporting the group, but they were fewer in number.

It just happened that the same week KISS appeared at the Five Seasons Center, the Wayne King Orchestra—he was known as the "Waltz King"—appeared at the Paramount Theatre. I couldn't resist taking the opportunity to take a jab at the anti-KISS letter writers. This is the Outlooks column that appeared in the *Gazette* the following week:

KING spells evil

Letters to the editor are a wonderful part of our culture. They are written to express opinions, to promote beliefs, to inform, to persuade. Some are laudable. Some are laughable. Their impact is questionable.

Readers tend to enjoy those letters in which the opinions expressed are similar to their own. They correspondingly dislike, or even become infuriated, by those to which they take exception.

Here are four letters to the editor representing opposite views on a controversial musical group which appeared in Cedar Rapids recently.

To the Editor:

I wish to protest the appearance of Wayne King at the Paramount Theatre here last week. Everyone knows that KING really stands for Knights in Nude Grossness. I know because I have a friend who saw it in the Wall Street Journal. I hear members of the orchestra actually enjoy standing nude while in the shower.

The worst part is the type of music the Wayne King orchestra brought to our community and the bad influence it had on our older people. It is no secret that the band features the waltz—a form of music which encourages people of opposite sexes to touch each other while moving their bodies in a synchronized motion to the pulsating three-quarter beat of the music. I hear their rendition of "The Waltz You Saved for Me"—which featured a stoical saxophone solo—was particularly disgusting.

Those who wish to join me in this protest may sign a petition I am circulating to demand that the City Council prohibit appearances by such saxophone wielding waltz groups in the future.

To the Editor:

I think the idea that Wayne King's music is part of a devious capitalistic plot to overthrow the recording industry is nonsense. These rumors are obviously being spread by young radicals who don't realize the Wayne King concert was really just good adult entertainment. It was not a bad influence on our community's senior citizens, as some have contended.

And the idea that KING stands for anything crude or vulgar is ridiculous. The word KING means just that—King, a male ruler of a nation or state usually called a kingdom; a male sovereign; a monarch. Also, it is the orchestra leader's last name.

To the Editor:

How can civilized people allow such performances as that of the Wayne King orchestra here in Cedar Rapids?

First, every member of the orchestra wore a sport jacket and tie! Second, the band members remained seated throughout most of the performance, only standing for occasional solos! According to an article in the New York Times, these are obvious signs of a leaning toward Satanism.

Further evidence of this link with the devil was noted by an acquaintance of mine who actually saw a band member eating a piece of devil's food cake before the performance.

To the Editor:

According to People magazine, the name KING is not meant to represent anything erotic or vulgar, such as nude showering. It is really representative of noted kings of the past, such as King Tut, King Lear, King Kong, King Pin, and King James Version.

And how can anyone believe such a group has any ties

with Satanism? Sure, some members of the band may have a devil-may-care attitude, and one or two may have raised the devil after a performance, but this does not mean they are into Satanism. It only means they are human, like you and me and Vincent Price.

I hope this is the end of the Wayne King controversy.

Of all the guest columns I had written for the *Gazette* over the years, the Wayne King piece was by far my favorite. It must have been a favorite of the *Gazette*, too. They reprinted it in a special advertising issue a few weeks later.

In late 1984, the *Gazette* asked some "prominent" citizens to tell what their New Year's resolutions would be for 1985. Somehow, I was included on the list.

Heading the list was John Ely, one of the city's most distinguished citizens. John turned 101 that year. He said simply, *"I hope it's all for the best, not only for me, but for everyone."*

Peggy Whitworth, executive director of Brucemore, was not quite five feet tall and got a lot of good-natured ribbing about her small stature from friends. *"I resolve to be tall,"* she declared.

Denny Frary, KCRG's prime-time weatherman, *"resolves to provide everyone with exactly the kind of weather they want throughout the new year."*

Barry Norris, KGAN's director of television operations, said, *"I resolve to help Mayor Don Canney become more outspoken. I think he is too much of an introvert, and I'm going to help him make his views better known."*

Tom Ecker, author of the *Gazette's* "Wuzzles" and "Crypto-Quote" word games, lets his fascination with words shape his resolution: *"I resolve to reduce the number of redundant phrases that I tend to use repetitively over and over."*

In the summer of 1991, I had the good fortune to be a participant in a river rafting adventure, a seven-day trip through the Grand Canyon. I wrote two articles for the *Gazette* and took color photographs to illustrate the two pieces. The main article was titled "Shooting the rapids." The sidebar article was "Raft riders rock, roll in roaring waters."

In the main article, I pointed out that this was a completely new experience for me. I had never been on a river raft, had never camped out, and had never worn a backpack. I couldn't remember ever going without a hot bath or shower, even for twenty-four hours. I've always said, "To me, roughing it is a Holiday Inn with black and white television."

When I became the school district's Information Director in 1985, I made a number of changes. One of my first ideas was to get rid of the mailed version of *The Window,* the school district's three-times-a-year information publication and replace it with an eight-page tabloid to be included as part of the *Gazette.* We decided *The Window* should come out on Mondays, when the *Gazette* was the smallest of the week, and a day when there were no other news or advertising inserts.

Previously, *The Window,* which cost $2,000 an issue just for postage, was considered junk mail and was thrown away by almost everyone who received it. Our idea was to make *The Window* look like part of the newspaper, filled with news, photos, and graphs, with everything subtly favorable to the school district. The cost of production was less than half the cost of the mailed version, and contained 60 percent more space.

In order to put *The Window* together in the *Gazette's* composing room, I had to learn to "cut and paste," using an X-acto knife and an electric-powered waxer. My teacher was Joe West, a longtime composing room employee at the *Gazette.* Joe laid out the first issue of *The Window* in February 1984. After that, we did the layout, with Joe there to help us when we needed it.

We produced *The Window* in the *Gazette* until my retirement in 1993. We considered it to be a very effective way to get our message out to the public.

In 1995, the big controversy in Cedar Rapids was over "The Tree of Five Seasons." It was to be a six-story-high, stainless steel structure to be placed in a downtown park next to the river. The project was to be privately funded, so cost wasn't the issue. The problem was how the structure would look. One person described it as "an upside-down egg beater."

So I decided to join the debate. Following is my letter to the editor that was printed in the *Gazette* on November 13, 1995:

To the editor:

The City of St. Louis has had wonderful success promoting its image with a huge metal arch. It stands in the park along the Mississippi River for all to see as they approach the city from the east. The St. Louis Arch is called "The Gateway to the West."

We could do the same in Cedar Rapids, constructing a smaller metal arch, say six stories high. It would stand in the park along the Cedar River for all to see as they approach the city from the south. The Cedar Rapids arch would be called "The Gateway to Waterloo."

The fund drive for the Cedar Rapids arch project will require a large support group, which I feel could be spearheaded by a team of local podiatrists. We could call them the arch support group.

The only serious problem I see for those in favor of the arch project will be the raft of letters to the editor from the project's arch-enemies.

In 1996, the Atlanta Committee for the Olympic Games selected me to be one of the torchbearers in the Olympic Torch Relay across the United States. The Olympic flame, which was kindled at the Temple of Hera in Olympia Greece, was flown to San Francisco, where the U.S. portion of the relay began.

At that time, I was making plans to run for the Iowa Senate in the 1996 elections. My son, Kerry, came back to Iowa to help me work out an effective plan for winning the election. We thought it would help that my new book, *Olympic Facts and Fables,* would be released in July 1996, four months before the November elections.

But then I learned there was a rule prohibiting carrying the torch and using the event for self-promotion. So, I decided to forgo running for office so I could carry the torch. In a front-page article in the Cedar Rapids *Gazette,* titled "He'll run, not run," I was quoted as saying, "I'm giving up four years of public service for four minutes with the torch. I can run for office again but carrying the torch is a once-in-a-lifetime opportunity."

Nationally, torchbearers followed a three-month, 15,000-mile, zigzagging route across the United States, ending when the stadium cauldron was lit during the opening ceremonies of the 1996 Olympic Games in Atlanta. Nationally, the relay included 5,500 United Way-chosen "community heroes." I was chosen as one of the forty-six "heroes" from Eastern Iowa, fourteen from Cedar Rapids.

The flame was scheduled to arrive in Cedar Rapids on the night of May 30 with the lighting of a small

Preparing to carry the Olympic torch through a part of southeast Cedar Rapids

cauldron on May's Island in downtown Cedar Rapids. But there was a big dispute over who would be the final torchbearer. The Atlanta Committee had selected Ron Steele, television news anchor at KWWL in Waterloo, an NBC network affiliate. NBC would be televising the 1996 Olympics.

KCRG, one of the two Cedar Rapids television stations, and the *Gazette* both complained that the final torchbearer should be from Cedar Rapids, since the flame would overnight in Cedar Rapids and wouldn't pass through Waterloo until the next day.

I was approached by Sondy Daggett, co-chairwoman of the Cedar Rapids Olympic Torch Relay celebration, who asked me if I'd be willing to be the final torchbearer, if she could convince the Atlanta Committee to have me replace Ron Steele. However, the best Sondy could do was have me run next to Ron as he carried the torch on its final leg onto May's Island. That meant I would get to run in the torch

relay twice, once on its final leg onto May's Island, and again early the next morning when I would be the fourth runner to carry the flame through a portion of southeast Cedar Rapids.

When Ron Steele and I reached May's Island with our torches, we were accompanied on both sides by Georgia state police officers on motorcycles. But the wildly cheering crowd of more than 46,000 people narrowed our path so the motorcycles had to drop out.

People on both sides of our narrow path reached out to touch us as we passed by them on our way to the temporary stage on the island. There we were greeted by the Cedar Rapids mayor and other dignitaries as Ron touched his torch to the small cauldron on the stage and transferred the flame.

The Olympic flame had officially arrived in Cedar Rapids for its only overnight stay in Iowa. You might wonder where a flame spends the night. It stayed in a room at the Holiday Inn on Williams Boulevard SW.

Running with the Olympic torch—twice—were two of the greatest thrills of my lifetime.

In the year 2000, I began sending Olympic "postcards" to the *Gazette,* which were printed daily during the time of the Olympic Games. During the past five summer Olympics (Sydney, Athens, Beijing, London, and Rio), eighty-one of my personal postcards or vignettes have appeared in *The Gazette.* They each contained unique, folksy stories that didn't appear anywhere else in newspapers.

For the Games in Australia, they were called "Postcards from Sydney." They actually looked like postcards, complete with a postage stamp which was my picture. That year, each postcard finished with a P.S. called "Today's translation from Aussiespeak." One example was "Put the chook in the molecule mauler," which means "Put the chicken in the microwave oven."

In 2004, the postcards were sent from Athens. Again they contained folksy stories, but each P.S. was "An Olympic fact from the past." An example was, "At the 1960 Olympics in Rome, the champion in the light heavyweight boxing competition was a brash young fighter named Cassius Clay, who later changed his name to Muhammad Ali. At ringside, encouraging the young fighter, was singer and boxing enthusiast Bing Crosby."

The 2008 postcards, which were sent from Beijing, followed the same format as the previous cards, including the P.S., "An Olympic fact from the past." One example was "At the Los Angeles Olympics in 1932, the three U.S. female springboard divers were all ordered to their locker room by a Hungarian official, who said their swimsuits were too revealing. The suits were banned for 'overexposure of the spinal column.' The three women changed to conventional suits and then went on to take all three medals in the event."

For the 2012 Olympics in London, we got a little fancier. Besides the typical postcard copy, we included the other side of the picture postcard, which appeared above "The Daily Olympic Postcard." The picture, which almost doubled the amount of space used, was of a London scene that related in some way to the postcard's copy. The P.S. was "Today's translation from Britspeak." An example, on the final day, was "Cheers, London. I'm low on dosh. It's time to take

My Olympic torch is mounted on a special plaque commemorating the run through Cedar Rapids.

the carriageway out of here," meaning, "Goodbye, London. I'm running out of money. It's time to hit the road."

In 2016, we sent sixteen daily stories back from Rio, but they were short vignettes, not postcards. Each story was called "Eck's Communication." In the final story, I wanted to finish by telling of the kindnesses offered by the Brazilian people to Carol and me on the crowded transportation lines. I wrote: "Every time Carol and I get on a train or bus, people are quick to give up their seats for us. I'm guessing it's because we appear to be old. I think it's a nice gesture. Carol says she's a little offended."

48

Talking at Sea

My wife, Carol, was the first one who suggested I become a lecturer on cruise ships. I had already been on six cruises as the tour escort for AAA Travel. It was March 1998, and we were escorting another AAA group on a Princess cruise, this one through the Panama Canal.

There was a professor on board who was advertised as an expert on memory development. The professor announced to one and all that if we'd come to his two lectures, we would never forget anyone's name again. Carol and I attended both lectures. Since neither Carol nor I can remember the professor's name, we just refer to him now as "Memory Guy."

After the professor's second talk, Carol said to me, "You could do that." She didn't mean I could do memory talks. She meant I could do talks on the history of the Olympic Games.

The next year we were escorting a group from KCRG-TV in Cedar Rapids on a Princess cruise to Alaska. One of the ship's lecturers was a very talented naturalist named Brent Nixon. After one of his talks, we asked him whom we should contact at Princess if I wanted to become a lecturer. We were surprised that he not only gave us the name of the woman who booked lecturers, Penny Johns, he also gave us her address and phone number, and said we could use his name as a reference. And he had no idea if I could do the job or not.

When we contacted Penny, she asked us to send her a list of recent speaking engagements and a videotape. Putting together a list of speaking dates was easy, but finding a videotape was not. I finally sent her two tapes—one was the comedy portion of a biomechanics talk that was several years old; the other was a tape of an appearance I made on *Newton's Apple,* a nationally televised PBS program from 1991. The tape was nine years old. I also sent her a copy of my latest book,

Olympic Facts and Fables.

Penny seemed to be satisfied with the tapes. We requested back-to-back cruises for January of 2000, from Auckland, New Zealand, to Sydney, Australia, and back, on the Sea Princess. We got both cruises, which meant we'd be away from home for four weeks. We did five forty-five-minute talks on each of the two cruises.

I always began the first lecture of each cruise by introducing Carol, who would sit in the first row. I explained that it was her job to listen to what I said and to correct me whenever I made a mistake, just like at home. I also explained that Carol moved from Oregon to Iowa and had to get an Iowa driver's license. On the form she had to fill out, it asked, "Color of hair." She put down, "Whatever's on sale."

In those days, we carried a slide projector and a thick three-ring binder with plastic sleeves with pockets holding the slides. There was room for twenty slides per sleeve, and there were more than thirty sleeves in the binder. The projector's slide tray held only seventy slides, which meant the average screen time for each slide was a long thirty-eight seconds.

During the next five-and-a-half years, we lugged the projector and bulky binder of slides on twenty-two cruises, to countries on all seven continents. We had definitely found the best way to see the world. As of this writing, we have visited more than half of the recognized countries in the world. In one forty-two-day period, without planning it, we visited all seven continents.

We met many other cruise lecturers during the next few years. One of our favorites was John Maxtone Graham, who was an expert on nautical history. One of John's sayings was, "Beware the pox. Beware the Ides. Beware the man with a box of slides."

Our next cruise was a month later on the Holland America line, not Princess. It was their "around the world" cruise on the Rotterdam, and we were told we could have any segment of the cruise we wanted. We selected the segment that began in Papeete, Tahiti, and ended in Wellington, New Zealand.

The other lecturer on the Rotterdam was actor Ernest Borgnine, who entertained his audience by showing one of his old movies, and then giving insight on some of the behind-the-scenes events associated with the movie. He came across as a truly nice guy. Besides Borgnine, we got to hang out with other entertainers, including comedian Shelley Berman and pianist Roger Williams.

Late in 2001, I lectured on a Panama Canal cruise on the Crown Princess. Also on the cruise were two other people from Cedar Rapids, Charlie Raines and his wife, June. Lecturers work only on sea days, so Carol and I were always free to do whatever we wanted on port days.

In Cartagena, Colombia, Charlie, June, Carol, and I decided we would take a taxi to see the sights. We noticed that taxi drivers had name tags so they could receive commissions anytime they stopped at a store where the taxi's customers bought something.

We were approached by a short, middle-aged man who didn't speak English, but obviously wanted to drive us around in his friend's new taxi. His name tag, which he had just manufactured, was a piece of masking tape with the name Luis printed on it.

When we got into the taxi with Luis, if was obvious to us that he didn't know how to drive. He drove only in second gear, which caused the car to lurch and

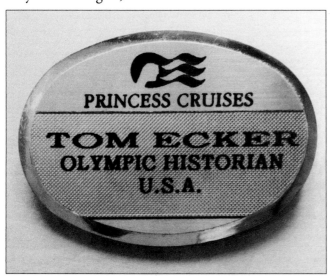

The badge I wore while lecturing on Princess ships.

the engine to die often. His only word in English was "Attention," which he used whenever he wanted to point out something of interest.

The tour ended when Luis pulled the taxi into a store's parking lot and sideswiped another car, causing considerable damage to both vehicles. We later commented that Luis had probably not earned enough that day to cover his expenses.

Our next assignment was the inaugural cruise of the *Star Princess.* The cruise began in Singapore and stopped in several Asian ports before arriving in Honolulu. We got off in Honolulu, even though the cruise continued to Los Angeles. We had to fly to New York. We had tickets to the Broadway production of *The Producers,* with the original cast. We couldn't miss that.

Our next cruise was my gift to Carol. I booked us on the final cruise of the original "Love Boat," the old *Pacific Princess,* from New York to Rome. When I told Carol about it, she asked, "You mean we're paying for a cruise?" The *Pacific Princess,* which was the setting for the long-running television series, "The Love Boat," had been sold and was being delivered to its new owners in Europe.

During the cruise, I wrote four articles, featuring highlights of our port stops in New York, Bermuda, Gibraltar, and Rome. Carol took the accompanying photographs. The articles appeared in the Cedar Rapids *Gazette* during the two-week crossing.

When we were at sea, the ship's cruise director was contacted by the Princess office in Los Angeles to let him know I was on board. They wanted him to ask me to give a talk on the Olympics. I agreed to do it. Without notes or slides, I did a half-hour Olympic talk in which I used some of my most interesting and most humorous material. I was interrupted by laughter several times. The cruise director was very happy with the performance and paid me with a bottle of wine.

The next month, we signed on with the *Royal Princess* and cruise director J.J. King and his very funny assistant, Scotty Roberts. It was the first of many cruises with J.J. and Scotty. This one started in Fort Lauderdale, went through the Panama Canal, and then visited six ports on the west side of South America.

The next month, again cruising with J.J. and Scotty on the *Royal Princess,* we had the most eventful cruising experience of our lives. We somehow survived a deadly hurricane on the south Atlantic Ocean. We sailed from

Cruise Director J. J. King

the Falkland Islands, off the east coast of South America, heading north toward Puerto Madryn, Argentina.

The hurricane hit us at about 9 p.m. and lasted for twenty hours. When it was at its strongest, the sea produced ninety-foot swells, causing considerable damage to the ship. The captain told us that in his thirty-two years at sea, the waves were the steepest he had ever seen. He also told us that the ship had to "face" the waves, which meant we were heading in the wrong direction.

A dining room window was knocked out. One of the ship's propellers was broken. More than half of the stateroom television sets were smashed. There were broken bottles and glasses everywhere. The breakable items in the ship's boutique were destroyed. The grand piano in the lounge was flipped upside down. Some passengers, fearing the ship would break apart, sat up all night in the stairwells with their life jackets on.

I don't know how many passengers were ill during the ordeal, but there were many reports of people with broken bones. The ship's doctor and nurse were very busy that day.

We missed the port of Puerto Madryn, but we made it to Montevideo, Uruguay, where the ship was met by representatives of Lloyd's of London. On the dock were many containers of supplies that had been flown in to replace the things that had been destroyed. That night, after the replacement items were loaded on the ship, we sailed the short distance to Buenos Aires, Argentina, our final destination.

We had four more cruises in 2003, two of them with J.J. and Scotty on the *Royal Princess*. The first was a trans-Atlantic crossing from Fort Lauderdale to Rome, by way of North Africa. One of the female passengers, whom we dubbed "Biker Lady," was traveling with her boyfriend, who looked like a motorcycle gang member. Both were heavy drinkers, and both appeared to be "trashy," at best.

One night, after the evening's entertainment was over, Carol and I were sitting at a bar, having a drink with J.J. He answered his phone, and all we heard from J.J. was, "Oh, my God." He left immediately. Later we learned that Biker Lady was so drunk she mistook the area under a stairway as the women's rest room. She had just peed on the carpet under the stairway. The next day, Biker Lady was confronted by the captain, who told her she would have to quit drinking or be removed from the ship.

In August 2003, we were on another trans-Atlantic cruise, this one from Copenhagen, Denmark, to New York City. Before the ship reached the port of Reykjavik, Iceland, there was an outbreak of norovirus among the ship's passengers and crew. At that time, it was the biggest outbreak of norovirus in cruise history. There were so many people who were ill, the ship had to miss ports in Greenland and Newfoundland.

Carol and I were not affected (or infected) because we knew the norovirus is not an airborne virus. You have to take it into your mouth to be affected. We were very careful.

When we docked in New York, a day early, the dock workers refused to unload the luggage at first, fearing they might contract the virus. When Carol and I disembarked, we were met by a huge group of journalists, many with cameras, wanting to get first-hand stories on "the sick ship." The journalists, who were behind a fence, pleaded with people to come to them for interviews. Carol and I were interviewed by CNN and Fox News, but we're not sure now which one of us was on which of the news networks.

In November 2003, we sailed from Papeete, Tahiti, to Sydney, Australia, on the new *Pacific Princess*. When we arrived in Tahiti, Carol took a nap in our cabin while I watched a movie in the cabaret lounge. The movie, *Plots with a View,* was a story about an undertaker in Wales named Boris Plots, who was in love with the village constable's wife, Betty. There was a line in the movie that really surprised me. I couldn't wait to tell Carol. The undertaker said to Betty, "You and I could be dancing on a Princess ship to Tahiti." What a coincidence. We later bought a DVD of the movie, but its name had been changed to *Undertaking Betty*.

In the summer of 2005 we finally entered the twenty-first century. We purchased a powerful computer and the best projector available. Although it was still a lot to carry, we were able to put all of our shows in PowerPoint. We not only had the still pictures as before, we now were able to use film clips, some with sound. Suddenly, it was much easier to change the images on the screen, and the images were much clearer and brighter. And we were no longer limited to seventy images. In some forty-five-minute talks, we had as many as 120 slides and film clips.

We did nine more cruises for Princess before we decided to retire. We had seen most of the world, which was one reason for quitting, but also it was get-

ting to be a bit of a hassle. There was a new woman booking lecturers for Princess. It became obvious that she was happier if her lecturers were booked through agents, reducing her workload. Agents charge lecturers $50 to $100 a day, depending on the ship, for the privilege of lecturing.

We had always been booked by Princess, which meant we didn't have to pay anything for the cruise, and we usually had outside officers' or entertainers' cabins. Those booked through an agent had to pay for the cruise and had inside cabins. Plus, we always received generous shipboard discounts when we were booked by Princess.

Our final Princess cruise was in May 2007. We had been under contract for that cruise for several weeks. Yet the cruise director was not informed of our arrival until the day we arrived. We were told there wasn't a

Disembarking a Princess ship in Portugal in 2006.

cabin available for us. Finally, they moved a musician from his outside cabin to an inside cabin in the entertainers' quarters, and they gave us the outside cabin.

So we decided to call it quits. It was a good run—thirty-one cruises in seven-and-a-half years, visiting the seaports of fifty-eight countries on all seven continents. It was a very good run.

Our retirement didn't last long. In 2011, we were recruited by the Cunard Cruise Line to do Olympic lectures on the three "Queens," the *Queen Elizabeth,* the *Queen Mary,* and the *Queen Victoria.* Our first assignment was a trans-Atlantic crossing on the *Queen Victoria,* from Fort Lauderdale, Florida, to Southampton, England, with seven port stops in Europe before arriving in England.

We did six more cruises on the Queens before finally giving up on the lecturing business. The most fascinating of those cruises was from Dubai to Athens on the *Queen Elizabeth.* We didn't know it beforehand, but we would be spending ten days in waters known for pirate activity. The ship's captain, who later said the ship had to outrun and outsmart the pirates, provided us with the following warning:

"*Queen Elizabeth* will be transiting the Indian Ocean, Gulf of Aden, and the Red Sea, an area well documented in the world's media for piracy. We will be passing through the area using an internationally approved transit corridor, under the protection of an International Military task force, including the UK Royal Navy."

We were told that the pirate boats, usually disguised as fishing vessels, would have trouble boarding our ship because the cruise ship is so much faster—more than twenty-three knots (about twenty-seven mph). Many of the ship's outside lights were turned off after dark, and we were required to close our cabin's curtains at night. Crewmembers even taped black plastic bags to some of the outside windows on the lower decks.

But during the day, we enjoyed watching some of the pirate ships trying, without success, to slow down some of the ships in the area. We even saw a Royal Navy frigate that had been called in to assist one of the merchant ships.

But the most impressive pirate deterrents we saw on our ship were three large anti-pirate LRADs (Long Range Acoustic Devices) that were on the main deck—one on the port side, one on the starboard side, and one aft. Each sound machine was manned by a Filipino woman. If anyone approached the ship without permission, the machine would broadcast a warning in six languages. If the warnings weren't heeded, the machine would send out a *deafening* sound that would actually blow out the eardrums of those approaching.

We really enjoyed the ten days we spent dodging pirates and were almost sorry to see it end when we transited the Suez Canal and sailed into the Mediterranean Sea.

Afterword

It's a great feeling to finally finish this book, after struggling with it for seven years. It would not have been possible without the continuing support of my wife, Carol, and the amazing editing of the manuscript by longtime friend, Mary Sharp. Mary suggested I finish the book by revisiting the 1996 Olympic torch run.

On May 26, 1996, the *Gazette* devoted three full pages to the running of the Olympic torch through Cedar Rapids, complete with biographical sketches and color photos of all of the Eastern Iowa torchbearers. My sketch read:

Tom Ecker

- *Age: 61*
- *Home: Cedar Rapids*
- *Occupation: Retired administrator, Cedar Rapids School District*
- *Background: A Waverly native who has lived in Sweden, and in Cedar Rapids for twenty-nine years, pioneered equitable sports for girls in public schools before equity was mandated. He has written nineteen books—fifteen on sports and four on word puzzles—with the latest, "Olympic Facts and Fables," due out in July. He coached Sweden's track and field team in the 1968 Olympics and served on two technical committees for the Games in 1980 and 1984. He is a current member of the Cedar Rapids Rotary Club (and helped the club establish a medical clinic for the Tarahumara Indians in Mexico), Tanager Place, The Salvation Army, Cedar Rapids-Marion Arts Council, The Performing Arts Commission, and Crime Stoppers.*
- *Quote: "My approach to life and community service has been based on hard work and the phrase 'Pass it on.' You can never repay the many people who guide you along the way. You can only repay them by helping others later in life, when you are able to do so."*

Analyzing a loop film with track and field expert, Fred Wilt. Drawing by Al Rainovic, The Milwaukee Journal's *award-winning editorial cartoonist.*

194—

Wherever I Choose

An Unauthorized Autobiography

As told to a Dell Laptop

Afoot and light-hearted I take to the open road,
Healthy, free, the world before me,
The long brown path before me leading wherever I choose.

—Walt Whitman, "Song of the Open Road"

Tom Ecker

Big Fox
Publishing

Acknowledgments

The drama/comedy on the following pages covers nearly a lifetime. Now that the book is finally being put to bed, I'd like to acknowledge all the characters who have been part of this eighty-four-year experience. They are all mentioned at least once on the following pages. An important character who is not mentioned in the main text is my dear friend, talented journalist Mary Sharp, who copy-edited the manuscript and wrote the introduction. Another is photographer Darel D. Hein, a fellow student at Iowa who took the cover photo.

Although this book has largely covered the humorous side of life, as the manuscript was being finalized, I learned of the unexpected death of my longtime friend, Hans Lagerqvist of Sweden. Hans is a main character in several of this book's chapters. As soon as I learned of his death, I wrote the following tribute to him:

"Hans and I met at the Olympic Stadium in Stockholm in July, 1964. I was a visiting American coach and he was a twenty-four-year-old Swedish pole-vaulter. Since most American pole-vaulters were retired at age twenty-two, after finishing college, I figured Hans was too old to be pole-vaulting. But he was such a nice guy; I decided to work with him anyway.

"Hans had trouble keeping his legs up before reaching the crossbar, so we put the bar up to seventeen feet (5.18 M) and had him repeatedly vault and kick the crossbar with his feet. Little did I know that Hans would be clearing the crossbar at seventeen feet with his entire body a few years later. He vaulted seventeen feet, 8-1/2 inches (5.40 M) in 1972, at the age of thirty-two.

"The afternoon we met, Hans invited discus thrower Lars Haglund and me to the Lagerqvist home for dinner. That was the night I offered the two athletes a travel deal. If they could get to Bowling Green, Kentucky the next spring to train with my Western Kentucky athletes, I would provide them with food and lodging for as long as they wanted to stay. They stayed for six weeks, and that trip changed all our lives.

"Since that time, Hans and I have gotten together to talk and laugh whenever we could. Several times he came to Iowa to visit me. I have visited Hans in Sweden at least once each year for the fifty-five-years we have been friends. We have also gotten together in Florida, Thailand, Hungary, Finland, Australia, Germany, and South Africa.

"I have always described Hans as my best friend. But over the years, I have learned that he is the best friend of everyone who has known him.

"Rest in Peace, my friend."

—Tom Ecker

Editing by: Mary Sharp and Deb Schense.
Cover by: Deb Schense, Photo permission by The University of Iowa
Printed in the U.S.A.
Big Fox Publishing
P. O. Box 170
North Liberty, IA 52317
www.bigfoxpublishing.com
Logo created at Logomakr.com